IMAGES
of America

SANTA FE SPRINGS

ON THE COVER: Martha and Walter Nimocks, pictured some time in the 1890s with family and friends, gathered around the fountain in their formal garden. After purchasing the property from the Hawkinses, the original owners who developed the site, the Nimockses made many changes to it, including the creation of the formal garden, construction of a very ornate and expensive Carpenter Gothic–style carriage barn, and a windmill with tank house. (Courtesy Nimocks Family Collection.)

IMAGES
of America

SANTA FE SPRINGS

Santa Fe Springs Historical Committee

ARCADIA
PUBLISHING

ISBN 978-0-7385-7576-6

Published by Arcadia Publishing
Charleston, South Carolina

Printed in the United States of America

Library of Congress Control Number: 2011921759

For all general information, please contact Arcadia Publishing:
Telephone 843-853-2070
Fax 843-853-0044
E-mail sales@arcadiapublishing.com
For customer service and orders:
Toll-Free 1-888-313-2665

Visit us on the Internet at www.arcadiapublishing.com

With sincere gratitude, we dedicate this book to the pioneers of Santa Fe Springs. It was those courageous individuals whose lives, fortitude, and imaginations created our rich culture and history.

Contents

ACKNOWLEDGMENTS

As with any worthwhile project and labor of love, it takes a dedicated group of individuals to create a quality product. This book is one such effort, and there are many people to acknowledge and to thank. First and foremost, this book wouldn't have even gotten off the ground without the unanimous support and hard work of the Santa Fe Springs Historical Committee. We are grateful for the generosity and kindness of the Hathaway Ranch Museum and thank them for opening the image archives of Richard F. Hathaway to the committee. We are also indebted to the city staff members who enthusiastically helped the committee in locating and preparing historical photographs for this publication.

We were indeed fortunate to have the help and memory of former city manager Robert Williams. We also want to acknowledge the help of former residents Ted and Margaret Snyder and Francine Hathaway Rippy, who were a vital part of Santa Fe Springs history and who eagerly lent a hand and their memories to the project.

The Santa Fe Springs Historical Committee extends its appreciation to the city council for its support of this project and commitment to preserving the history of Santa Fe Springs.

All images used in this book come from the Hathaway Ranch Museum, Richard Hathaway Collection, unless otherwise noted.

INTRODUCTION

Before the first Spaniards settled in the Santa Fe Springs area, a native population inhabited the area for over 2,500 years. The people were known as the Tongva, and their villages dotted the Los Angeles basin. Tradition tells of a village that occupied the Santa Fe Springs area called Chokiishngna (Cho-keesh-ing-na), or Chokiish. The Tongva had developed a complex society of independent villages and towns that all prospered in the basin. Most villages were established adjacent to a water source, as was the case for Chokiishngna. Rivers, streams, ponds, and lakes, which are no longer present in Santa Fe Springs, provided plenty of water for wildlife and plants and allowed the Tongva to thrive.

By the time Manuel Nieto and his family had arrived on the Los Coyotes land grant, the village of Chokiishngna was gone, no doubt a result of Mission San Gabriel's forced proselytism and the Tongva's assimilation into what would become known as the "Gabrieleños." Another factor in their disappearance may have been the diseases that spread among indigenous people after the Spanish arrived on their shores. Validation for the existence of the lost village of Chokiishngna came when a stone map was discovered during the oil boom of the 1920s. The map, which showed etchings of a lake with a village of wigwams and other distinguishable landmarks, was claimed by Jesse Hathaway to have been sent to the Smithsonian Institute.

Manuel Nieto first came to California in 1769, when he was 35 years old, as a member of the Gaspar de Portola expedition. He was part of an elite unit of Catalonian *soldados de cuero* (leather jacket troops). Under the command of Capt. Pedro Fages, they marched northward in California to the Bay of Monterey. Nieto was eventually stationed at the Mission San Gabriel and remained there until his retirement in 1795. In 1784, while at the Mission San Gabriel, he petitioned and received La Zanja de Zacamutin, a land grant, to graze his small herd of cattle. As the years passed and his herds grew, Nieto realized he needed more land to sustain his livestock. Manuel had his eye on a neighboring tract of land called the Encino. Nieto petitioned Governor Fages for the desired tract, but he did not receive the Encino. Instead, he received the Los Coyotes concession of land. Years later, the Encino was given to the Franciscan Order, who subsequently built the San Fernando Mission in 1797. The abandoned Zacamutin tract was given to fellow soldado de cuero Jose Maria Verdugo when he petitioned for the concession in 1794.

The original size of Manuel Nieto's Los Coyotes land grant was 300,000 acres, but after a lengthy battle with the Mission San Gabriel over rights to the northern portion of his land, the grant was reduced by Gov. Diego de Borica to only 167,000 acres, still making it the largest concession granted by either the Spanish or Mexican government. The mission was not the only neighbor Nieto had disputes with; the Dominguez family had a decade-long dispute with Nieto over Nieto's claim to most of the livestock on the Rancho San Pedro.

Manuel Nieto was a very successful rancher. When he died in 1804, he was reported to be the richest man in California. After his death, Nieto's land was passed on intact to his wife, Maria Teresa Morillo, and his four children: Juan Jose, Maria Manuela, Jose Antonio, and Antonio Maria Perez. They lived there together on the ranch until 1834, when a claim was made on their land.

A decade after Manuel's death, for reasons unknown, the family gave Patricio Ontiveros permission to build a home just two miles southeast of the Nieto compound. After leaving the military, Patricio went to work for Mission San Juan Capistrano as mayordomo over cattle operations on grazing lands north of the mission. Archeological evidence from the adobe foundation site of the Ontiveros house in Santa Fe Springs Heritage Park supports the claim that cattle were slaughtered there for their hide and tallow. Ontiveros lived on the land until 1834, when he petitioned Gov. José Figueroa for possession of the land that he had been living on for 20 years. Going to court, the Nieto family fought the claim and won validation of the original land grant; as a result, however, they were required to divide the Los Coyotes concession into five smaller portions that were to be divided again between the surviving heirs. The land on which the original home was located became known as Rancho Santa Gertrudes and was given to Josefa Cota Nieto, widow of Manuel Nieto's youngest son, Antonio Maria Perez Nieto. The other four land grants were called Los Serritos, Los Coyotes, Las Bolsas, and Los Alamitos.

It seems Josefa Nieto lived on the ranch for only a short time—maybe 10 years—when she decided to sell Santa Gertrudes, her 40,000-acre ranch, to her niece Maria Dominguez and her niece's husband, Lemuel Carpenter. Carpenter's prosperity took a sudden downturn when, around Christmastime 1852, he borrowed $5,000 from John Downey, known as El Boticario. Carpenter was in town with his friends and was running short of spending money, so he signed a note with Downey for $5,000 at a 12.5-percent interest rate that compounded daily. In 1859, after several years of reissuing the note (each time financing a larger sum because of accrued interest), John Downey finally demanded payment on the debt, which had ballooned to over $100,000. Carpenter was unable to pay the loan in full, so Downey filed suit for the foreclosure of Carpenter's mortgage. The rancho was sold at a sheriff's auction in 1859, where partners John Downey and James McFarland acquired 17,602 acres of the land. They established the Santa Gertrudes Land Company, subdivided the land into smaller parcels, and began selling them off. Around the time of the foreclosure, unable to handle the shame, Lemuel Carpenter solved his problem by putting a gun to his head and pulling the trigger.

Even before Rancho Santa Gertrudes was sold off at auction, there was a moderate-sized community that had formed near the Nieto compound. This community was originally made up of ranch hands, their families, and family and friends of the Nietos. After Downey and McFarland acquired the ranch and started selling off the newly subdivided tracts of land, the community began to grow. An 1862 map of Los Nietos Township shows homes dotted along both sides of Norwalk and Puente Mills Road (now Norwalk Boulevard) and all the way down to Anaheim Telegraph Road (now Telegraph Road). This community came to be known as Los Nietos. By the end of the 1860s, a community also began to grow around the Four Corners area. There was a Banning Stagecoach stop that was soon followed by a small grocery store and mail drop. The next few decades brought more growth to the Four Corners area, and before the end of the 19th century, this area became known as Santa Fe Springs.

One

Native Americans to the Rancho Era

Lemuel Carpenter, a Kentucky fur trader, arrived in California in the 1830s. He opened a very profitable soap factory in El Monte along the San Gabriel River, now the Rio Hondo. Lemuel soon met and married Maria Dominguez, his second wife. The 1850 US Census recorded Lemuel's age as 42 years old and Maria's as 22 years old. The census also recorded their four children: Susana, age 11; José Antonio, age 9; Refugio, age 6; and Francisco, age 3. Another source, Hubert Howe Bancroft, writes in his book *The History of California* that Lemuel had five children from his second wife, Maria, and two from his first wife, Espiritu, a Native American. Bancroft claims that Refugia, Lemuel's daughter from Maria, married Judge Joseph E. Pleasants of Orange and became a schoolteacher at Los Nietos. It is not clear whether Refugia is the same child listed in the census of 1850 and Bancroft just misspelled the name or if she is the youngest child born after the census with a similar name.

After moving to the Nieto Ranch, Lemuel made many improvements to the house and ranch, reported to be valued at $5,000. It again became productive and provided the Carpenters with a nice income. Times were good for Lemuel and his family. Within a decade, however, a series of events would change everything.

The Nietos had begun selling portions of their land before it was subdivided in 1834. In 1830, Jose Maria Ramirez purchased 140 acres just east of the Nieto compound from Maria Theresa Nieto, Manuel's widow. In 1835, Governor Figueroa granted Juan Perez the title to Rancho de Bartolo, which was the northern portion of Santa Gertrudes continuing north into Whittier Narrows.

After the loss of the Carpenter Ranch and Lemuel's subsequent suicide, Maria Carpenter's residence was uncertain. She did not immediately leave the ranch, so John Downey filed a lawsuit to have her evicted; however, because he sensed ill will from the community, he dropped the suit. Maria and her children continued to live on 90 acres of the original ranch that surrounded her home.

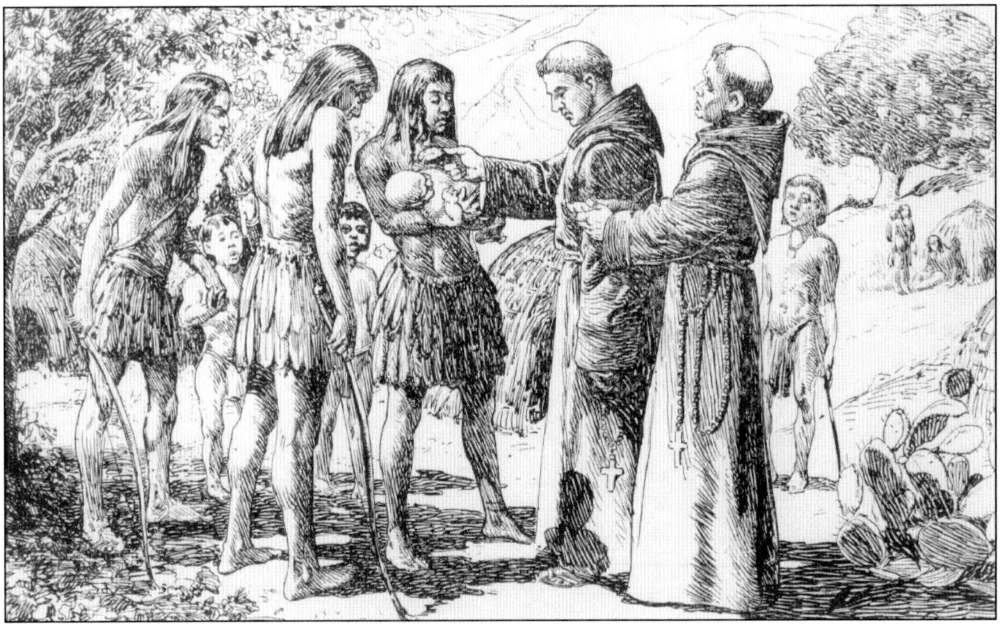

The local Tongva people were forced to convert to Catholicism. As a result, they were driven from their villages and made to live on the San Gabriel Mission grounds. It was not long before they were known as the Gabrieleños. There is evidence that Manuel Nieto had local Tongva working for him on his rancho. Above is an artist's depiction of a baptism of Native Americans by one of the mission fathers. (Courtesy Santa Fe Springs [SFS] Archives.)

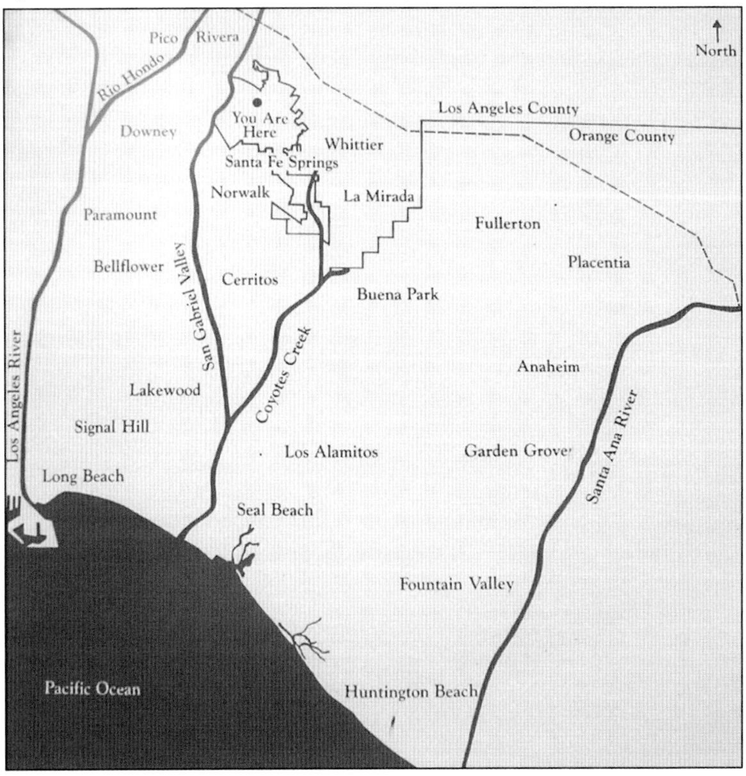

The 300,000-acre Los Coyotes land grant given to Jose Manuel Nieto was reduced to little more than half, or 167,000 acres, when the fathers of the San Gabriel Mission complained to Governor Borica that it needed the northern portion, La Zanja de la Puente, for its Tongva converts. Despite this, Manuel Nieto prospered on his vast empire, which today encompasses almost two dozen cities. (Courtesy SFS Archives.)

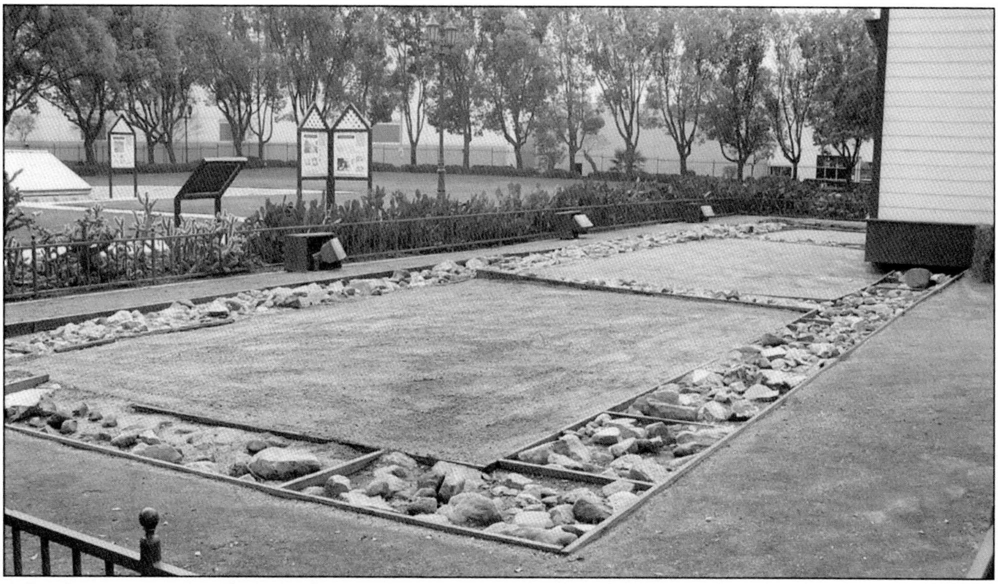

After being appointed mayordomo of Mission San Juan Capistrano, Patricio Ontiveros built his home on the location of what is now Heritage Park in Santa Fe Springs. Pictured is the stone foundation of his adobe house, discovered during the development of Heritage Park in 1987. Archeologists also discovered a trash pit that included artifacts providing a treasure trove of information about the period. (Courtesy Oblea Collection.)

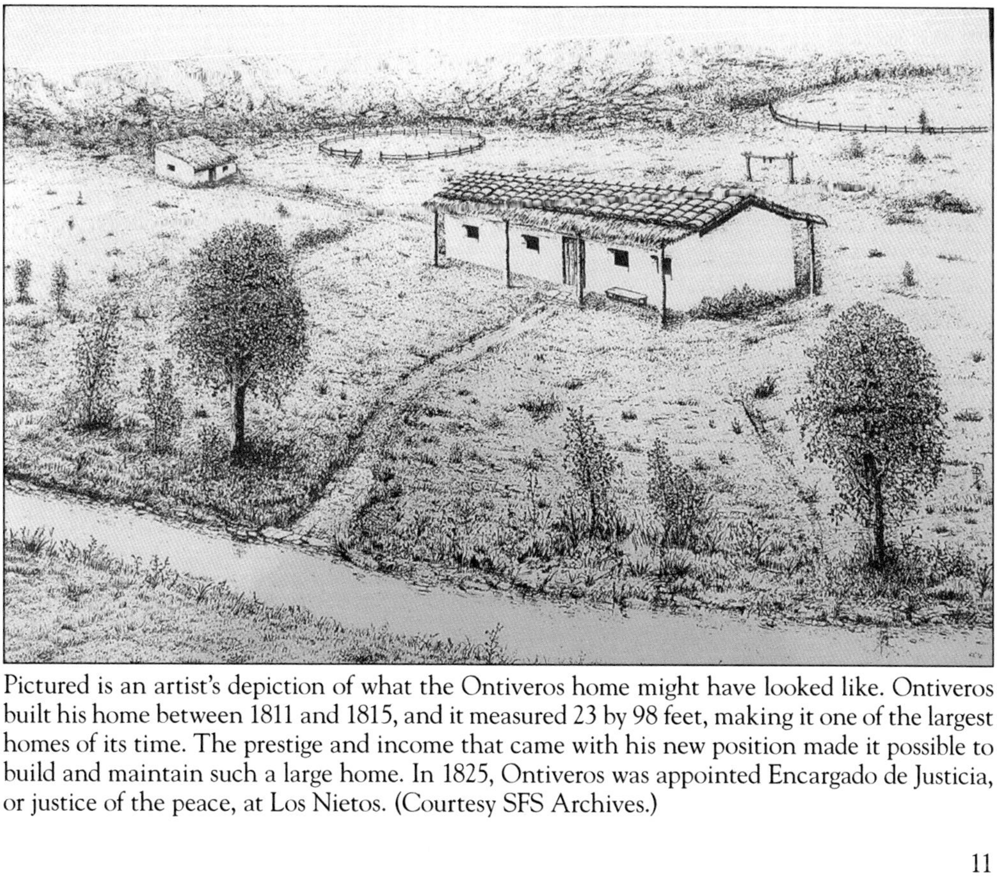

Pictured is an artist's depiction of what the Ontiveros home might have looked like. Ontiveros built his home between 1811 and 1815, and it measured 23 by 98 feet, making it one of the largest homes of its time. The prestige and income that came with his new position made it possible to build and maintain such a large home. In 1825, Ontiveros was appointed Encargado de Justicia, or justice of the peace, at Los Nietos. (Courtesy SFS Archives.)

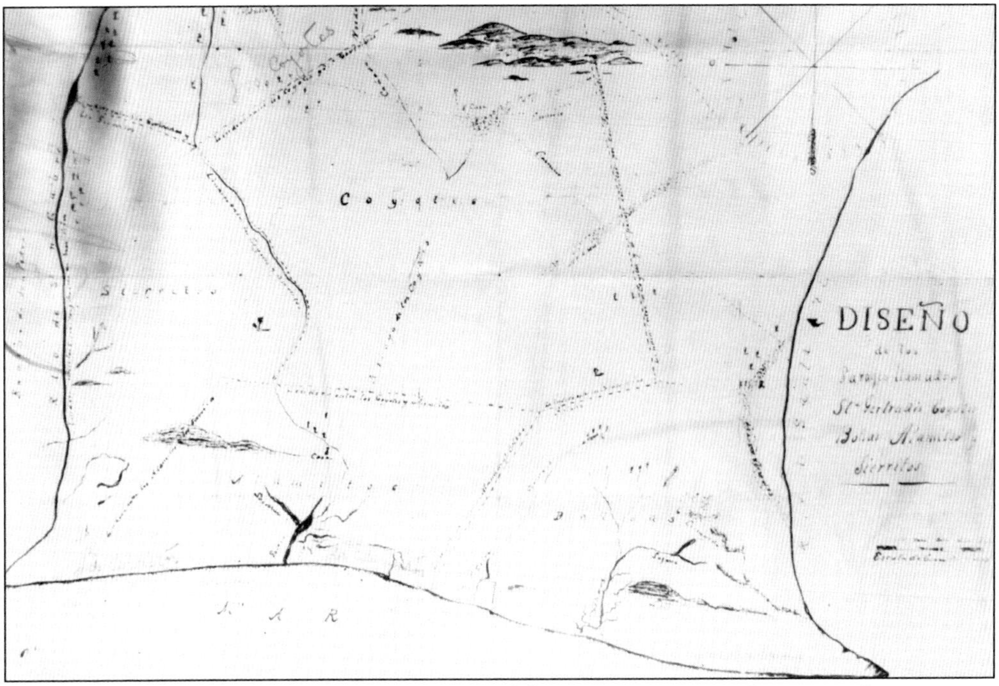

The surviving heirs of Manuel Nieto were successful in preventing several attempted acquisitions of portions of their land by Patricio Ontiveros, Antonio Machado, and Nacio Avilas, to name a few. In 1834, the land was granted again to the Nietos, but they were required to subdivide the large rancho into five smaller ranchos. The above 1834 *diseño*, or drawing, shows the subdivided Los Nietos Rancho with the names of five new, smaller ranchos. (Courtesy SFS Archives.)

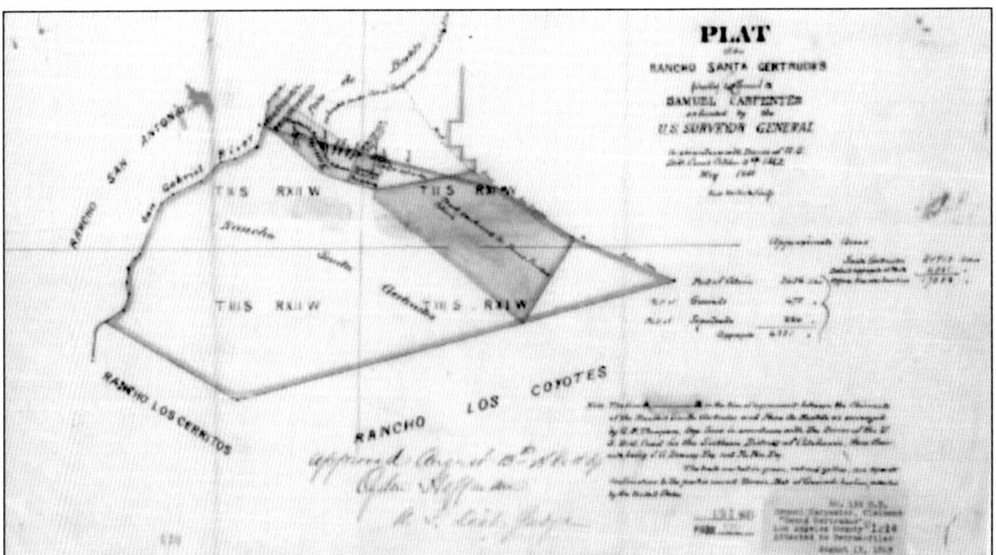

By the time of the auction, much of the original Rancho Santa Gertrudes had already been acquired by others. As far back as 1804, Juan Crispin Perez, with Nieto's permission, had been grazing his cattle on Nieto land. In 1835, with no objection from Josefa Nieto, Perez was granted the title to Rancho de Bartolo, which took the northern portion of the Santa Gertrudes ranch. Tomas Colima acquired an eastern portion in 1852. (Courtesy the Bancroft Library, UC Berkeley.)

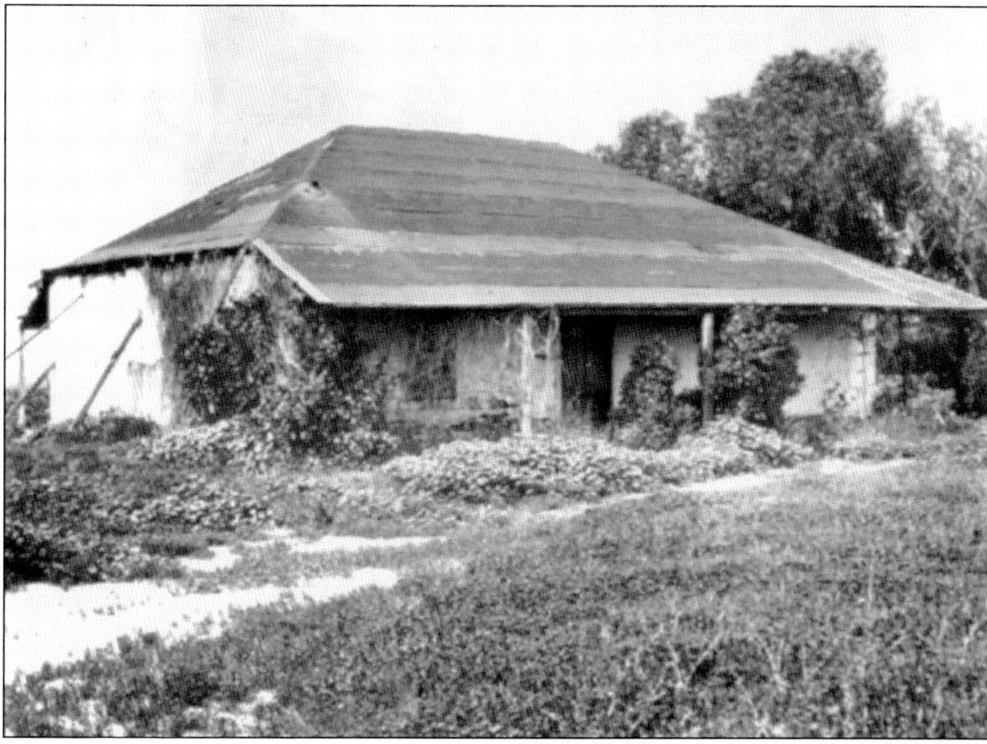

Pictured in 1920 is the Carpenter adobe. The original house, believed to have been built by Manuel Nieto, was located several hundred feet to the west of this one. The home was destroyed twice, first by the flood of 1867 and again in the flood of 1881. Each time they rebuilt their home, they relocated further east away from the river. (Courtesy Poyorena Collection.)

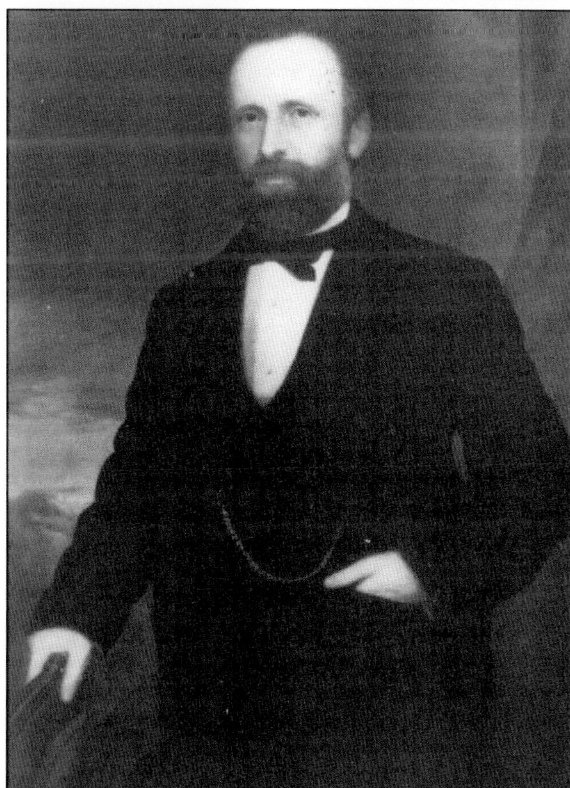

John G. Downey, a pharmacist, arrived in California around 1845. In 1849, he and Dr. James McFarland opened the first drugstore in Los Angeles. In 1852, after Downey became a US citizen, he married Maria Guirado. Downey was elected lieutenant governor of California in 1859 and a week later assumed the governorship when newly elected governor Milton Latham resigned to fill the recently vacated federal senate seat. (Courtesy Downey Historical Society.)

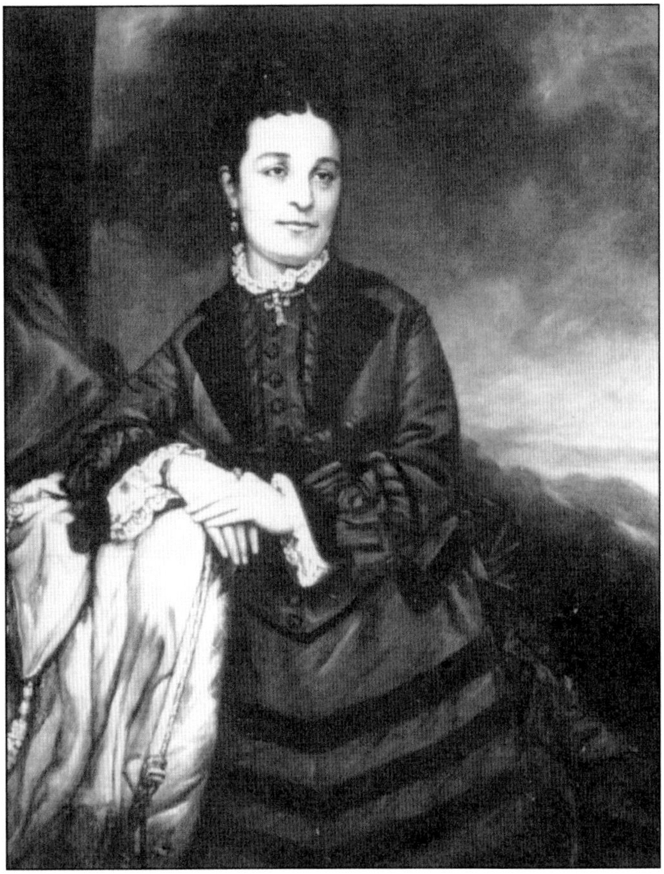

Maria Guirado Downey was 15 when she married John Downey in 1852. Maria was the sister of Los Nietos storekeeper and landowner Bernardino Guirado. Bernardino's store was on the south side of Los Nietos Road, west of Norwalk Boulevard. The Downeys had a home in Los Angeles and also maintained a home near her father where Downey oversaw his ranching operations. (Courtesy the Seaver Center for Western History Los Angeles County Museum of Natural History.)

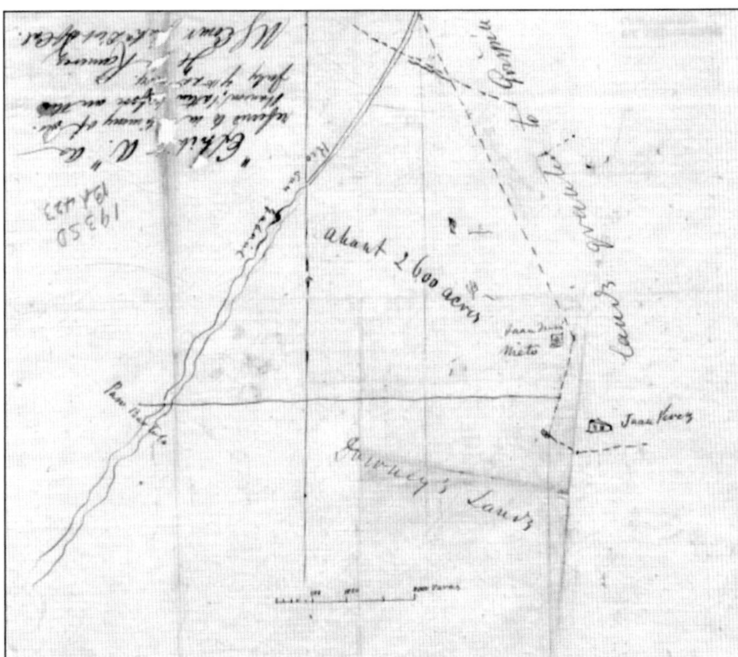

This 1864 map shows lands acquired by John Downey at the sheriff's auction of Lemuel Carpenter's ranch. By the time of the auction, Carpenter had already sold a large portion of his ranch. He sold the eastern portion to Jose Maria Ramirez and the western portion to Sheriff James Barton. (Courtesy the Bancroft Library, UC Berkeley.)

Two

EARLY COMMUNITIES

The cattle industry suffered a devastating blow during the 1860s. In 1862, the Los Angeles basin experienced so much rain that major flooding occurred, causing the San Gabriel River to cut a new course to the Pacific Ocean. Flooding was followed by a decade long drought, giving the knockout blow to the cattle industry. This was not the end of the area's economy, but the beginning.

With the subdivision of the land by Rancho Santa Gertrudes Land Company, the area began to take on a new look. Newly available land attracted people from all parts of the country looking for land of their own. It was not long before families were moving in and farms were springing up everywhere. The community of Los Nietos, which had been established earlier around the Nieto Ranch, was now becoming quite sizeable.

Nearing the end of the 19th century, a new community began to develop around the intersection of Telegraph Road and Norwalk Boulevard. A Banning Stagecoach stop at the intersection made the area even more desirable. With the stagecoach stop came a US mail drop in the small market. It is unknown whether the stagecoach stop attracted the market or vice versa. As time passed, this community came to be known by several different names, such as Fulton Wells, Iron Sulphur Springs, and Santa Fe Warm Mineral Springs. Finally, when the Achtison, Topeka & Santa Fe (AT&SF) Railroad put a train stop nearby, it became known as Santa Fe Springs.

In the early 1920s, a small Mexican American community was being established around the ruins of the Nieto family compound. It was a quiet, secluded area nestled between the railroad tracks to the north, the river to the west, and orange groves to the east and south. Some of them chose the area because of the fertile soil, evidenced by the healthy fields of corn and groves of walnut trees. The residents of this community, which came to be known as Flood Ranch, did not have much to start with, but they were able to build themselves comfortable homes out of virtually any materials they could find. Over time, the people of these three communities became close knit with strong ties to each other.

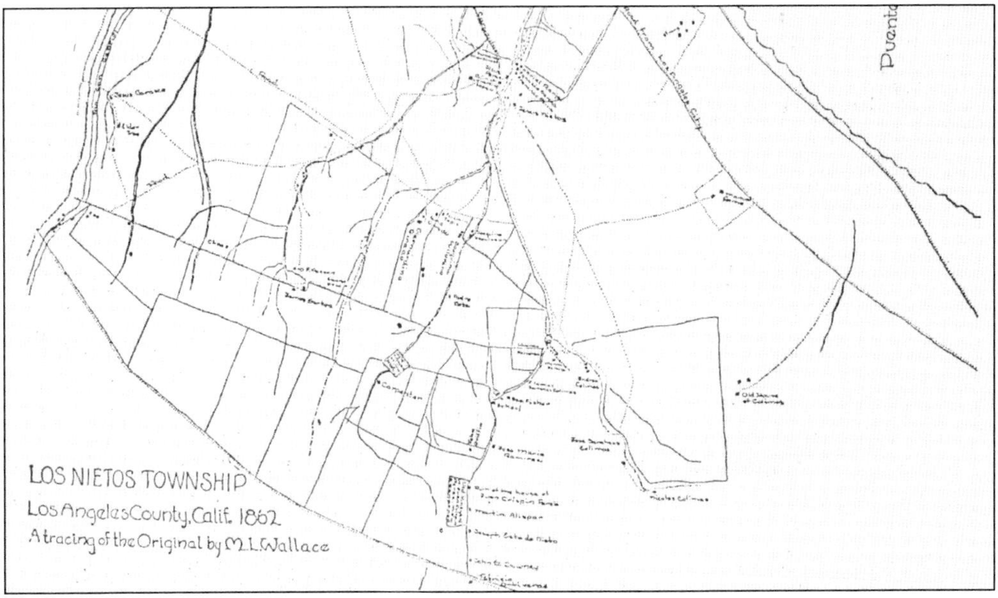

This 1862 map of the Los Nietos Township shows the changing face of Rancho Santa Gertrudes. By this time approximately 40 families were living in the township. The Carpenter Adobe is labeled with its vineyards just north of it. Also marked are the locations of the original Los Nietos School and the ruins of the Juan Perez Adobe and his old vineyards. John Downey's house is identified at the bottom of Norwalk, near Telegraph Road, the horizontal line at the bottom of the map. Just below Downey's place is the Ontiveros Adobe. The current course of the San Gabriel River differs from its mapped course in 1862, when it was only a creek shown running north and south in the middle of the map and was used mainly as an irrigation ditch. (Courtesy SFS Archives.)

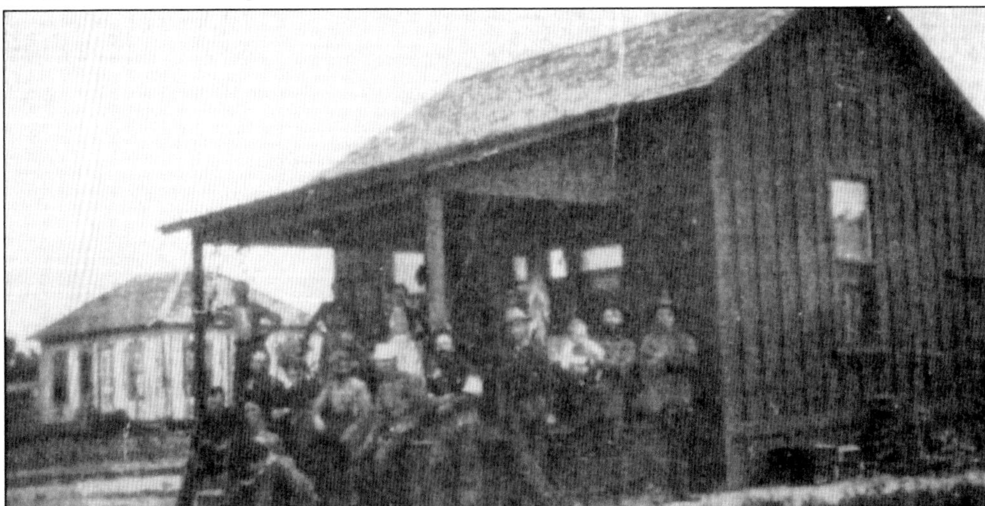

In the 1860s, more families began moving into the Los Nietos community. To help provide some of their needs, Bernardino Guirado (not to be confused with his uncle Bernardino Guirado, who purchased the Perez property in 1843) opened a store on the southern end of the township. The store was located on Carpenter Lane, now Los Nietos Road. The house in the back was sold to Reginaldo and Leonora Poyorena for $200. They moved the house in 1905 to its present location on Pasadena Street in Whittier. (Courtesy Whittier Historical Society, Whittier Museum.)

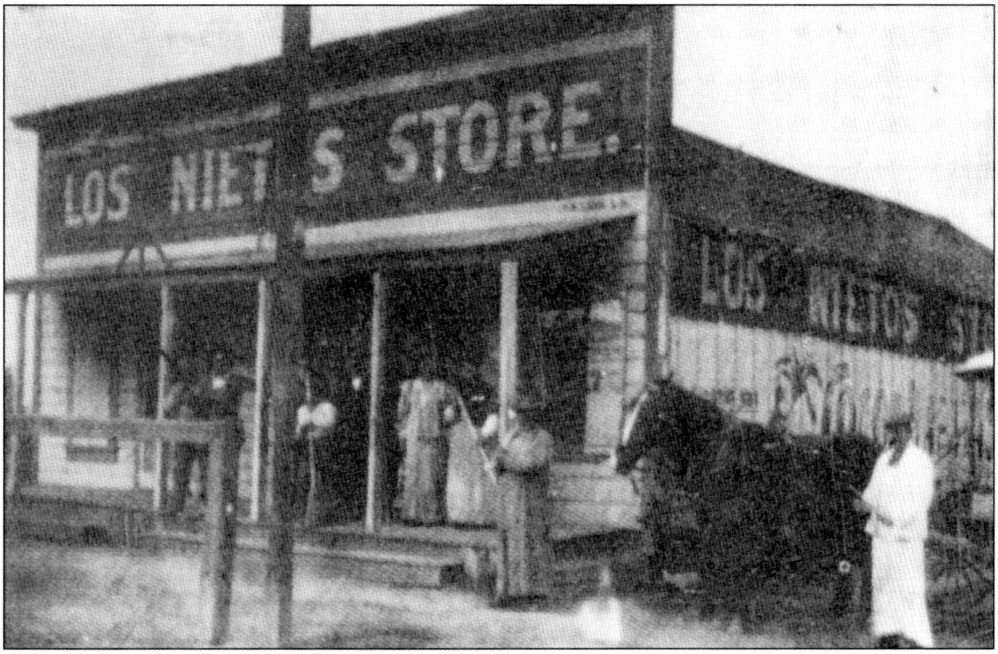

There were several small stores in the Los Nietos area. This store opened on Norwalk Boulevard in the early 1900s and was operated by Samuel Perkins and his wife, Grace. Perkins's father, James, came to Los Nietos in 1852. Samuel apprenticed and became a blacksmith. In 1924, Grace became the postmaster of Los Nietos. (Courtesy Whittier Historical Society, Whittier Museum.)

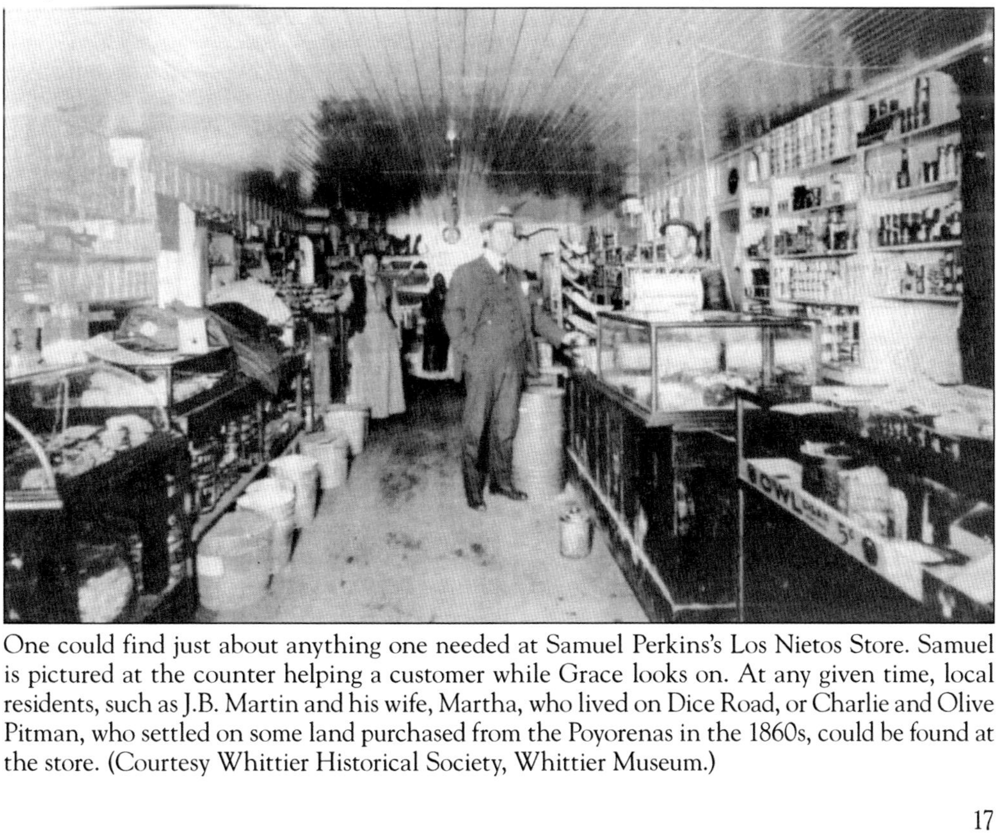

One could find just about anything one needed at Samuel Perkins's Los Nietos Store. Samuel is pictured at the counter helping a customer while Grace looks on. At any given time, local residents, such as J.B. Martin and his wife, Martha, who lived on Dice Road, or Charlie and Olive Pitman, who settled on some land purchased from the Poyorenas in the 1860s, could be found at the store. (Courtesy Whittier Historical Society, Whittier Museum.)

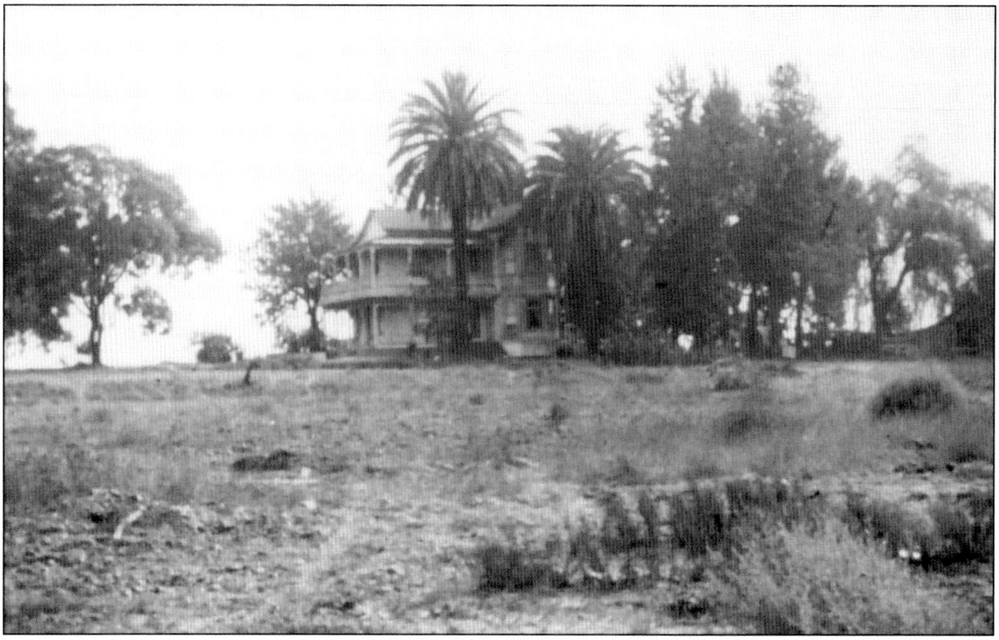

Storekeeper Bernardino Guirado built this two-story, Victorian-style house on Los Nietos Road west of Norwalk Boulevard in 1885 for his second wife, Maria de la Luz Sanchez. She was born in 1861 to Juan and Luisa Sanchez. Maria and Bernardino married in 1881, and their daughter Margarita Guirado was born on November 29, 1884. Guirado married his first wife, Edwarda Poyorena, on January 20, 1870. There is no record of any children or why his first marriage ended.

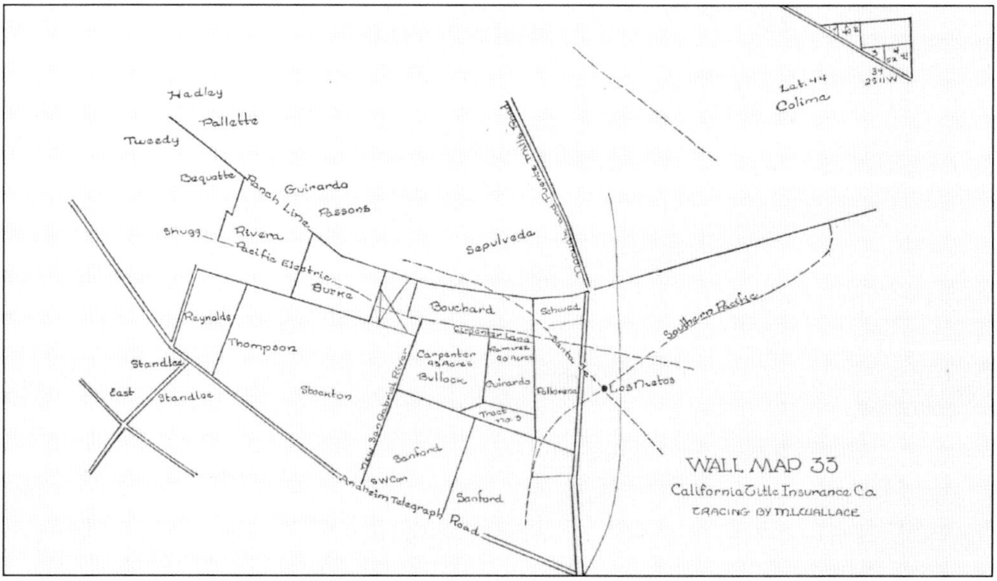

This c. 1895 map shows the land subdivided by the Santa Gertrudes Land Company. It was divided into many smaller parcels. The 93 Carpenter acres was later called Flood Ranch; the Ramirez and Guirado property is to the east; the Pollorena or Poyorena property is to the west of Norwalk Boulevard, south of Carpenter Lane (now Los Nietos Road); and to the south of these properties from Norwalk Boulevard to the San Gabriel River is the Sanford Ranch. To the west of the New San Gabriel River are many parcels with familiar names.

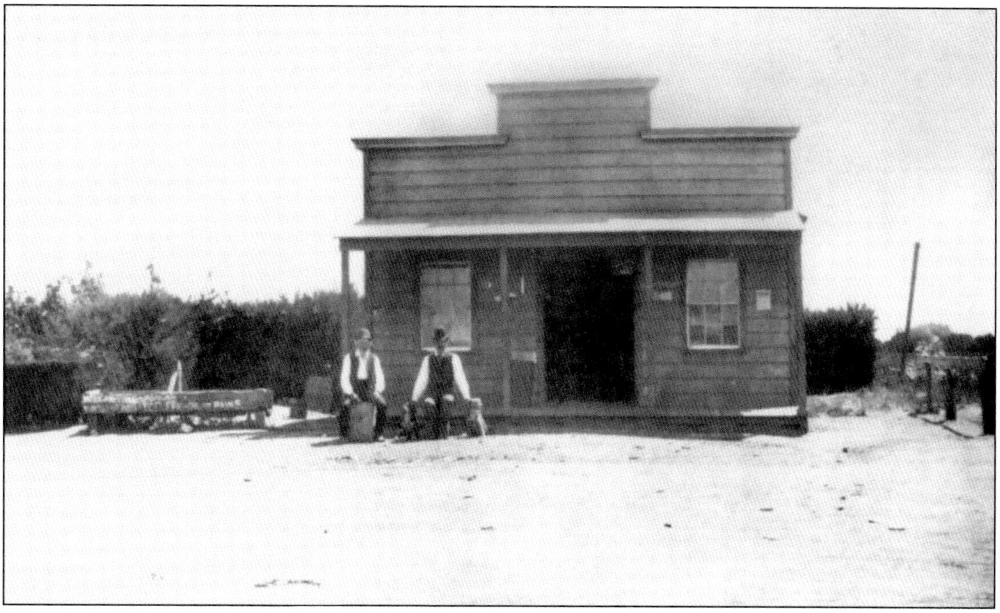

Martin and Maryann (born Kitterman) Koontz came to California by way of covered wagon and purchased one acre of land on the corner of what is now Telegraph Road and Norwalk Boulevard. A Banning Stagecoach stop came with the property, and it was there that they opened the Koontz Store. Sitting in front of the store in 1868 is Martin Koontz on the left with his son William.

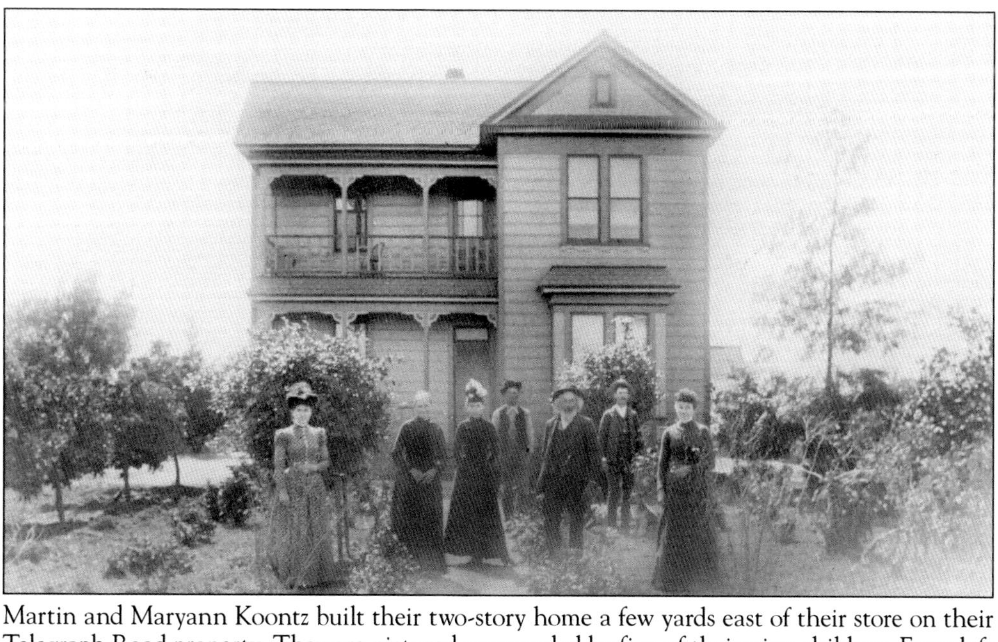

Martin and Maryann Koontz built their two-story home a few yards east of their store on their Telegraph Road property. They are pictured surrounded by five of their nine children. From left to right are Emma, Maryann, unidentified daughter and son, Martin, William, and Jennie. The family lived in this home until the mid-1920s, when the fires, smells, and noise created by the oil boom forced them out.

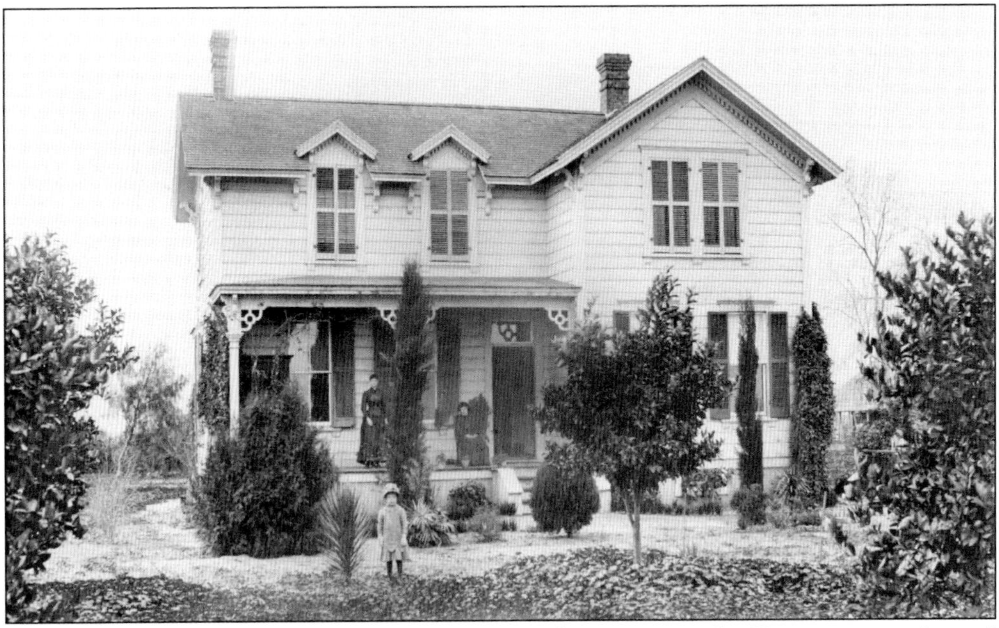

The Bakers came to Four Corners in 1867—about the same time the Koontzes arrived—and bought property on Little Lake Road, down the street from the Koontzes. They eventually built a two-story wood-frame house. Sitting on the porch is Elizabeth Baker, and to her right is daughter Mary. Standing in the front yard is Elizabeth's granddaughter Hattie Surbeck, daughter of Harriet and Bill Surbeck.

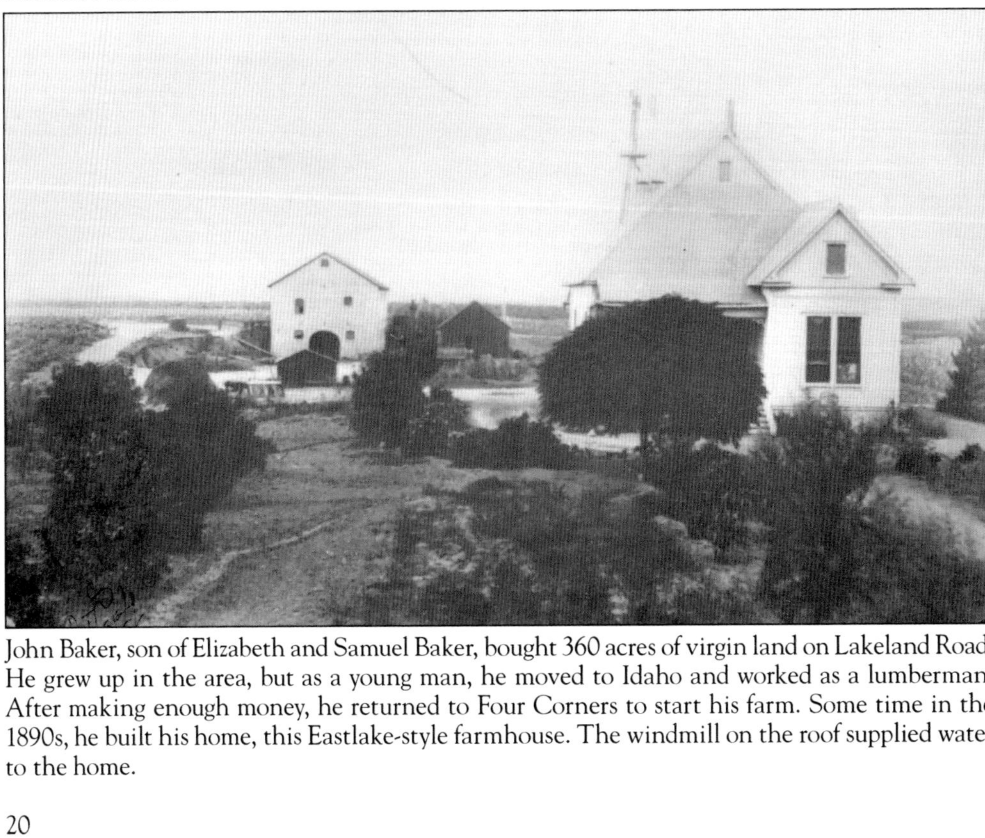

John Baker, son of Elizabeth and Samuel Baker, bought 360 acres of virgin land on Lakeland Road. He grew up in the area, but as a young man, he moved to Idaho and worked as a lumberman. After making enough money, he returned to Four Corners to start his farm. Some time in the 1890s, he built his home, this Eastlake-style farmhouse. The windmill on the roof supplied water to the home.

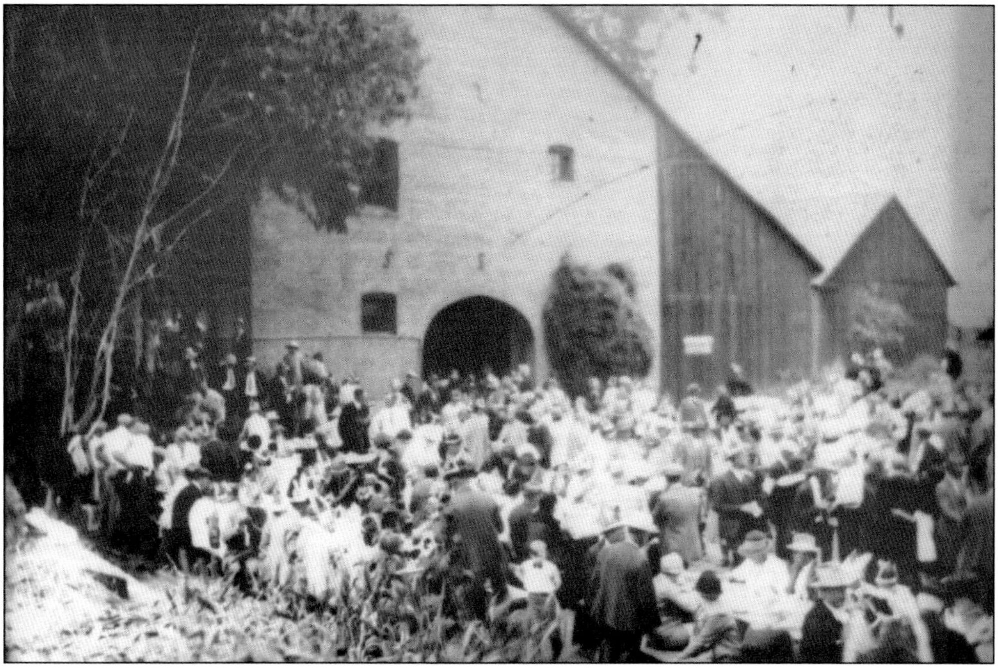

Not only did John Baker cultivate his walnut orchards, he also planted a vineyard and operated a winery. His winery became the venue of many community social events, as seen here. He became so successful that in the 1920s he founded the Norwalk Commercial and Savings Bank and became its major stockholder. He was one of the most prosperous people in Santa Fe Springs during the early 1900s.

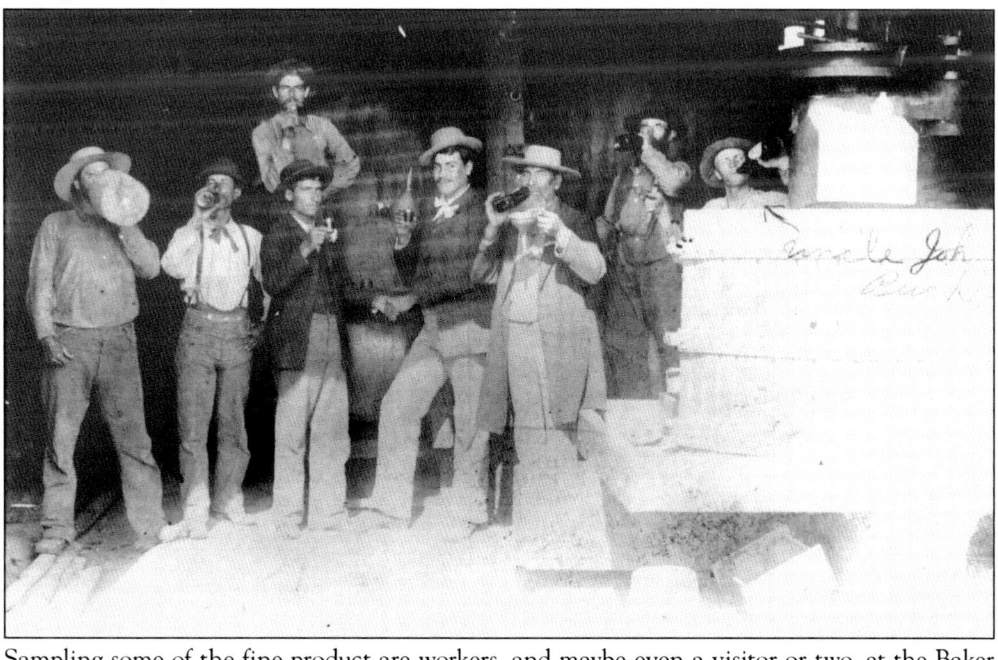

Sampling some of the fine product are workers, and maybe even a visitor or two, at the Baker Winery in this 1912 photograph. The winery was a well-known landmark in Santa Fe Springs for many decades. John Baker's daughter Leona Baker Meyer lived in the area up until the 1950s.

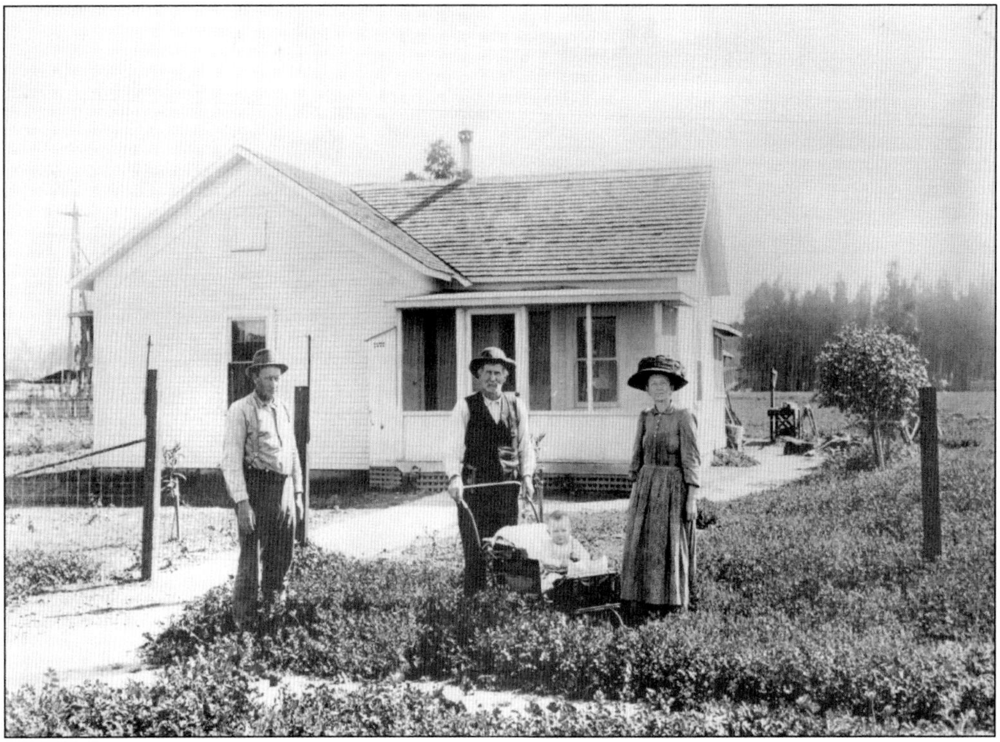

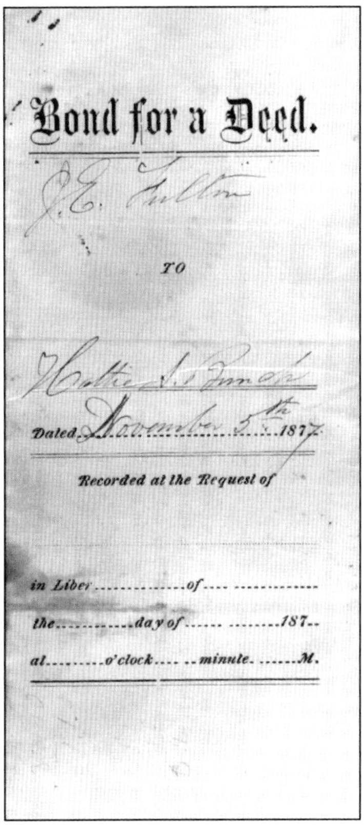

Bond for a Deed.

J.E. Fulton

TO

Hattie S. Finch

Dated November 5th 1877

Recorded at the Request of

in Liber ....of.... ....

the............day of...... ....187..

at.........o'clock..... ..minute. ....M.

The modest house pictured was the home of the Eagle family. This 1918 photograph shows Roy Eagle Sr. pushing a buggy carrying baby Roy D., and Ida Eagle is in the fancy hat. Also pictured is Roy Sr.'s brother. The Eagles held the mortgage to the Alexander ranch, located just north of Telegraph Road and east of Norwalk Boulevard, which was the location of a large oil strike in the 1920s.

In 1874, J.E. Fulton owned several hundred acres of land in the Four Corners area. One day, while drilling for water, he discovered a sulfur spring. To finance his plans to build a health resort around the spring, he began selling off portions of his property. One such sale is evidenced here in this bond for deed document from J.E. Fulton to who appears to be Hattie S. Finch, dated November 5, 1877. (Courtesy SFS Archives.)

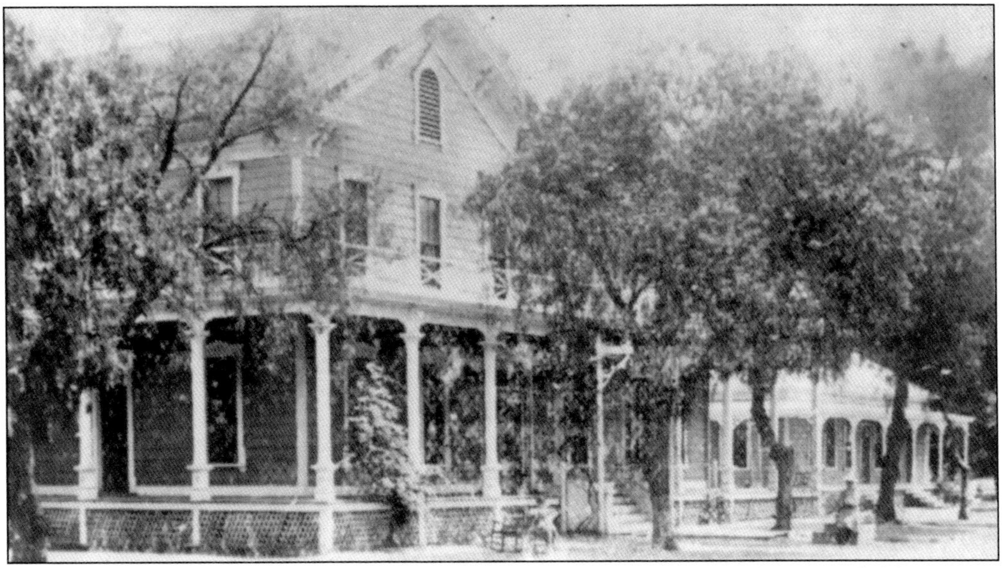

By the early 1880s, J.E. Fulton's health resort boasted a two-story hotel surrounded by private bungalows that each had indoor sulfur pools. The hotel had gas lights, ladies' parlors, billiard rooms, reading rooms, and lavish gardens. Tourists came from all over California and the nation seeking the curative powers of the mineral waters. The Southern Pacific Railroad named its nearby train stop Fulton Wells after Doctor Fulton's health resort. (Courtesy SFS Archives.)

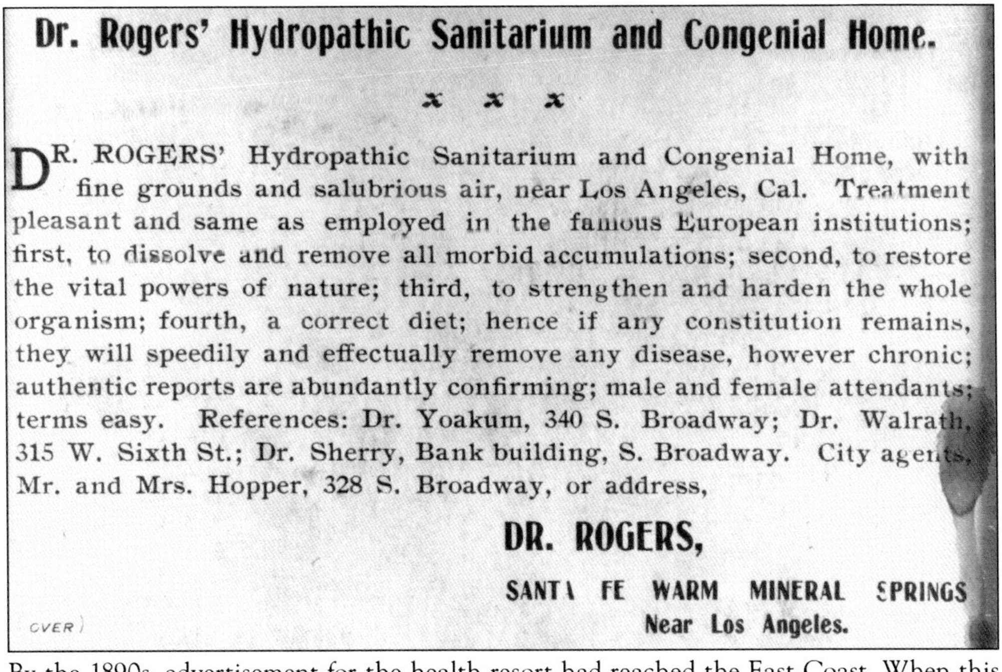

By the 1890s, advertisement for the health resort had reached the East Coast. When this advertisement came out, it seems the resort was owned by a Doctor Rogers and was called "Dr. Rogers' Hydropathic Sanitarium and Congenial Home." The resort treated as many as 400 patients annually, with illnesses ranging from rheumatism to liver trouble and skin diseases. The advertisement compared the treatments to those of the famous European institutions. (Courtesy SFS Archives.)

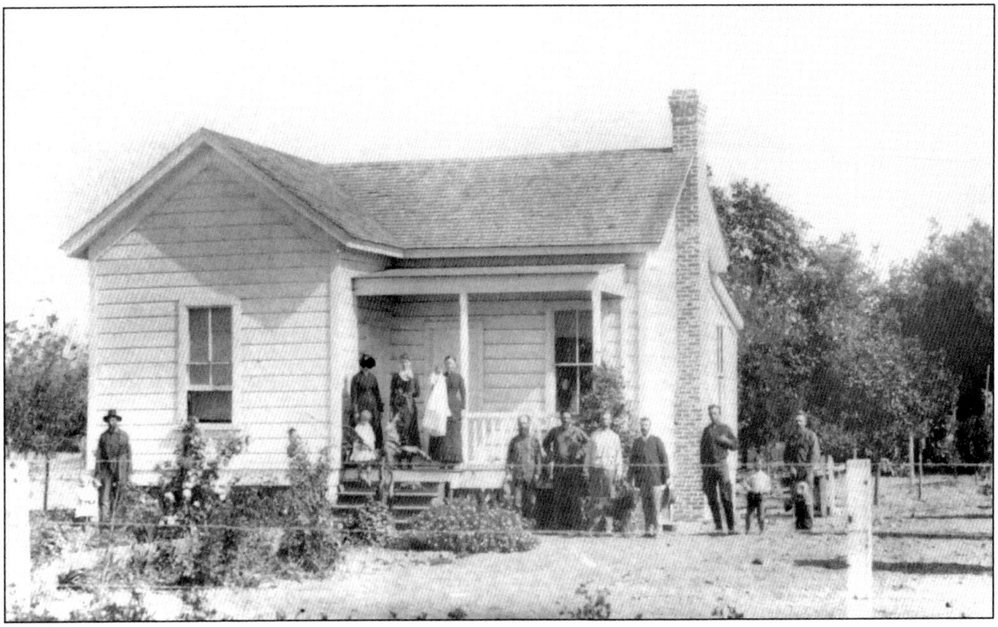

In this 1885 photograph, the Miller family is seen standing in front of their shiplap-style home, common in the area in the late 1800s. The back of the photograph identifies Francis Haddock on the porch holding Nellie. At the far left is Mr. Miller, and the little girl next to him is Bessie Miller Koontz. The home was located where the Paradise Memorial Park cemetery is now.

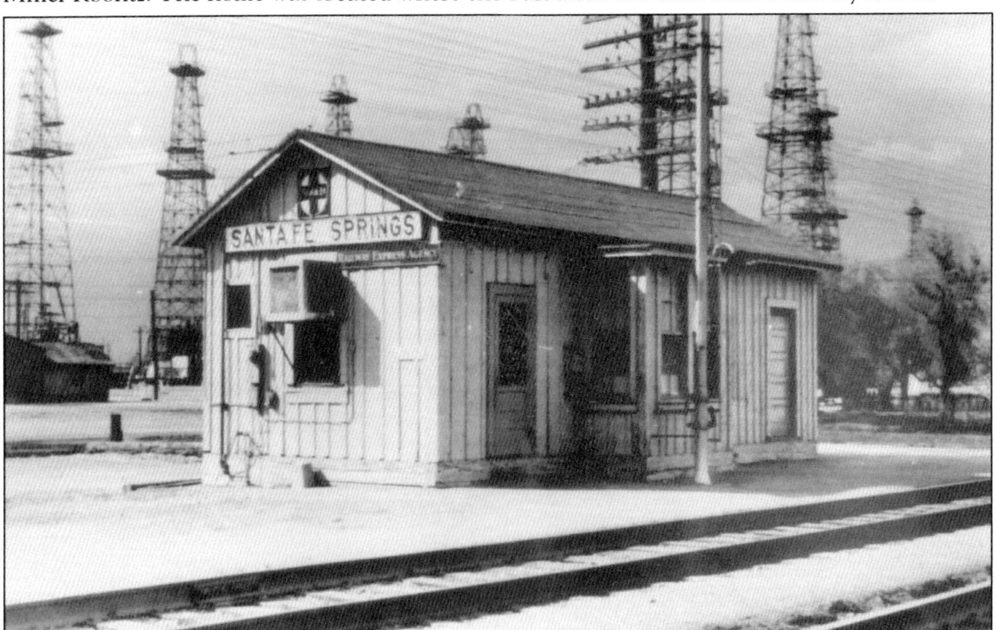

The railroad expanded to the West Coast and California, making travel safer and less expensive. People came from the east and south looking for good, inexpensive land, and they found it in Santa Fe Springs. The Southern Pacific Railroad came through the area in 1876 and built the Fulton Wells depot. The AT&SF came through in 1886 and named its depot Santa Fe Springs, seen in this c. 1960 photograph. (Courtesy SFS Archives.)

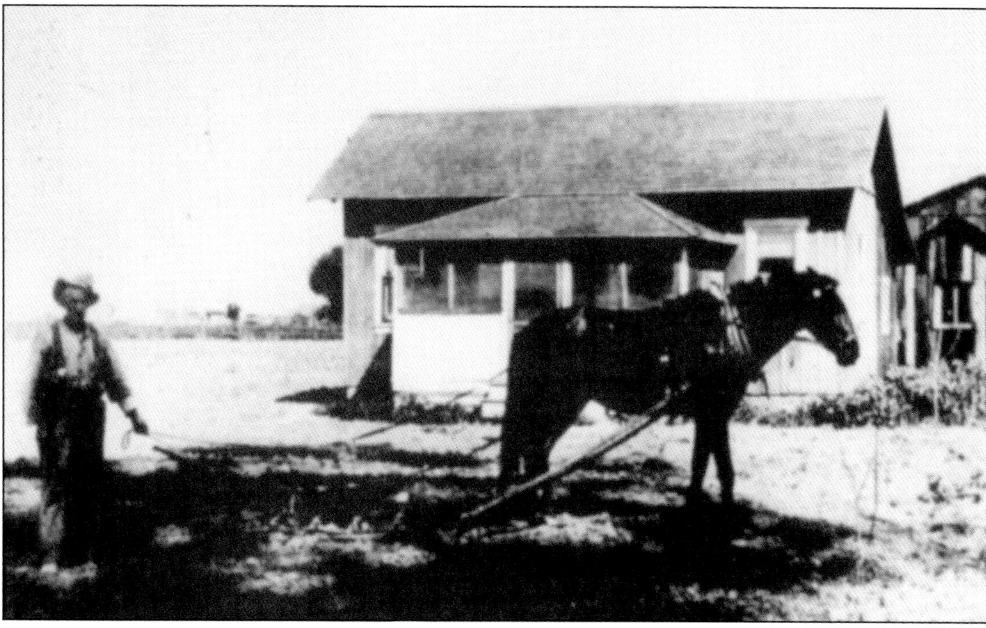

Franklin McCarric is pictured in front of his modest home on Doggett Avenue (now Bloomfield Avenue). He came to Four Corners in 1889 at the insistence of the Koontzes so that his two daughters could be raised by their maternal grandparents, aunts, and uncles. McCarric felt he could not raise his daughters by himself after his wife, Sarah Isabelle Koontz, along with their baby and young son died.

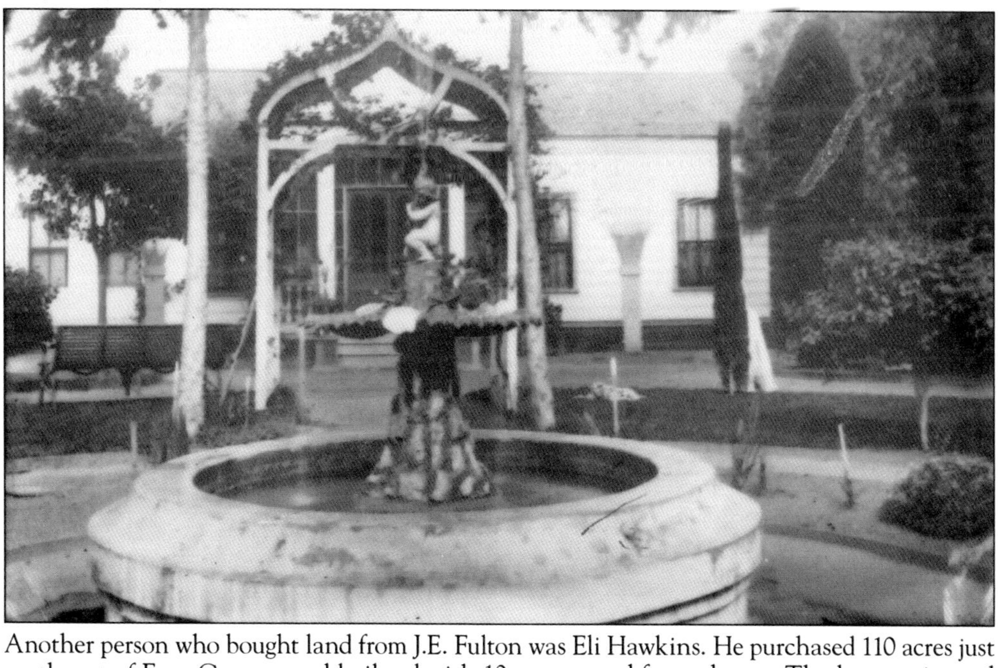

Another person who bought land from J.E. Fulton was Eli Hawkins. He purchased 110 acres just southwest of Four Corners and built a lavish 10-room wood-frame house. The house, pictured behind the fountain, boasted indoor plumbing and a basement. In 1878, he moved in with his wife, Mary, and their four young children: Edward, age 11; Effie, age 8; Eli W. Jr., age 2; and Alice, 10 months old. (Courtesy Nimocks Family Collection.)

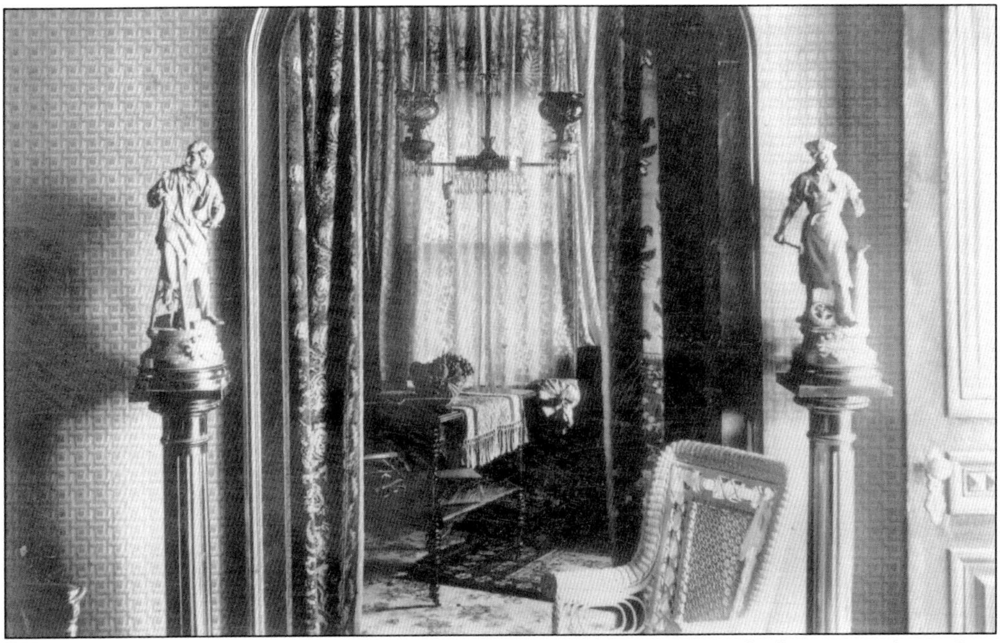

Shortly after moving in, baby Alice died; heartbroken, Eli's wife, Mary, died two years later. One year after burying Mary, Eli married a woman by the name of Susie. Two years later, Eli died on June 30, 1883, at the age of 50. It is not known if Susie had any children of her own or if she continued to raise Eli's children. (Courtesy Nimocks Family Collection.)

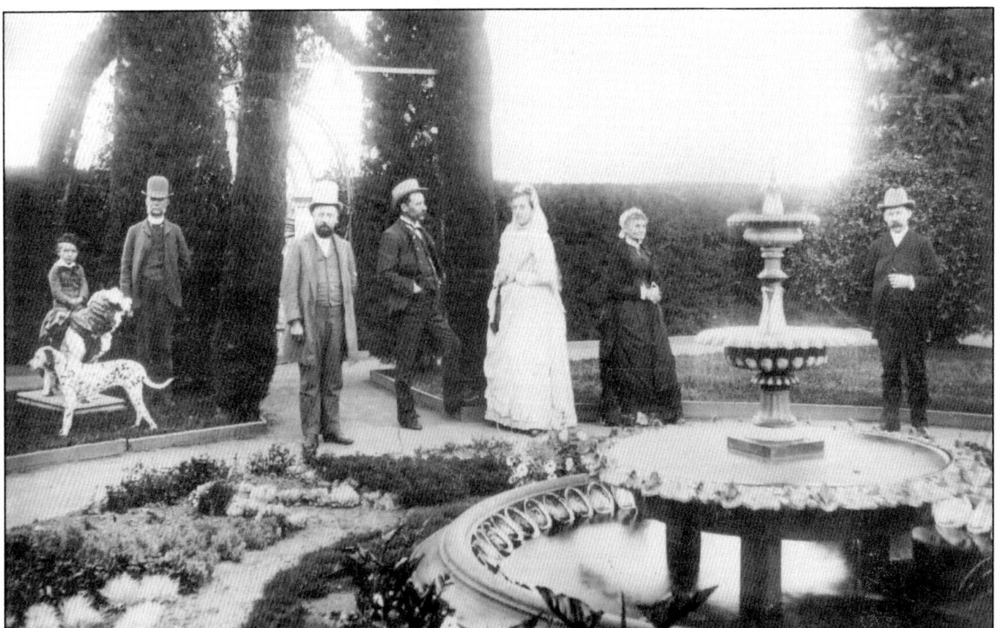

Susie and the Hawkins children lived on the estate for only a few more years. In 1886, the estate was sold to Martha and Walter Nimocks. After moving in, they made lavish improvements to the property. This c. 1890 photograph shows Walter and Martha standing in the formal garden they created, accompanied by family or friends. The garden was created with what were at the time rare and imported plants. (Courtesy Nimocks Family Collection.)

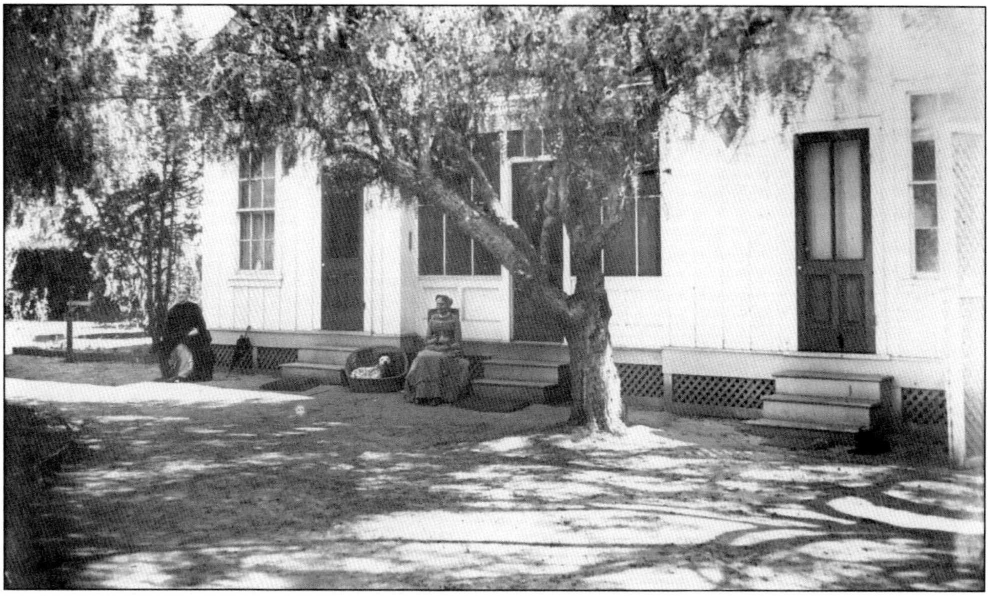

Walter was the publisher of the *Farmers Union* and the *Minneapolis Journal.* Martha was the grandniece on her mother's side of Stonewall Jackson. Befitting their status in society, one of the many improvements to the estate was to add on a servants' wing, which increased the size of the house by several hundred square feet. The Nimockses enjoyed collecting exotic plants from all over the world. (Courtesy Nimocks Family Collection.)

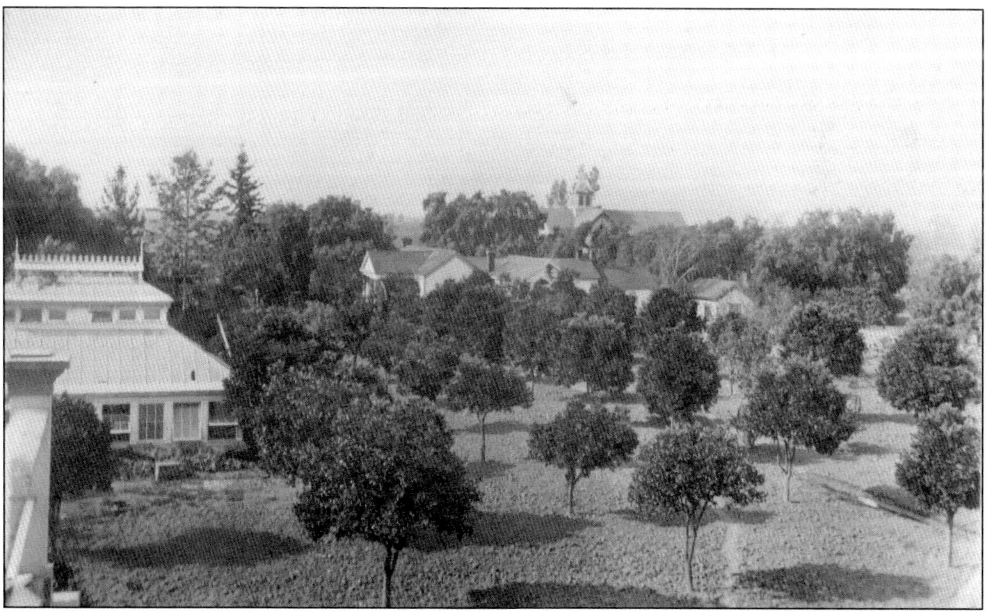

The Nimockses built a conservatory, or greenhouse, visible in the far left of this c. 1890 photograph. The conservatory provided an ideal environment for the young seedlings they collected from all around the world. The beautiful formal gardens became the showplace of the county, with people coming from all over to see them. (Courtesy Nimocks Family Collection.)

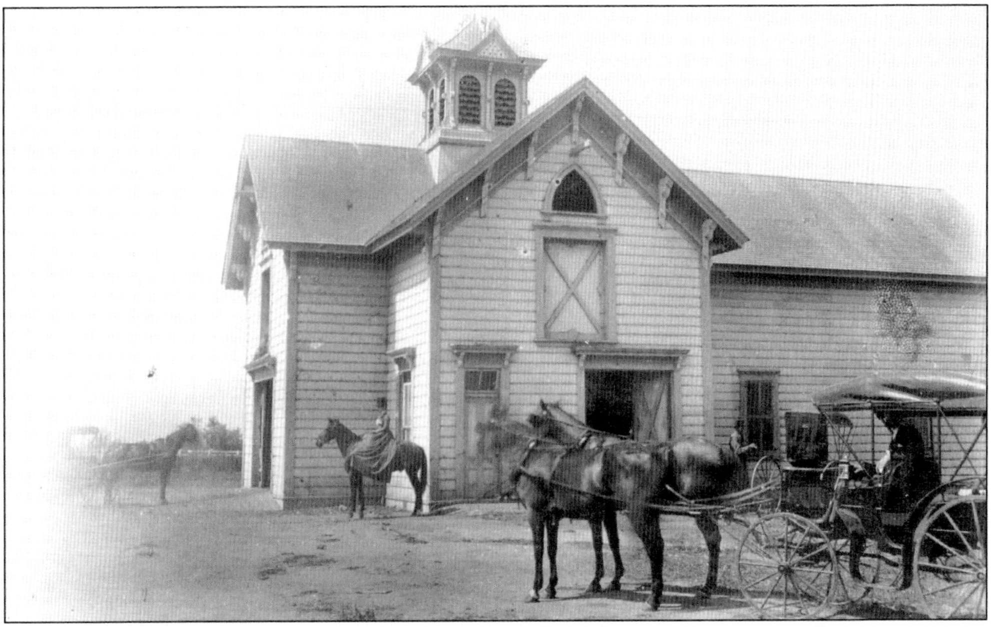

Another improvement to the new Nimocks estate was the construction of an expensive Carpenter Gothic–style carriage barn. It cost $5,000 to build, making it the most expensive barn of its day in Los Angeles County. The barn housed the family's carriages and the horses that pulled them and even had a place for a caretaker. In this 1890 photograph, the Nimocks family is preparing to leave for the day. (Courtesy Nimocks Family Collection.)

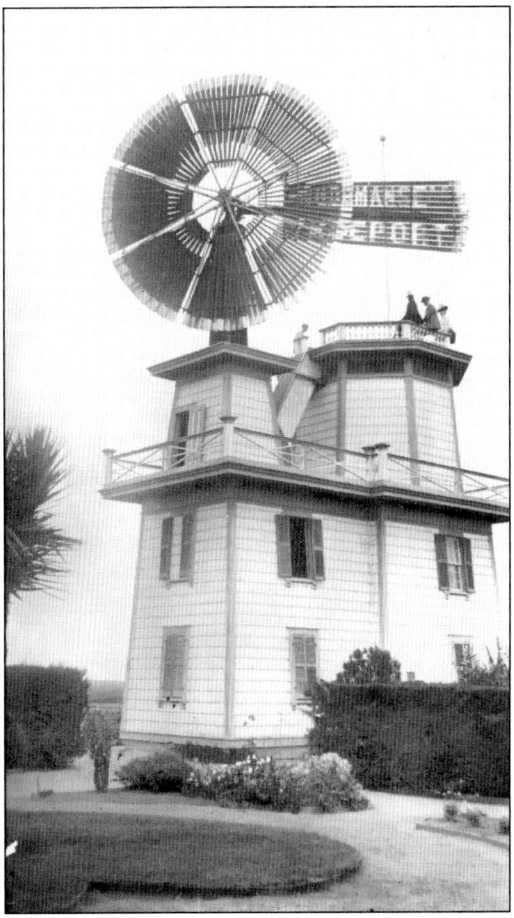

The Nimockses also made improvements to the nearby windmill. Walter had a structure built to enclose the windmill machinery and water tank. He also had a lookout platform built on top of the tank house, as seen in this photograph. It was a favorite place for guests to get a breathtaking view of the valley. The water tank provided water to the house and gardens by way of underground pipes. (Courtesy Nimocks Family Collection.)

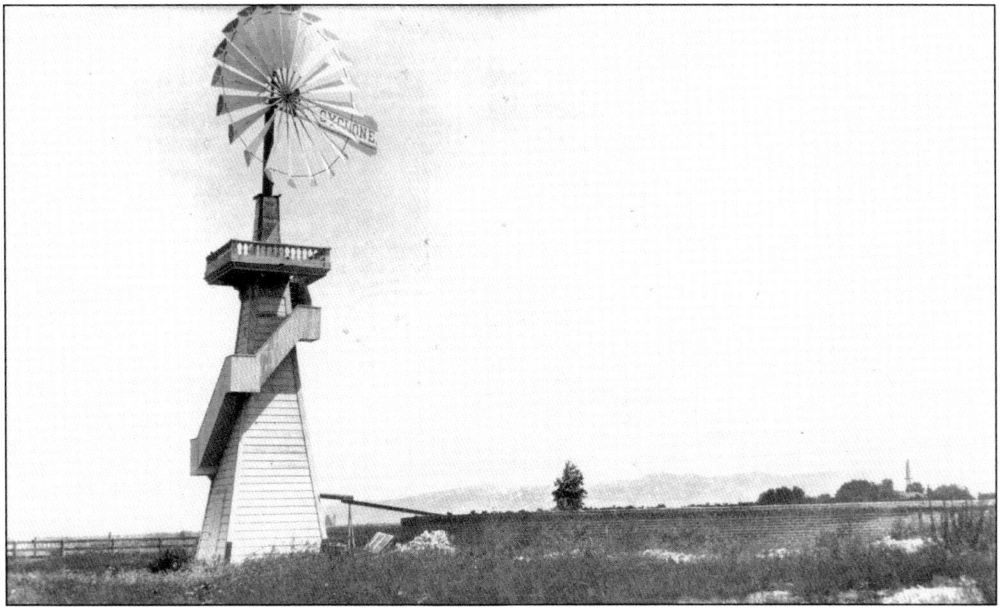

The Nimockses also had a water well and windmill constructed on the northeastern edge of their property. This well supplied water to an above-ground reservoir that provided water for the estate's agricultural needs. This windmill also had a viewing platform at its top. The reservoir could be seen in later photographs of the corner of Norwalk Boulevard and Telegraph Road at Four Corners. (Courtesy Nimocks Family Collection.)

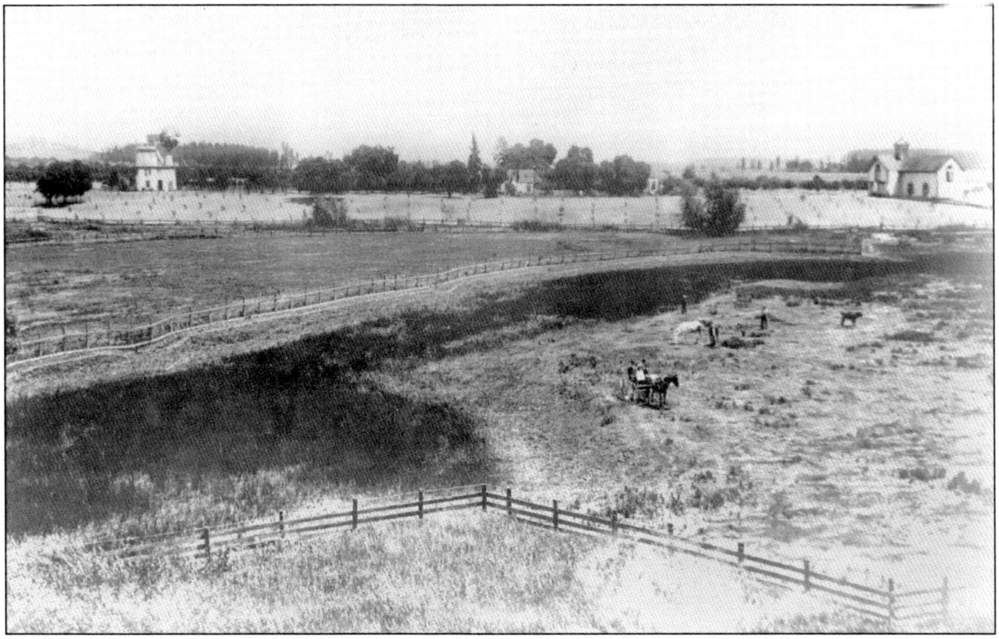

One of the main crops at the Nimocks farm was alfalfa, which provided a quick source of revenue for the estate. In this c. 1890 photograph, workers can be seen harvesting the crop. In the background, the carriage barn is on the right, the house is in the center, and the tank house is on the left. Their orange groves were behind the house and windmill. (Courtesy Nimocks Family Collection.)

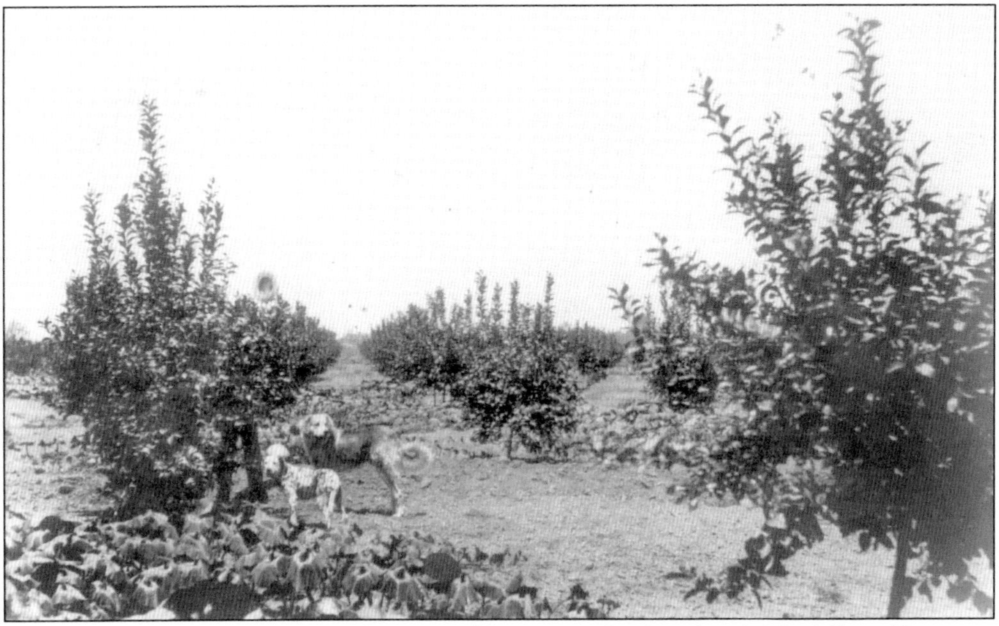

In the late 19th century, cattle ranches were all but gone. The drought of 1864, followed by severe flooding in the winter of 1867 and 1868, had dealt a heavy blow to the industry. As a result, agriculture had taken over as the main source of income for the people of Santa Fe Springs. One of the main crops grown in the area was citrus, and, since it grew well, almost every ranch had an orchard. (Courtesy Nimocks Family Collection.)

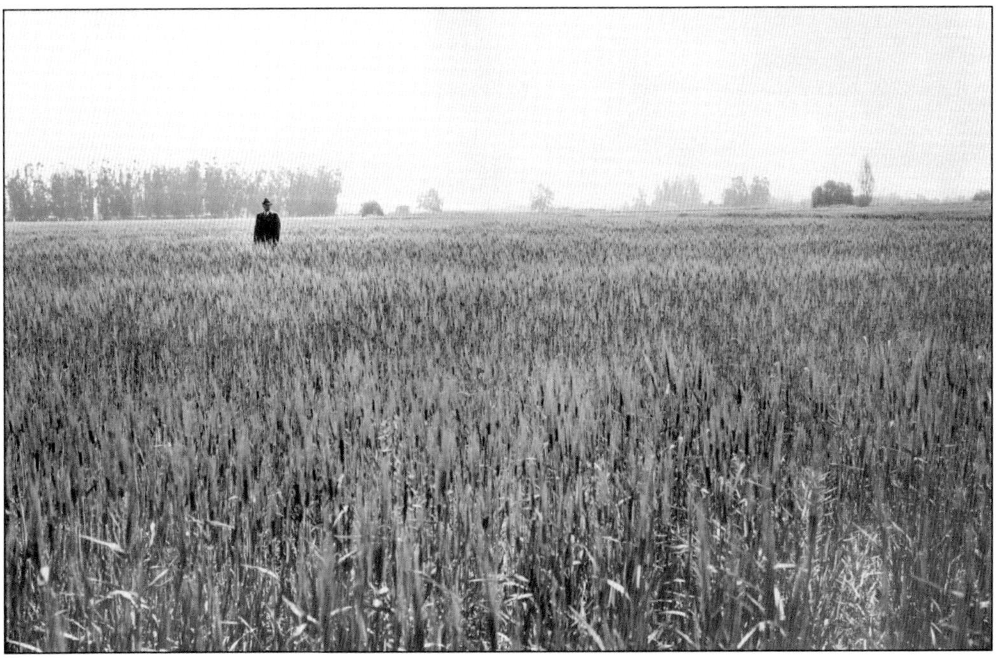

Citrus was not the only crop that flourished in the rich soil of Santa Fe Springs. Corn stalks grew tall and walnut trees were plentiful. Grains were another crop that was easy to grow in the area. Here, H.L. Emerson stands in the middle of a barley field located near the corner of Lakeland Road and Shamrock Road (now Pioneer Boulevard).

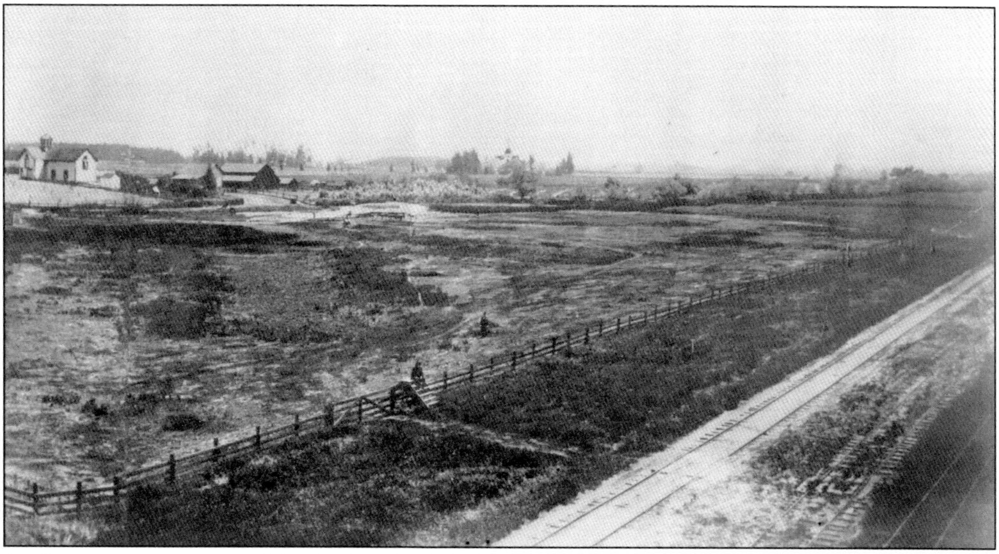

In this panoramic view of the back side of the Nimocks estate, ranch hands can be seen working on the field in the center of photograph. To the left is the carriage barn, and the utility barns are to the right. The photograph was most likely taken from the top of Southern Pacific's Fulton Wells Depot or the top of a local water tower. The tracks can be seen in the lower left-hand corner. (Courtesy Nimocks Family Collection.)

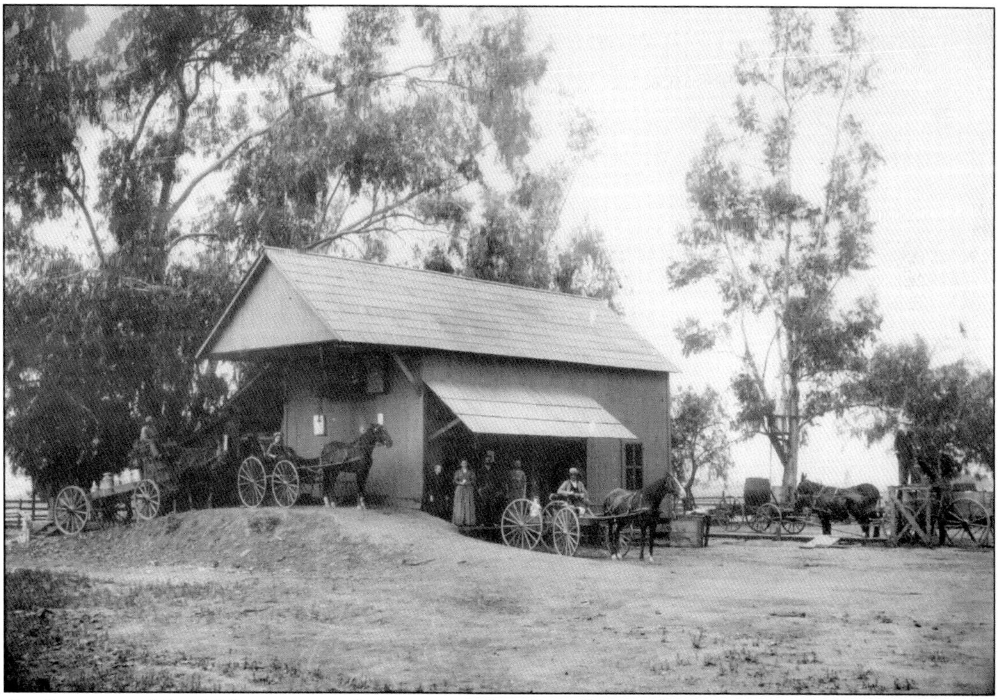

At the turn of the 20th century, there were only a few places where farmers could take the milk from their cows to be processed, and the O'Connell Buttery was one of the nearby ones. It was where local farmers took their milk to separate the cream to make into cheese and butter. The buttery was located on the southern end of the C.B. Woodhead Ranch on Pioneer Boulevard just south of Lakeland Road.

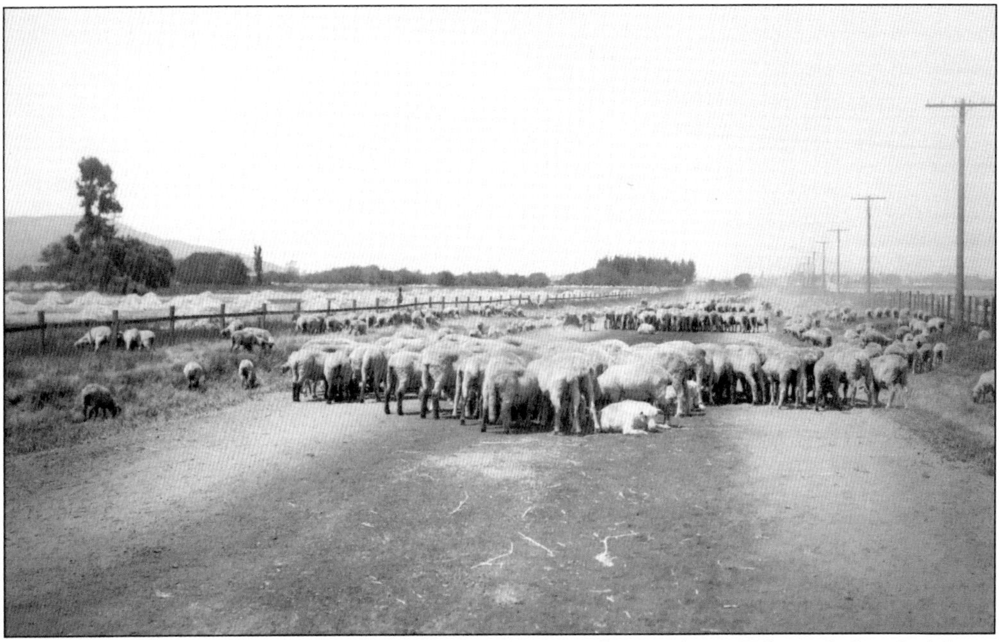

Large flocks of sheep were frequently seen traveling on the Anaheim-Telegraph Road. After a long day of grazing in the fields, Marius Meyer herds his sheep east of Four Corners back to the holding pens. They are pictured traveling leisurely eastward, grazing and stopping to rest along the way. Meyer immigrated to the United States with a few rams. He crossbred them with native sheep and produced better-quality wool than what was available in those days.

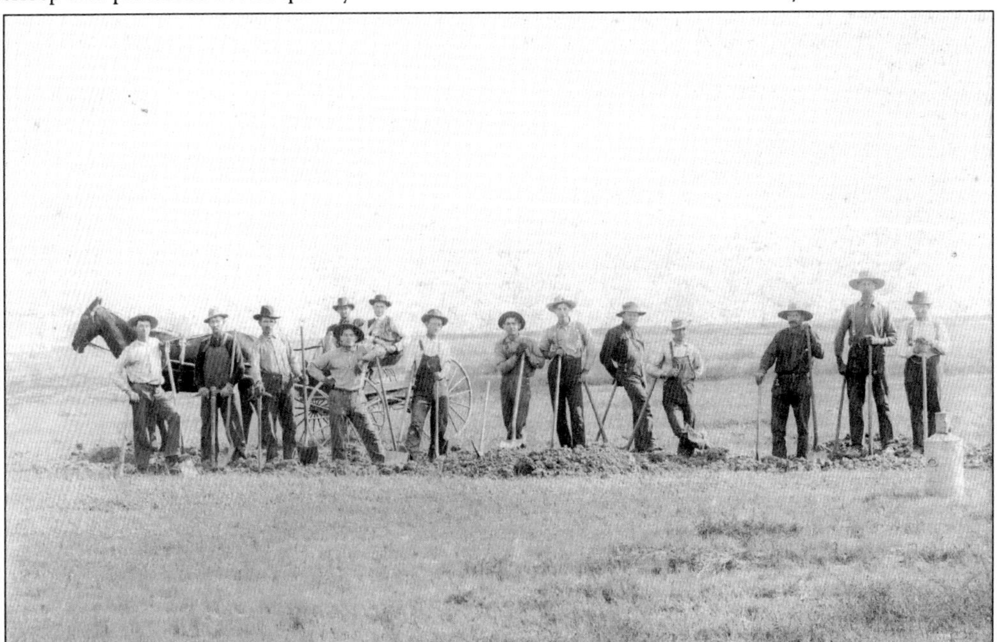

Not everyone worked in the farming industry. A crew of men digs what appears to be either an irrigation ditch or a trench, possibly to run underground pipe. The names of these men are not known, but it is known that this c. 1910 photograph was taken in the Santa Fe Springs area.

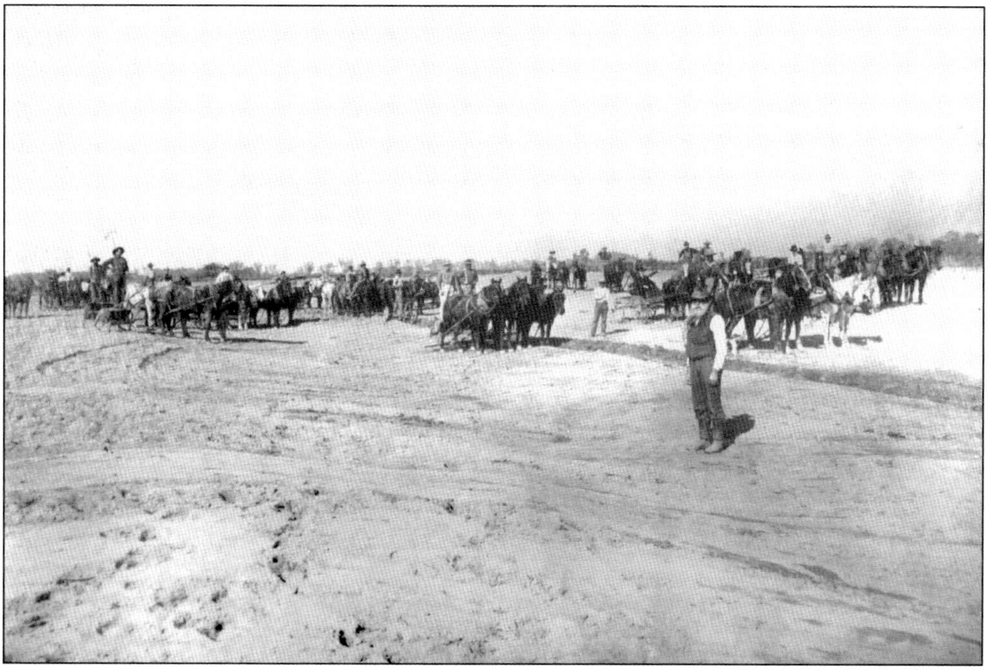

Towns to the south of Santa Fe Springs continually had problems with the new San Gabriel River flooding its banks during the rainy season. To alleviate the problem, Mr. Scott, a grocery store owner from Artesia, organized the local farmers and ranchers to cut a straighter channel to the sea. In this 1910 photograph, James Suelle (Sewell) leads teams of Fresno scrapers drawn by mules and horses into the riverbed near Florence Avenue.

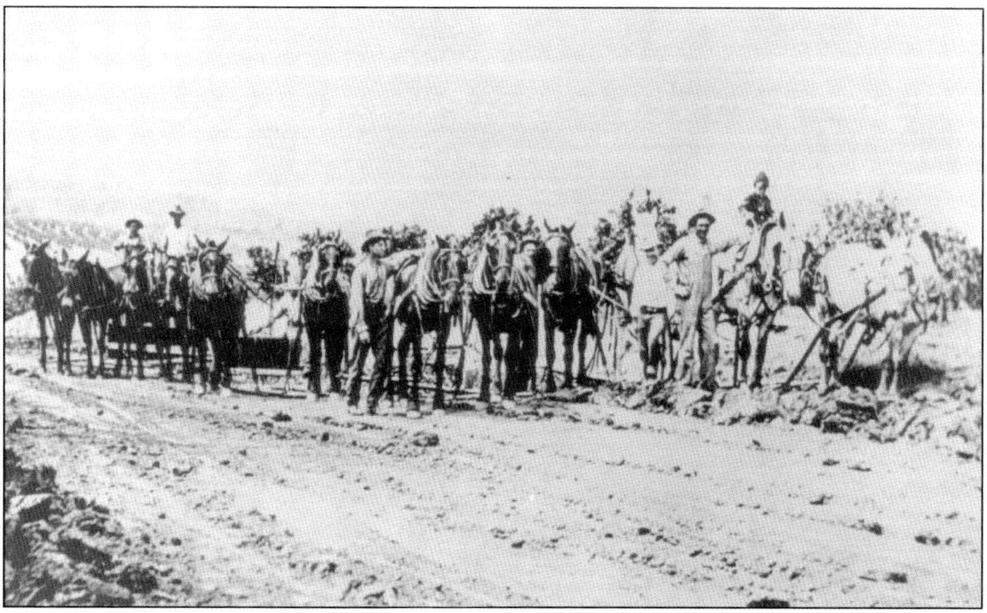

Heading east from the Santa Fe Railroad tracks, a road crew widens Telegraph Road in this 1915 photograph to facilitate safer and more comfortable automobile travel through the area. Some of the same scraper teams employed to cut the new San Gabriel River channel were put to work here five years later. (Courtesy Keene Collection.)

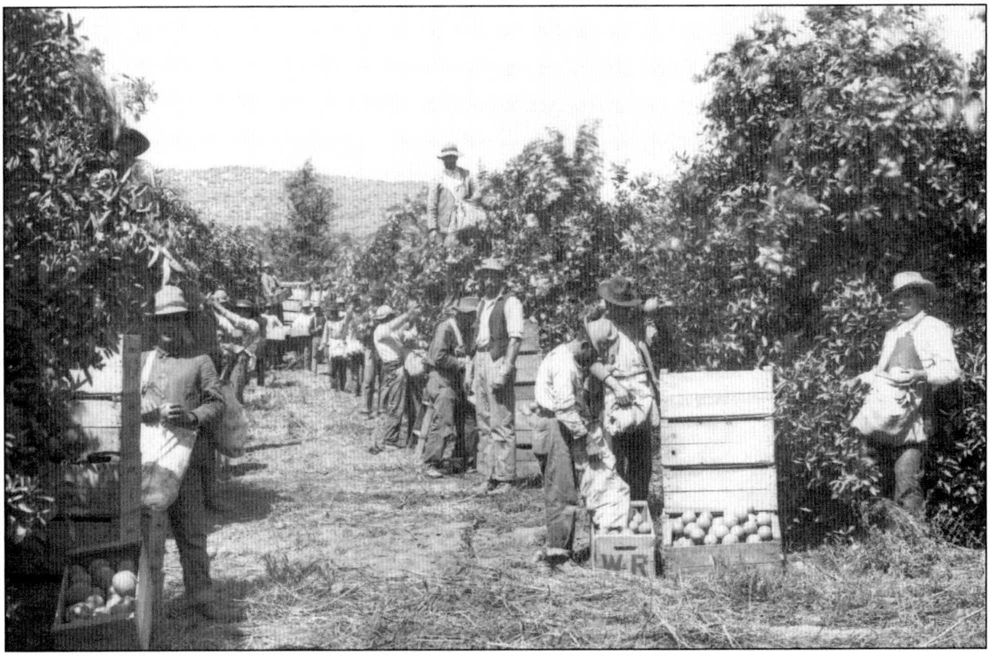

With agriculture being the principal industry, most of the workforce was employed by farm owners. The dominant crop of the region was citrus, mainly oranges. This c. 1920 photograph shows a large crew of men picking oranges at a local farm. Migratory crews were a common sight in the Santa Fe Springs area during the harvest season.

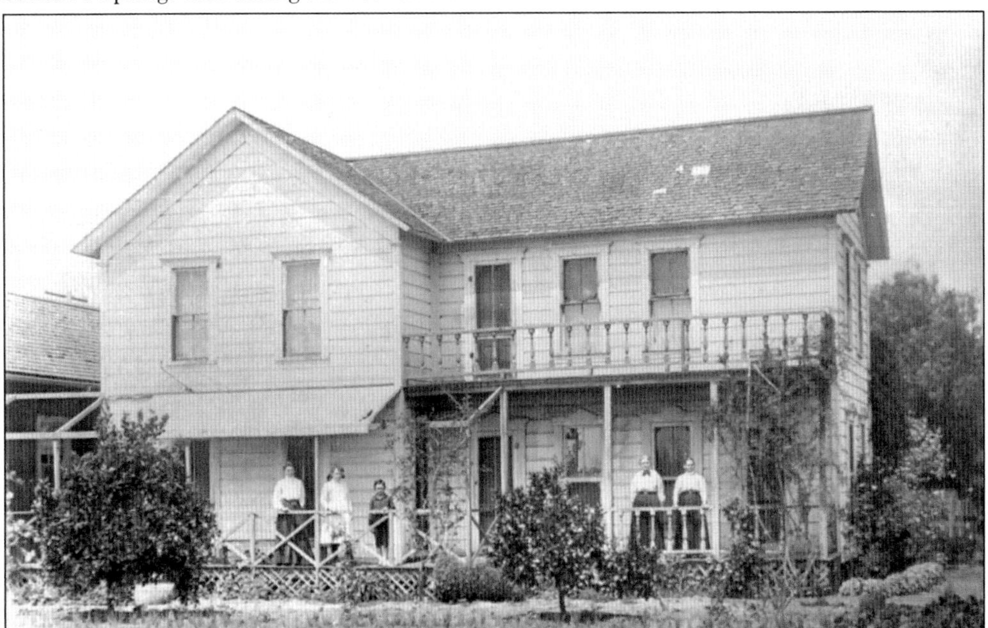

The Tiffany family was another longtime resident of Santa Fe Springs. They are pictured here on the porch of their home, which was located on Clark Avenue in the Four Corners area. In this c. 1918 photograph, Tellie Tiffany is at the far left with her two children, while the children's grandmother and aunt stand on the opposite end of the porch.

One of the first churches to be founded in Santa Fe Springs was the First Methodist Episcopal Church. Founded in 1886, it was located on Gardner Avenue just south of Telegraph Road in the Four Corners area. Inset in this c. 1911 photograph, on the left, is the first pastor, W.C. Cowan (1886), and on the right is the second pastor, R.H. Haddock (1911).

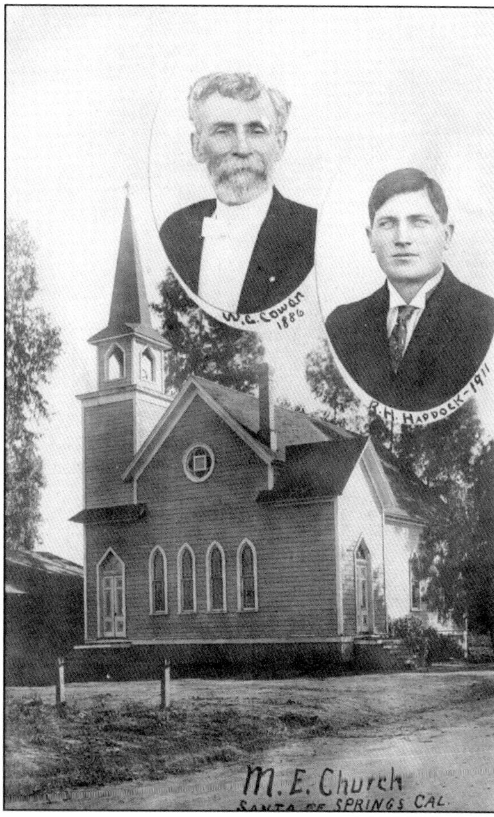

Many families from Santa Fe Springs attended the First Methodist Episcopal Church. In this 1911 photograph, they are celebrating the church's 25th anniversary. Pastor Cowan and his wife are standing in the center of the back row. Pastor Haddock is sitting in the front row, far left, with his wife and children. The original building, pictured here, burned down in 1924, but a new church was built on the same location.

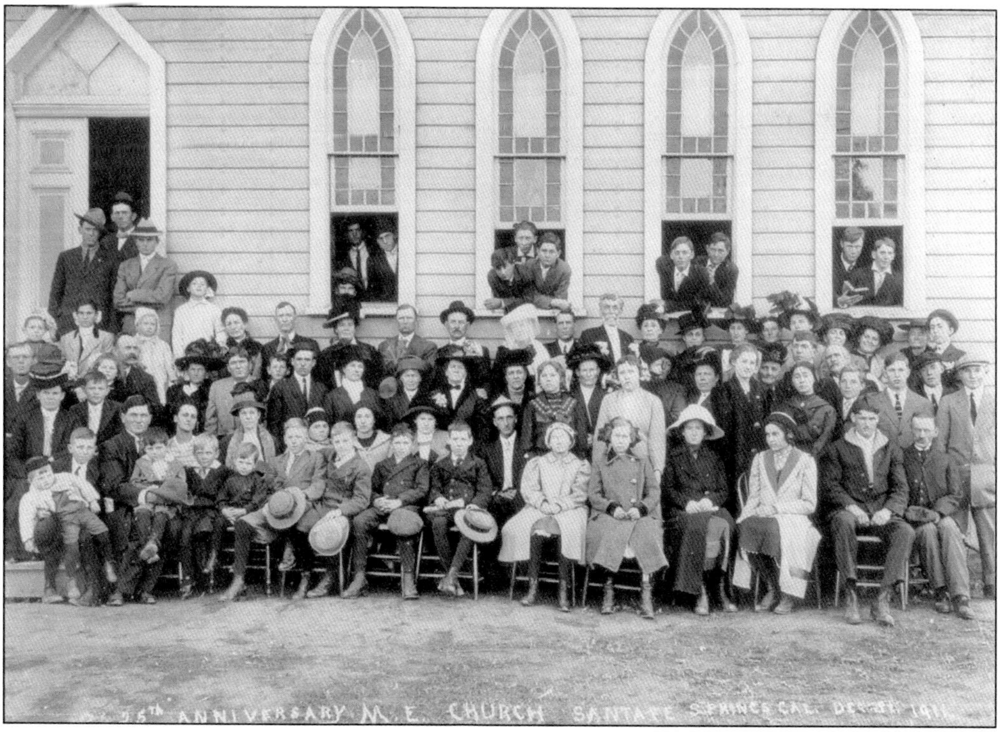

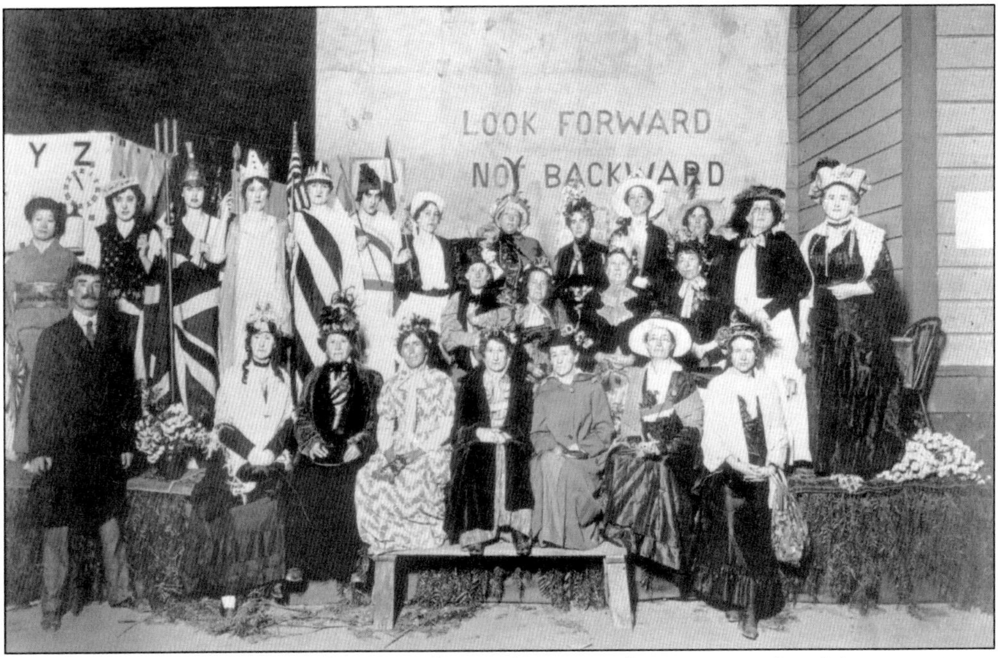

The Methodist church became the center for social events and community plays. Many prominent ladies of Santa Fe Springs, young and old, performed in the lighthearted 1919 play called *The Old Maid's Convention*. The play ended in a rousing patriotic pageant and the singing of the National Anthem. Emma Koontz is in the back row on the far right.

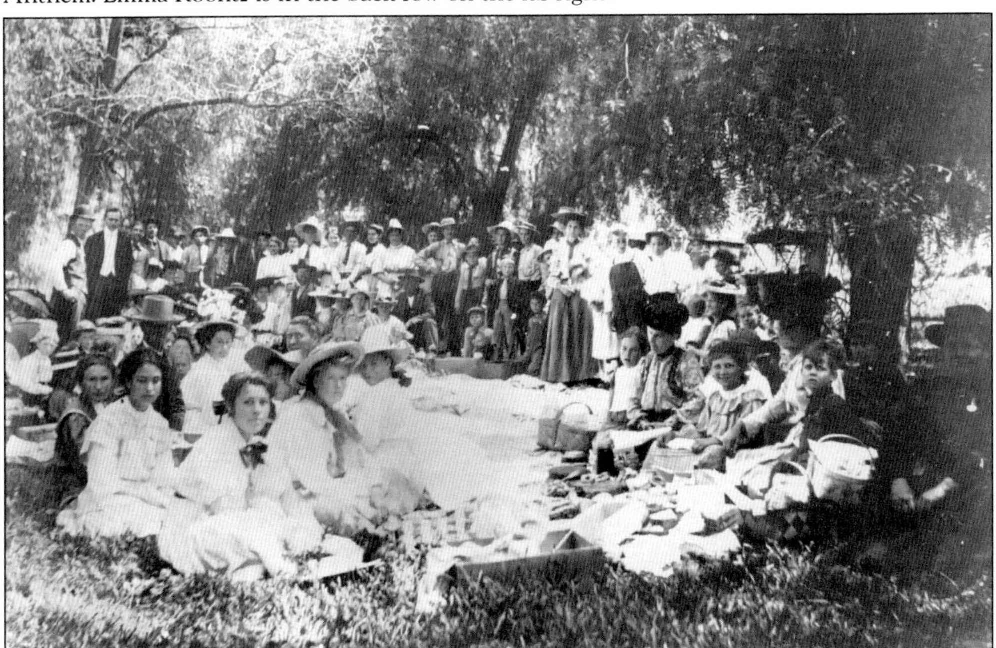

Not all the social events were at the church. In this c. 1910 photograph, the community gathers for a picnic. Some of community's favorite places for a picnic were the banks of the San Gabriel River, in the Whittier hills, or in the middle of a shady grove of trees. Some of the families identified at the picnic are the Couches, Houghtons, Coopers, Ledfords, McAlpines, and Hammertons.

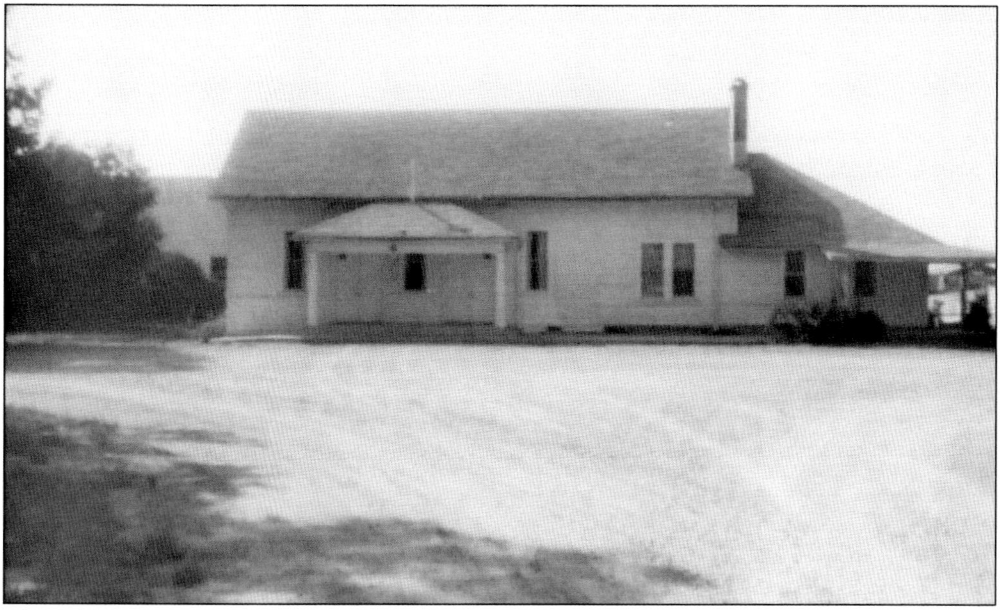

This Bible Missionary Church was located on Painter Avenue at Los Nietos Road and held services from 1972 until the mid-1990s. The German Baptist congregation built the church in 1886 on land it had purchased from the Hazzard family. It called itself the New River Congregation and was well-known for the congregants' Quaker-like mode of dress. They held services in Santa Fe Springs until 1972 and then moved to the San Joaquin Valley. (Courtesy SFS Archives.)

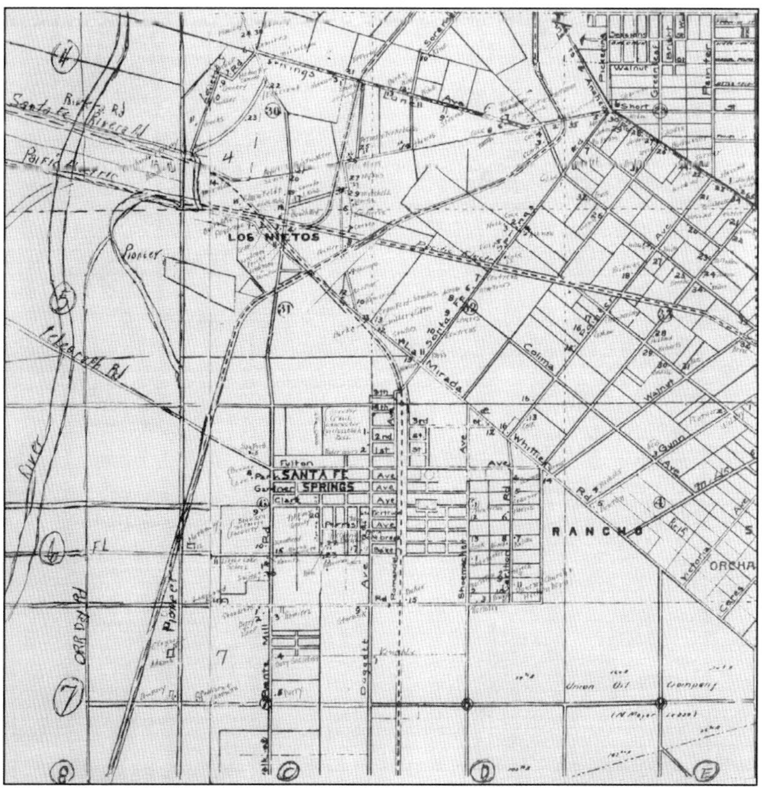

By the turn of the 20th century, many new families were calling Santa Fe Springs home. This rare 1902 map of the Santa Fe Springs area shows the township that Santa Fe Railroad was hoping to develop. With a magnifying glass, one may also be able to make out some of the old familiar street names and the location of many of the early families of the area. (Courtesy SFS Archives.)

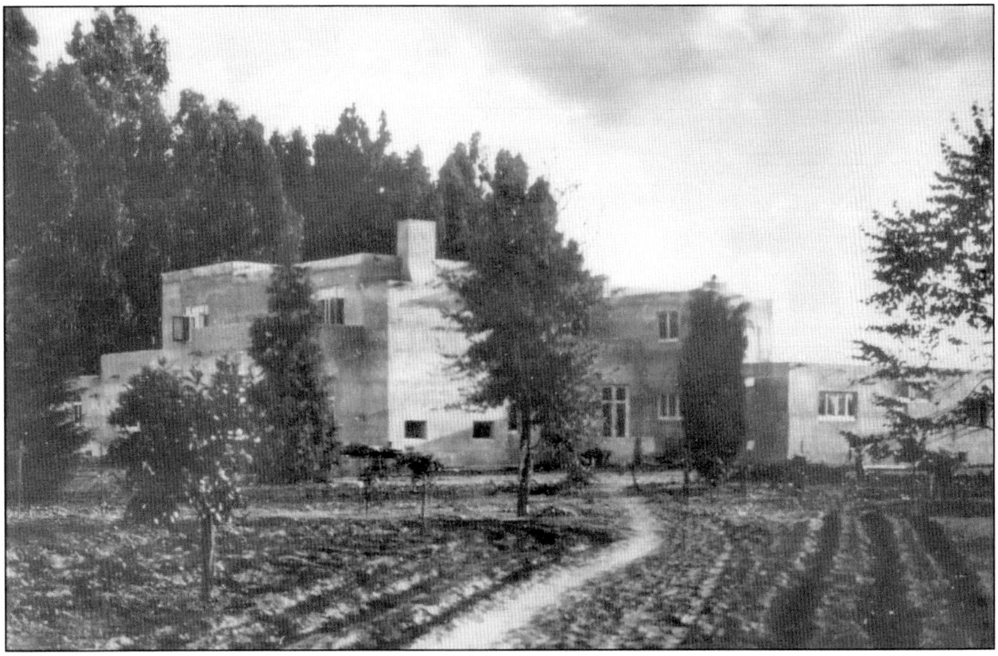

In 1919, construction started on an 8,000-square-foot home for Chauncey and Marie Clarke. The Clarkes moved to California in 1904 and shortly after began purchasing properties in Downey, Pico Rivera, and Santa Fe Springs. They chose the middle of the 62-acre citrus grove in Santa Fe Springs as the site of their country home. (Courtesy SFS Archives.)

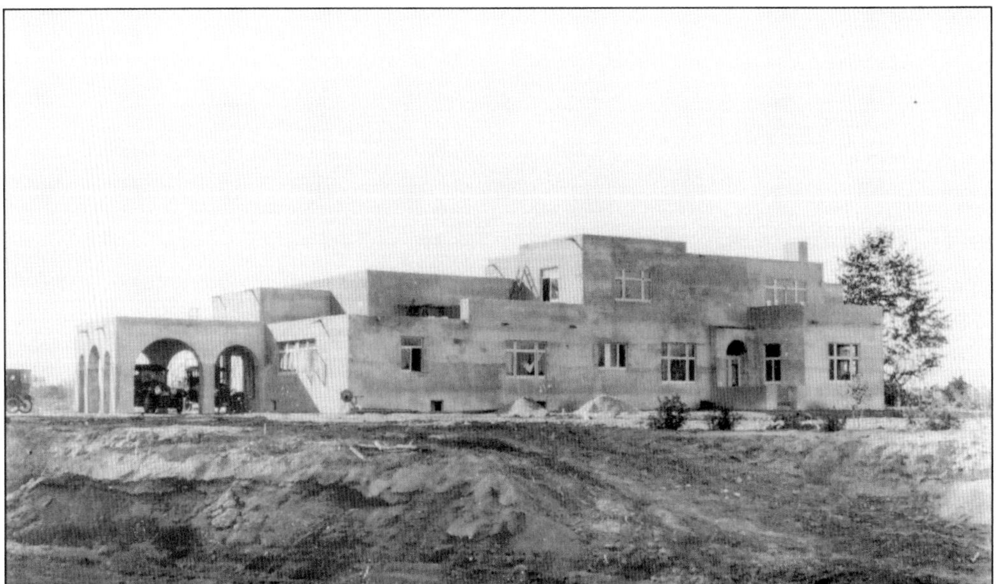

The Clarkes hired architect Irving Gill to design and build their country home. Gill built this elegant house in an unusual style for the era. Using Mediterranean-inspired and Mission Revival architecture, he designed this house devoid of ornamentation. Irving Gill pioneered innovative construction techniques, such as concrete tilt-ups, undecorated wall surfaces, built-in closets, skylights, and low-maintenance interiors. (Courtesy SFS Archives.)

Marie Rankin, an only child, was born in 1868 in Afton, Iowa. Her father, a mining engineer, moved the family to Phoenix, Arizona, for the many work opportunities the city offered. Maria's father encouraged her to excel in many pursuits that at the time were considered masculine. Marie frequently rode horseback with him to the mines on prospecting trips. "She could ride a horse with as much grace, and shoot as accurately, as Annie Oakley," a lifelong friend of hers once said. (Courtesy SFS Archives.)

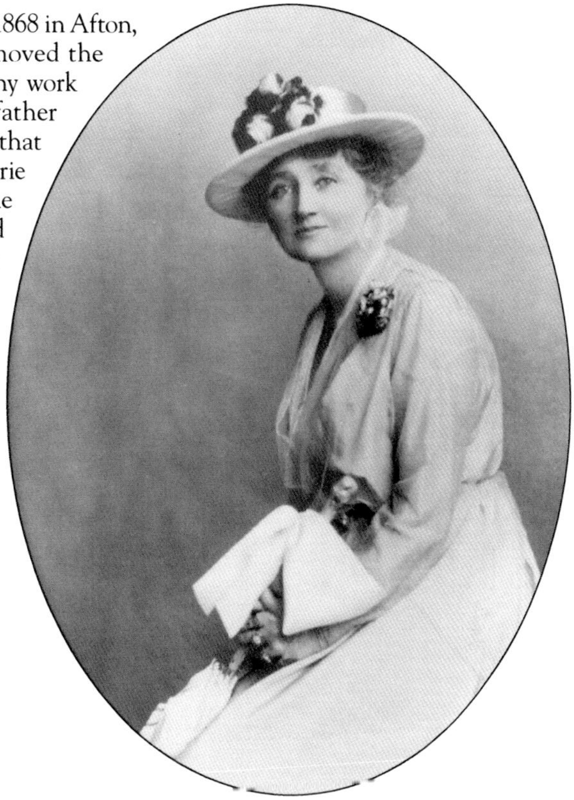

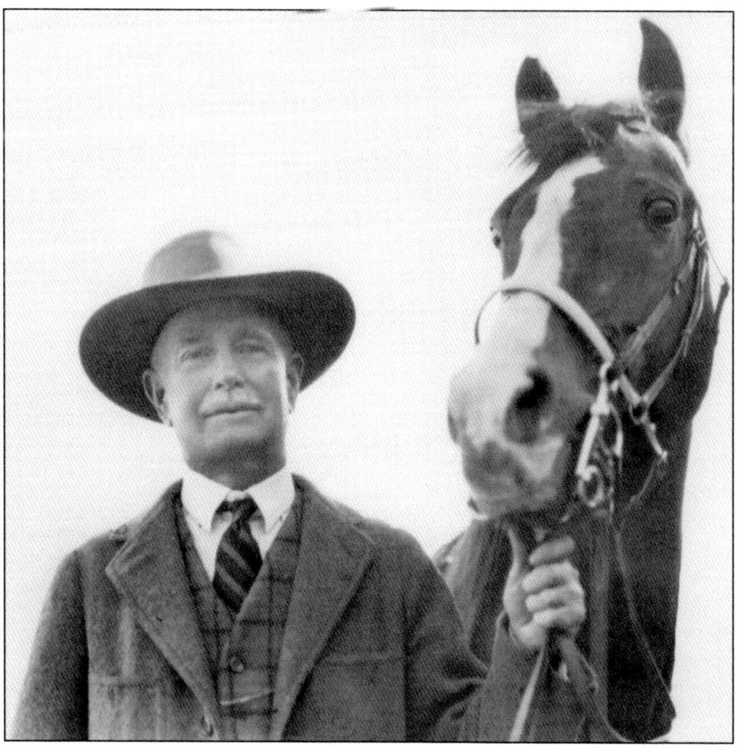

Chauncey Clarke was born in 1858 in Peoria, Illinois, where his family made a fortune by developing the Clarke Distilleries. In the 1890s, Chauncey moved to Phoenix, Arizona, for his health. Suspecting he would find gold, he began purchasing hundreds of acres of desert land. As he had hoped, he established a very successful gold mining enterprise on that desert land. One of Chauncey's other passions was raising purebred Arabian horses. (Courtesy SFS Archives.)

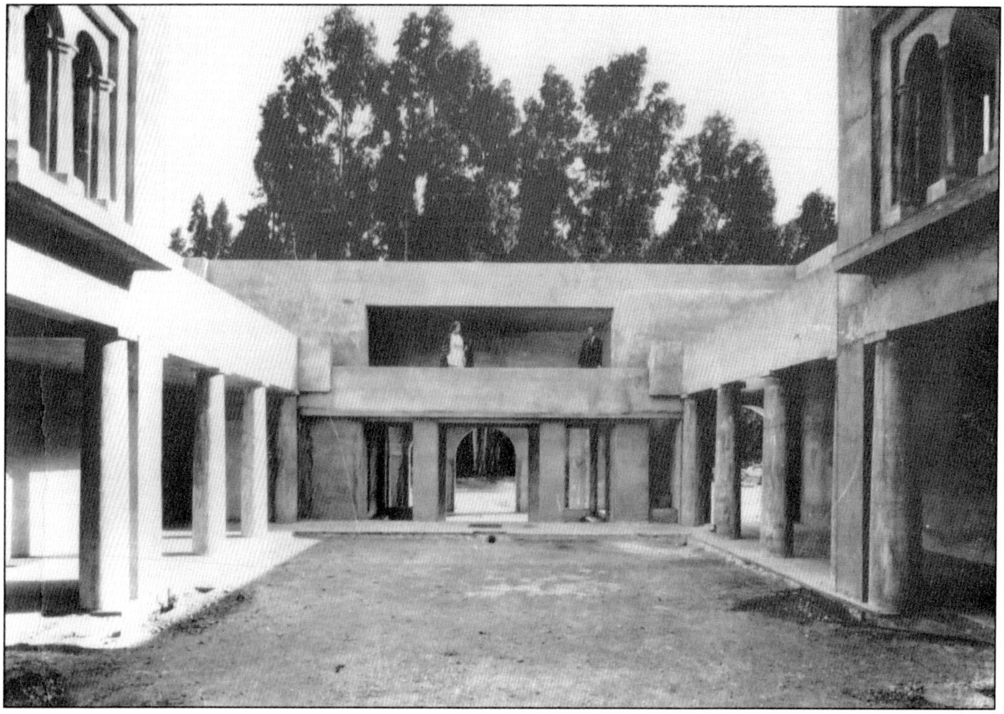

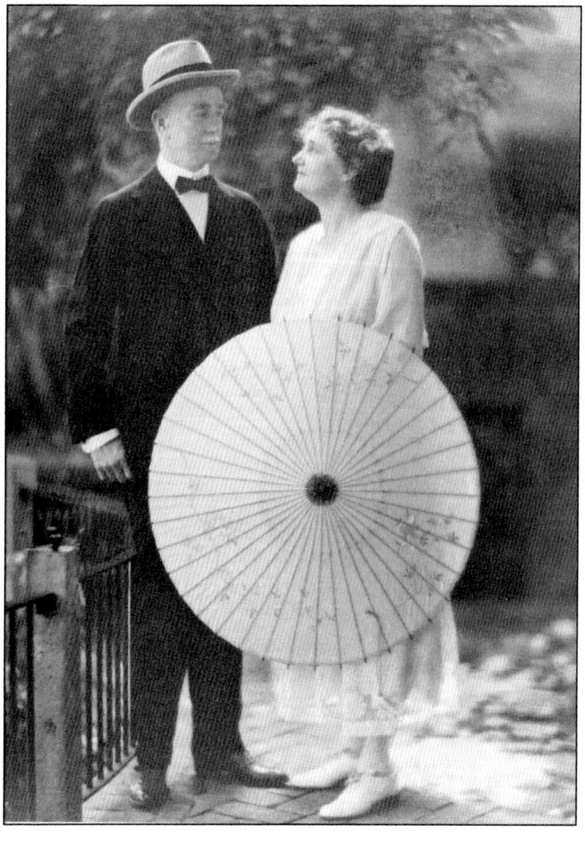

While riding horseback on his mining property, Chauncey Clarke met the high-spirited Marie Rankin. They were married in 1894, and their first home was in Peoria, Arizona, a city founded by Clarke. The Clarkes moved into their newly completed country home in 1921. Not long afterward, they discovered oil on their property. The smells and noise of oil production made it necessary for them to move, so they built another home on their property in the Coachella Valley. (Courtesy SFS Archives.)

Although they lived in their Santa Fe Springs home for only a short time, they sometimes entertained friends and showed movies outdoors in the courtyard. They were married for approximately 33 years when, in 1926, Chauncey Clarke died. Marie Rankin Clarke died in 1948 and left their home to her cousin James Siemon, who lived there until 1986, when he sold it to the City of Santa Fe Springs. (Courtesy SFS Archives.)

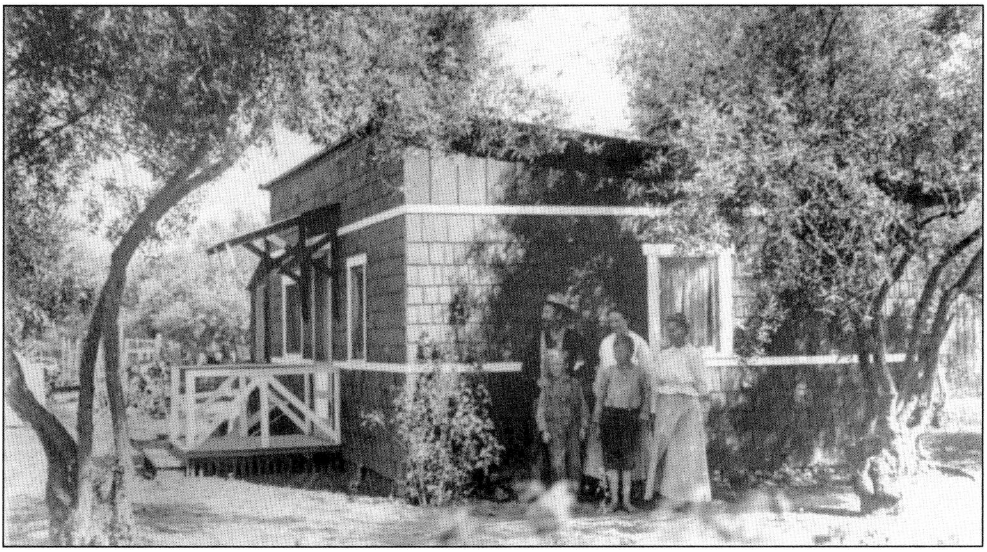

The Nordstrom family came to Santa Fe Springs in the late 1800s. In this 1908 photograph, the family is standing in front of their modest shingle-sided home. According to the inscription on the reverse side of this photograph, the house was located on Telegraph Road, but according to a 1902 map, it was located on Shoemaker Avenue just north of Lakeland Road. From left to right are (front row) sons Edgar and Oswald; (back row) John Nordstrom, his wife, Christina, and their daughter Esther.

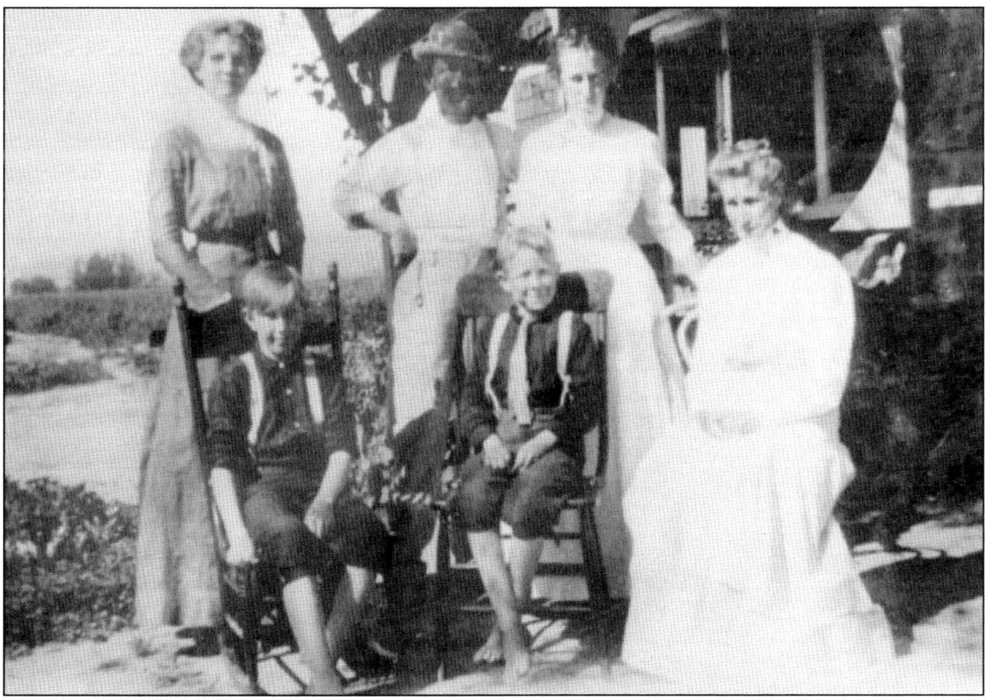

Taken in 1911, the family had grown from the previous photograph. From left to right are Laura McKiel, wife of Steve McKiel; John Nordstrom; daughter Esther, who was married to or would soon marry Harry McKiel; and Christina Nordstrom. In the front are Oswald and Edgar Nordstrom. This is not the John Nordstrom of the department store family.

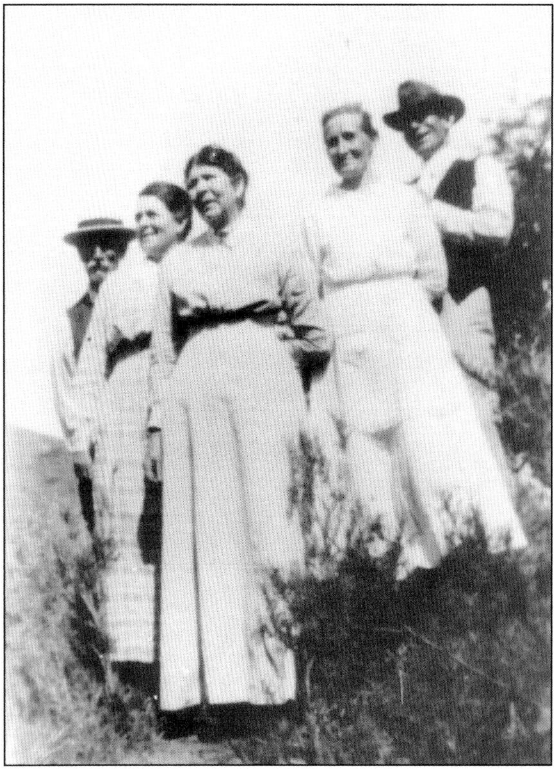

Just as today, families and friends gathered for leisurely weekend outings. These three Santa Fe Springs families, the Bakers, McKiels, and Nordstroms, enjoy a picnic in the Whittier Hills in 1918. From left to right are John Baker, his wife, Julia McKiel Baker, Frances Wood McKiel, and Christina and John Nordstrom.

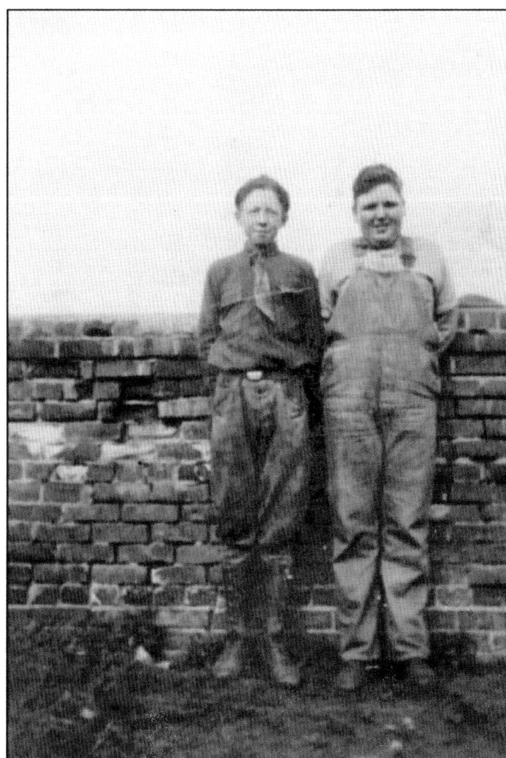

The 1920s brought about many changes for the Santa Fe Springs area, but not for all. To the young people of Four Corners, life went on as usual. Two of the area's local boys are pictured standing by the Nimocks reservoir at Norwalk Boulevard and Telegraph Road. On the left is Richard "Skinny" Langan, and on the right is Wellington "Fat" Wheeler, as they were known.

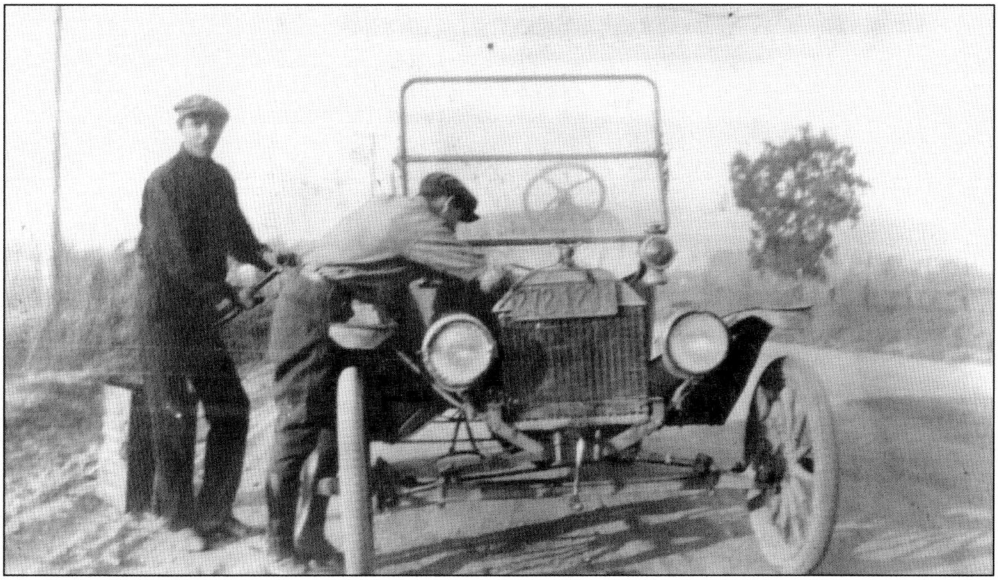

Much has not changed in nearly 100 years. The hand-me-down cars of teenage drivers take a lot of work to keep running. Here, local boy Richard Langan is working on his Tin Lizzie, or Model T, that had stranded him and his friend Pat Nelson on Norwalk Boulevard. Pat's father owned one of the local grocery stores.

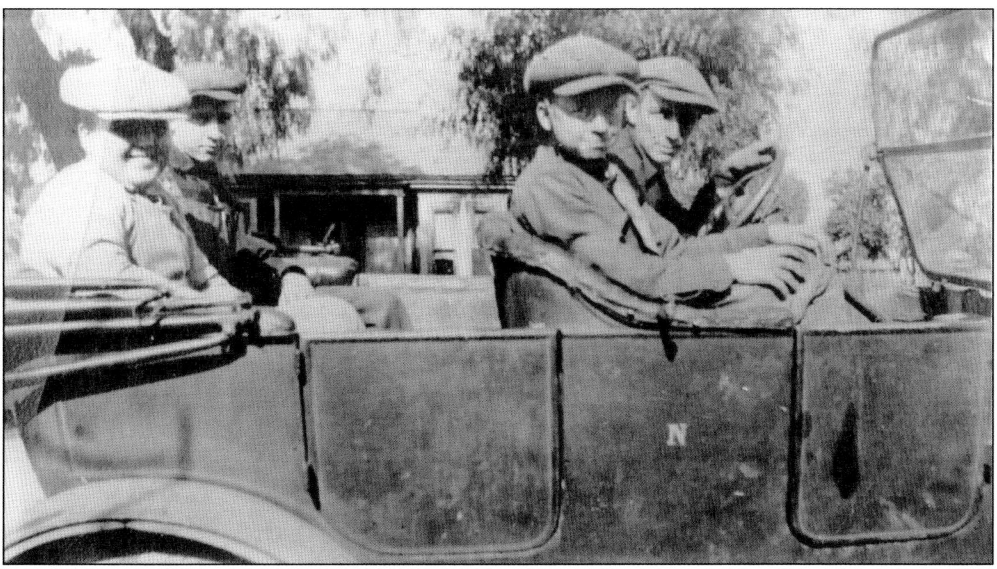

Pat Nelson drives around in his car with friends, very likely cruising for "chicks." Hanging around with friends is still a favorite pastime with today's youth. Sitting shotgun is Albert Ellis, known as "Red," who would open up a hot dog stand on Telegraph Road not long after this photograph was taken. Wellington "Fat" Wheeler and Richard "Skinny" Langan are in the back seat.

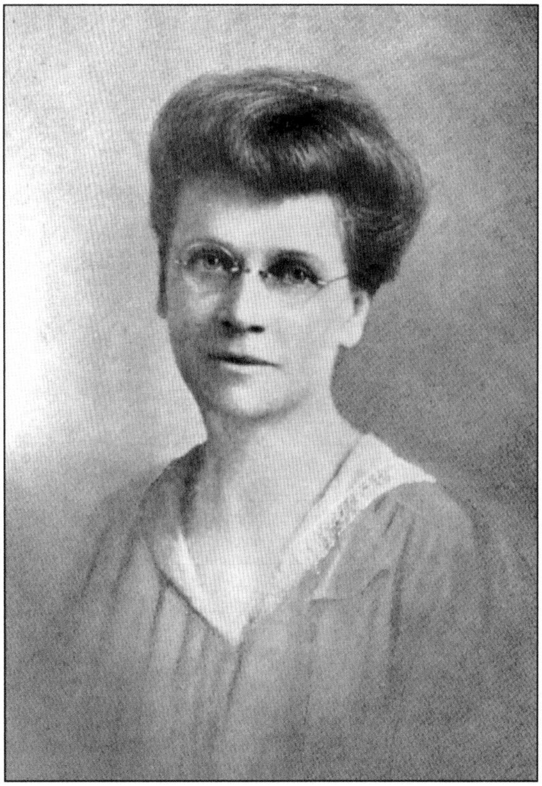

Margaret Frances Campbell Slusher was born in 1879 in Livermore, California. In a 1960 newspaper interview, Margaret stated that she was only 12 years old when she started earning her own way. At 15, she went to work for a laundry service in Los Angeles, and in 1907, she started her own laundry business. Her business prospered during World War I, when she received a contract to do the laundry for Fort MacArthur. (Courtesy SFS Archives.)

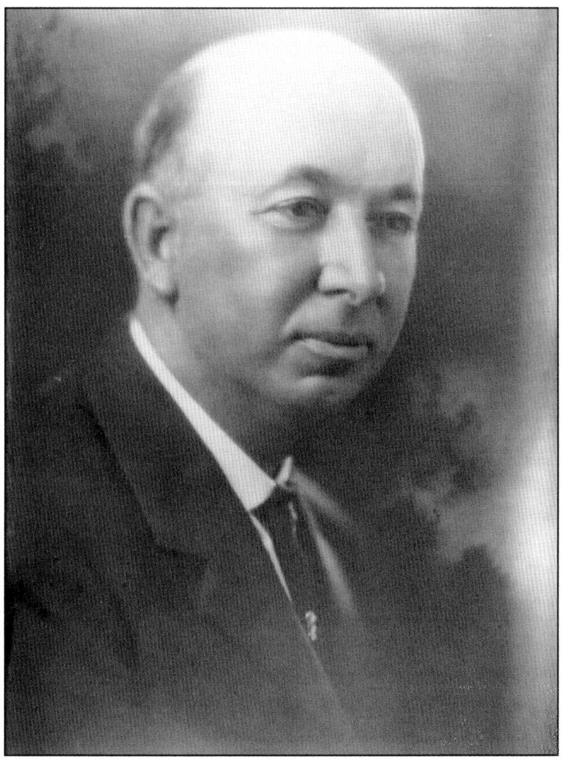

Not much is known about Silas Slusher, but it is known that he was an engineer for the Southern Pacific Railroad and retired when he and Margaret bought the Nimocks estate in 1919. He and Margaret met in Los Angeles and were married in 1902. The Slushers bought the estate from Eugene Overton, and just months later, oil was discovered in the Santa Fe Springs area. The house burned down in 1941. (Courtesy SFS Archives.)

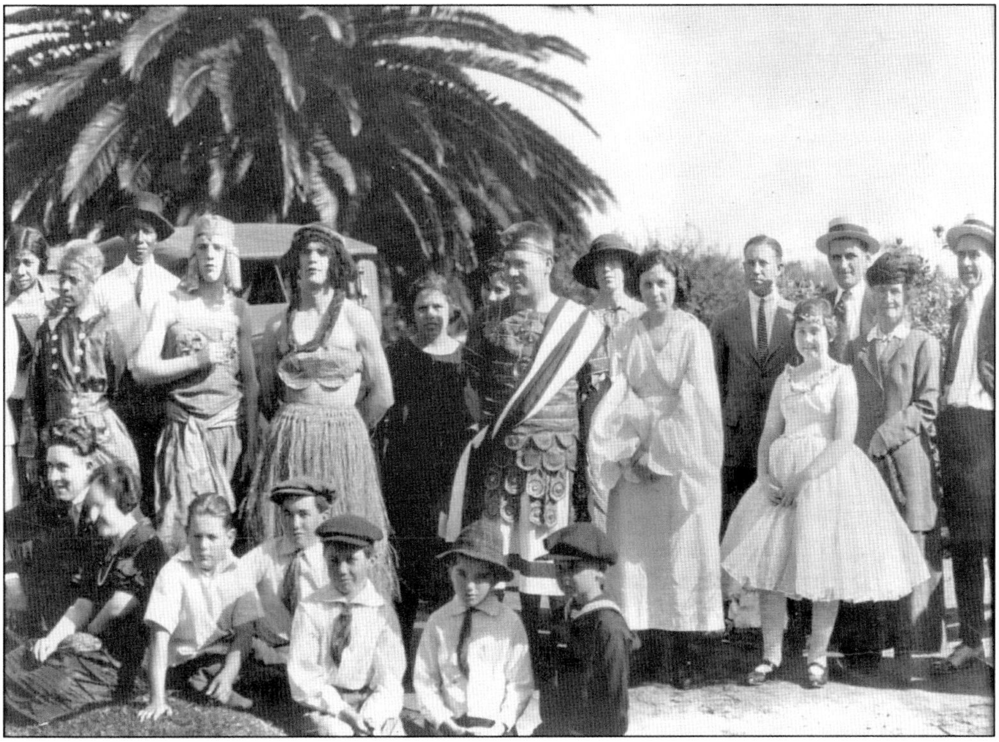

The Slushers enlarged the house and restored the gardens that had been neglected by its previous owners. They loved collecting exotic animals, including monkeys, and even had a tamed eagle named Mike. The large aviary they built for their collection of rare and exotic birds still stands at Heritage Park. The Slushers loved entertaining, and in 1922 Margaret held a costume party for the employees of her former laundry business. (Courtesy SFS Archives.)

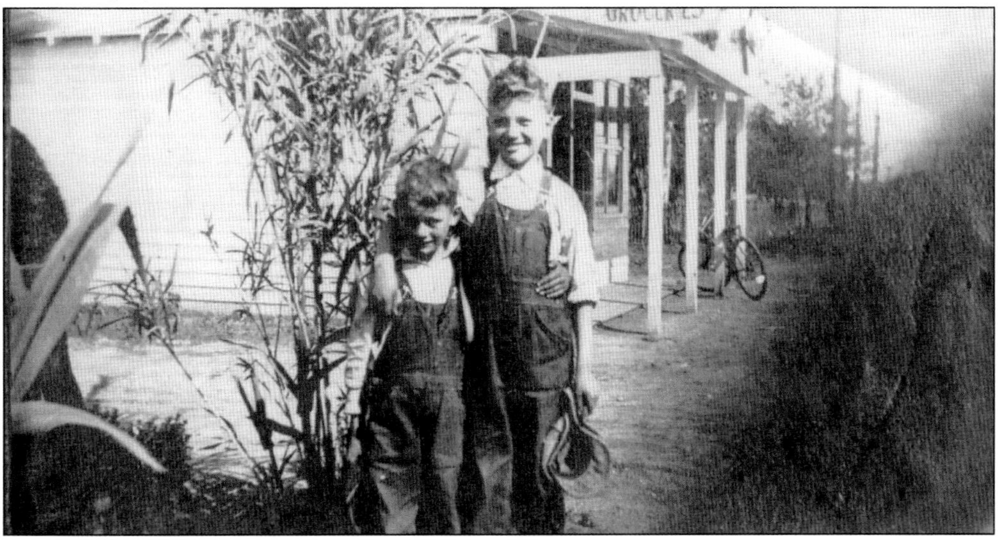

In 1920, the population in Santa Fe Springs was large enough to support several small grocery stores. Two young local boys are standing in front of Nelson's Grocery Store. It was located on the Walker property on Norwalk-Puente Mills Road (now known as Norwalk Boulevard). One source claims that this store was owned by Bob Frazier and was called Frazier's Grocery Store.

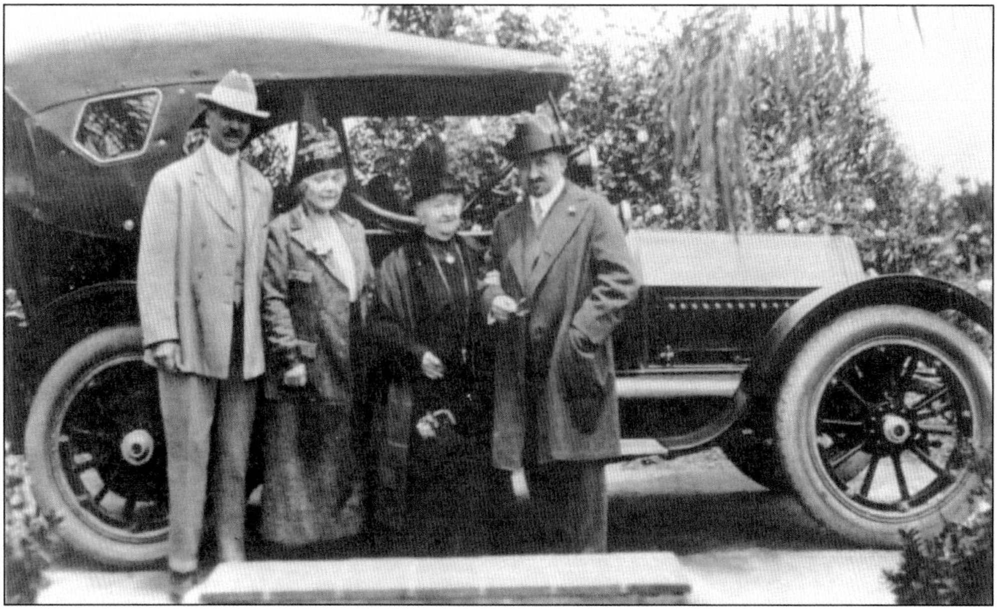

William and Gertrud Matern moved to Santa Fe Springs in 1915 and built a one-story mission-style home on the 105 acres of land they had purchased. Their land was formerly part of the Sanford Ranch. This 1921 photograph shows, from left to right, William Matern; his wife, Gertrud; his mother-in-law, Ida Besser; and the German consul Emil Rodel. They are standing in front of their luxurious convertible automobile.

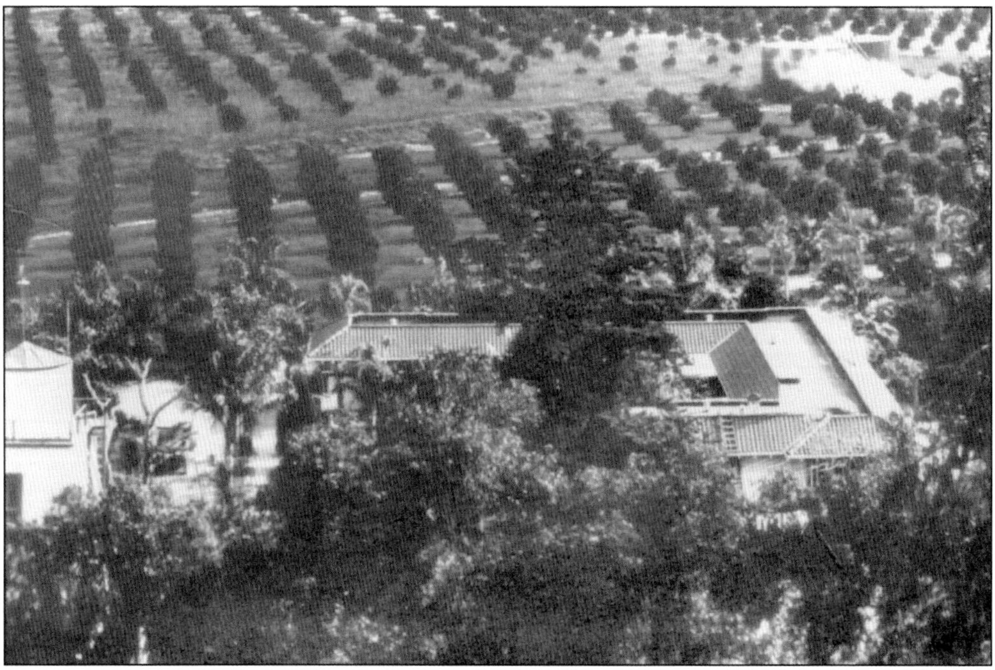

By 1917, the Materns had planted 7,000 orange, lemon, and grapefruit trees on their land. Tough times brought on by World War I forced them to sell some of their land and raise German shepherd dogs for profit. Within a year of the war ending, oil was discovered on their property, and it was not long before oil derricks were replacing the orange groves.

Lula Gertrud Ogelsby, pictured with her infant son Larry, recalled years later how she fell in love with the Matern estate at first sight. She was instantly taken by all the beautiful trees and flowers in the garden, and that it even had a waterfall. Some time around 1950, horse stables had been added to the property. Lula Ogelsby lived in the house until 1980, when it was torn down.

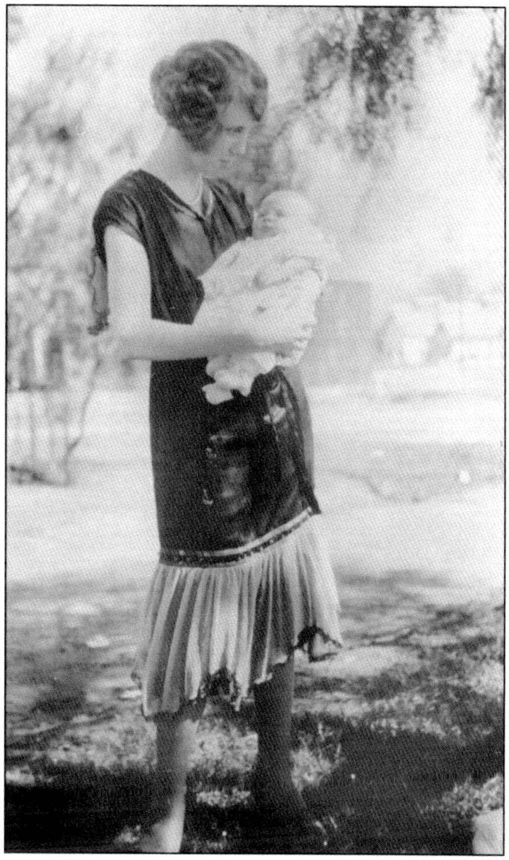

William Matern died in 1923, and Gertrud continued to live in the home until 1926, when she had to move away from the fumes and noise caused by the oil drilling. Her nephew Carl Besser and his wife stayed in the home and managed the ranch until they could not take the fumes and noise, either. Bud Ogelsby, here with his son and daughter, bought the home in 1931 from Gertrud Matern, but she retained ownership of the land.

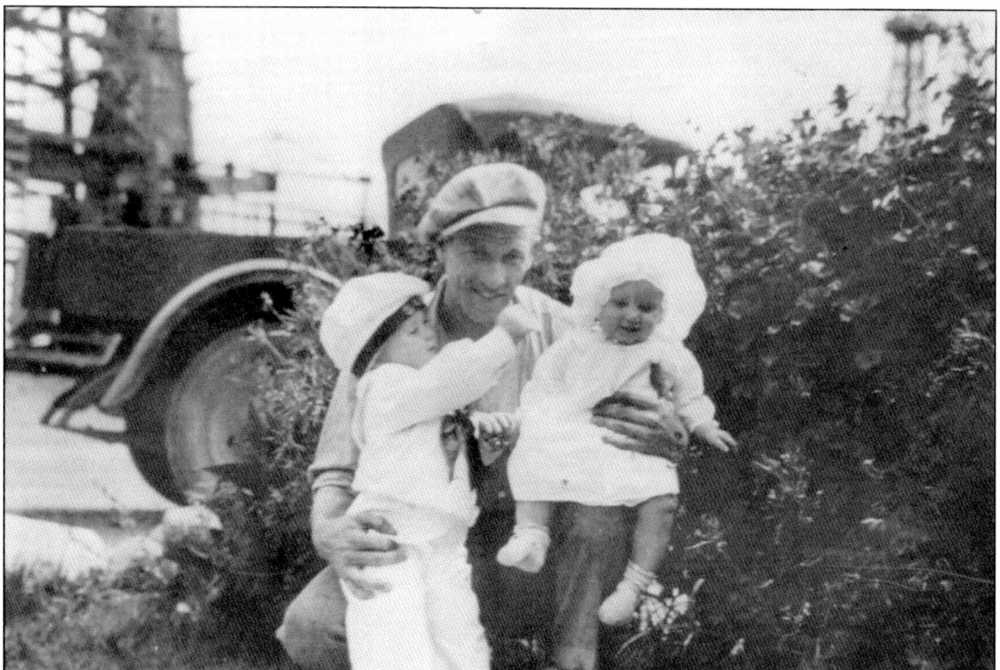

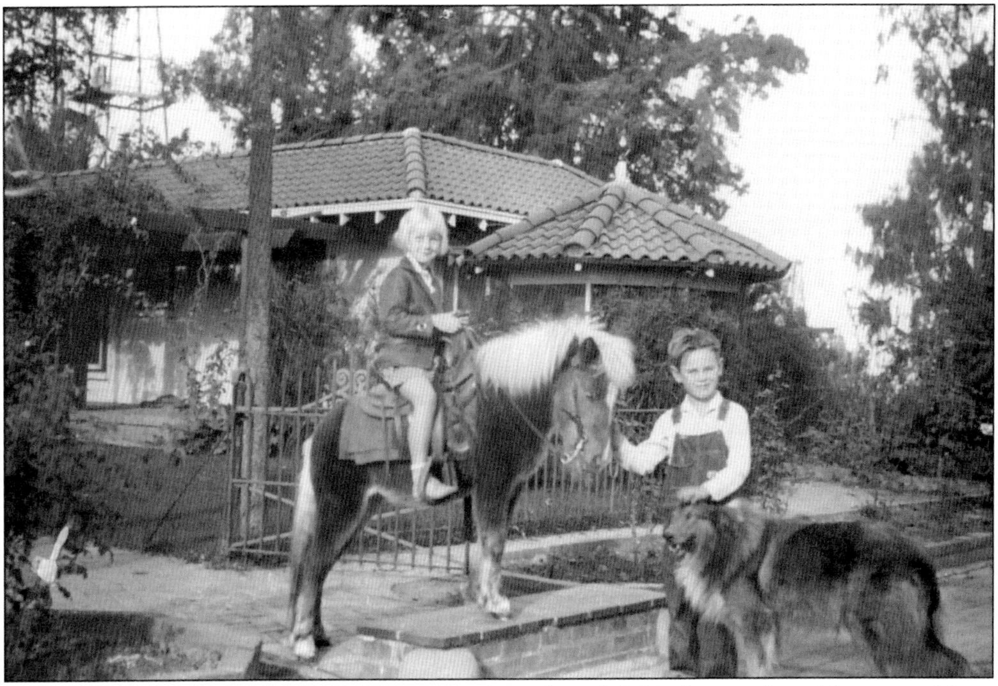

Bud Ogelsby came to Santa Fe Springs to work in the oil fields during the oil boom and later started his own independent oil company. Ogelsby's two children enjoyed an adventurous childhood playing in the orchards and oil fields. Pictured in front of their home is daughter Teta, ready for a ride on Tony the pony while her brother Larry stands by with Laddie Boy, their collie.

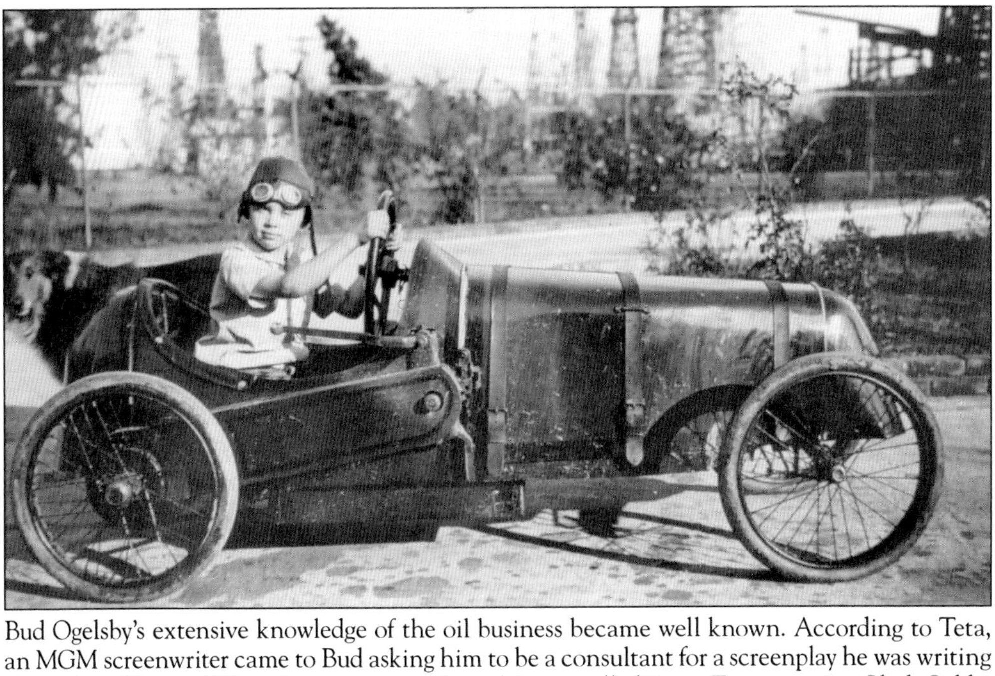

Bud Ogelsby's extensive knowledge of the oil business became well known. According to Teta, an MGM screenwriter came to Bud asking him to be a consultant for a screenplay he was writing about the oil boom. When the movie was released, it was called *Boom Town*, starring Clark Gable. Here, Larry is seated in his very own race car with the oil derricks in the background.

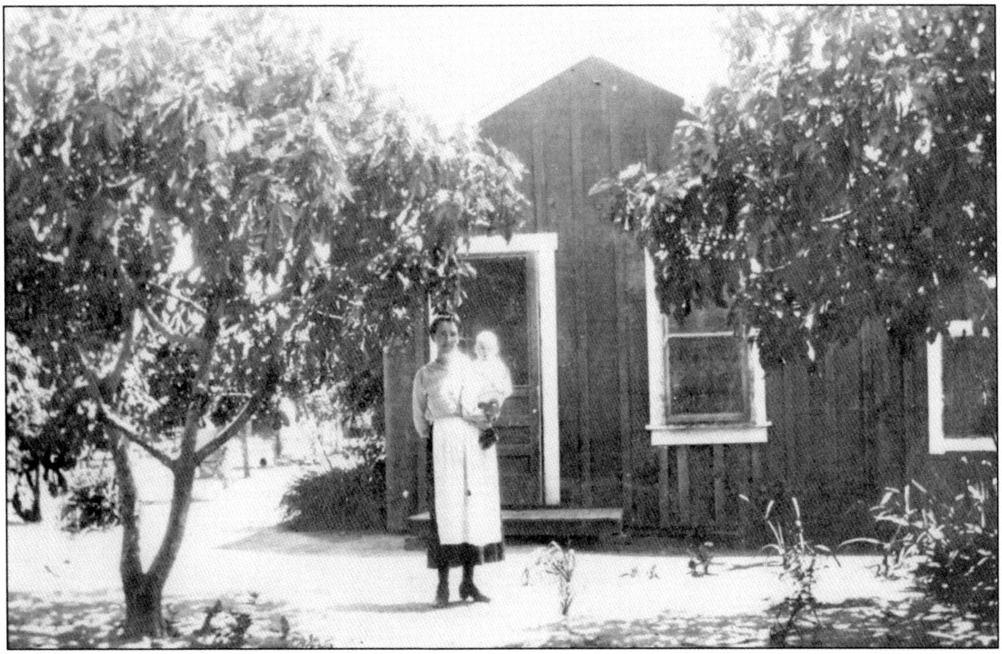

Tom and Josie Langan came to Santa Fe Springs after World War I. Tom was a veteran of the Spanish-American War. Josie Langan stands in front of her small, board-and-batten-style house with their infant daughter Josie in this c. 1915 photograph. The house is believed to have been located on Little Lake Road (now called Florence Avenue).

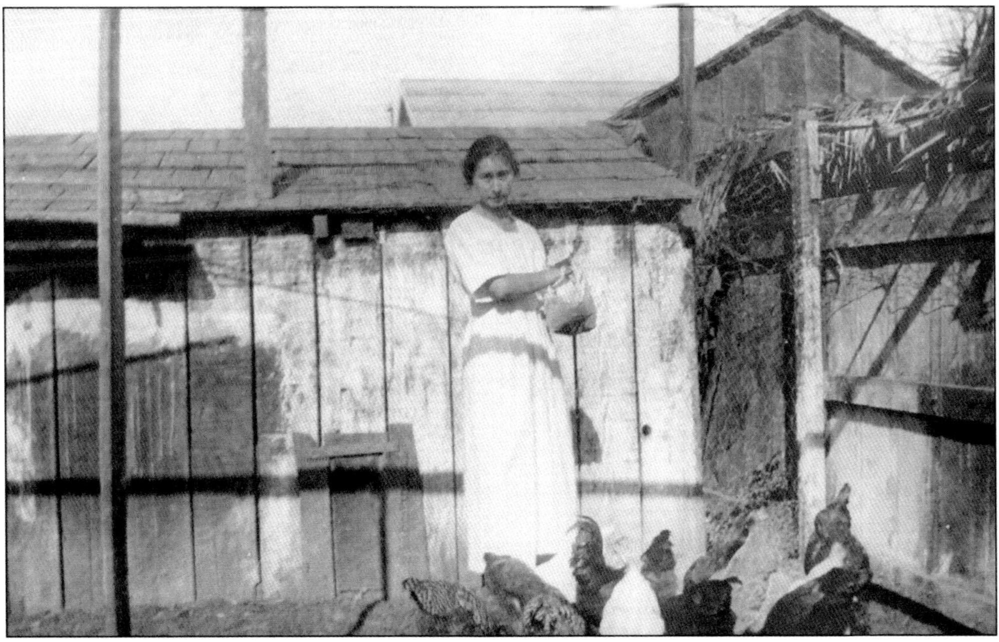

In this c. 1920 photograph, Josie Langan is in her backyard feeding the chickens. The look on her face seems to be saying, "Why are you taking my picture?" Though the Langans were not farmers, chicken coops were almost a necessity for early residents of Santa Fe Springs. Tom and Josie continued to live in Santa Fe Springs until they moved in the late 1930s.

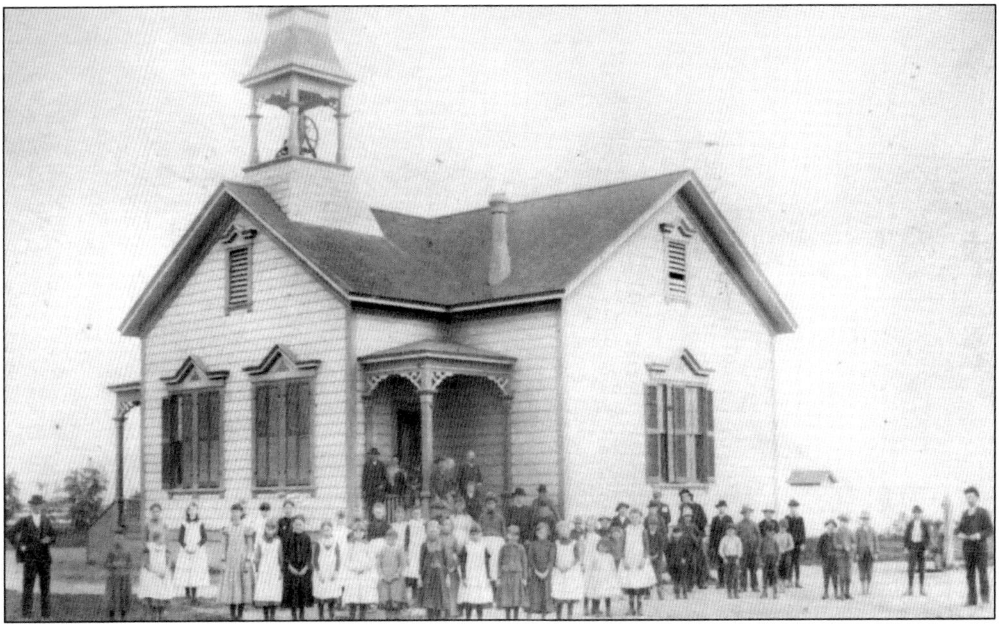

The first Little Lake Schoolhouse stood near the southern end of Little Lake. It was a one-room building of approximately 12 feet by 24 feet. One stormy winter, students were unable to make it to school because the bridge that crossed the lake had been washed out. It was then decided to relocate the school further from the lake. The original structure was replaced in 1882 with this two-room schoolhouse on Little Lake Road. The school bell was added in 1889.

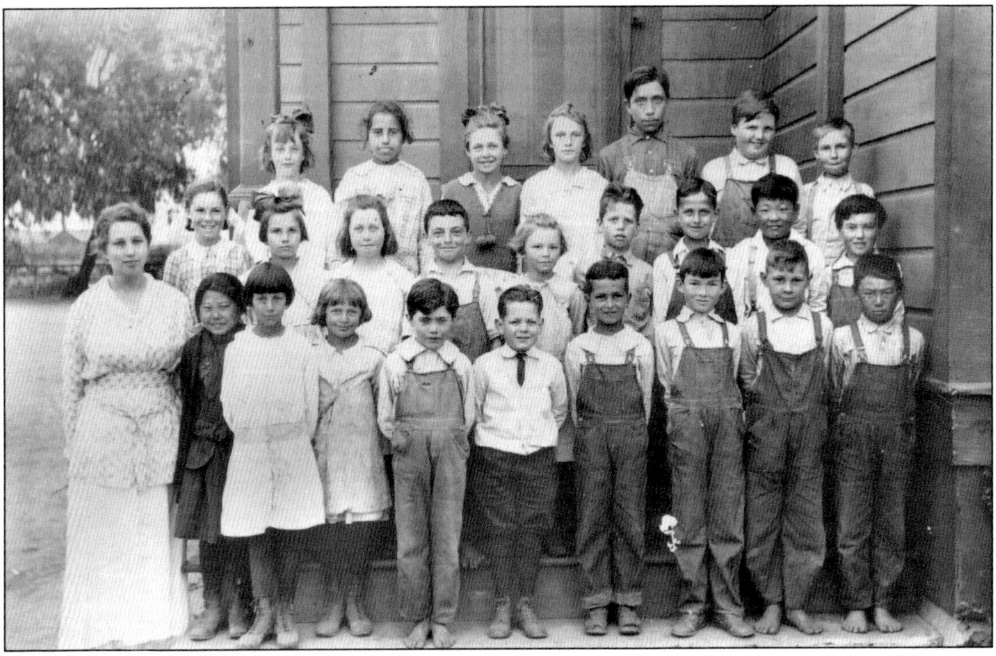

The Little Lake School District was formed from a part of the Los Nietos School District in September 1871 upon petition of W.L. Houghton and 28 other parents. In this c. 1890 photograph of a Little Lake class, the ethnic diversity of the Santa Fe Springs region is very apparent, much as it is today. The date and names of those in this photograph are unknown.

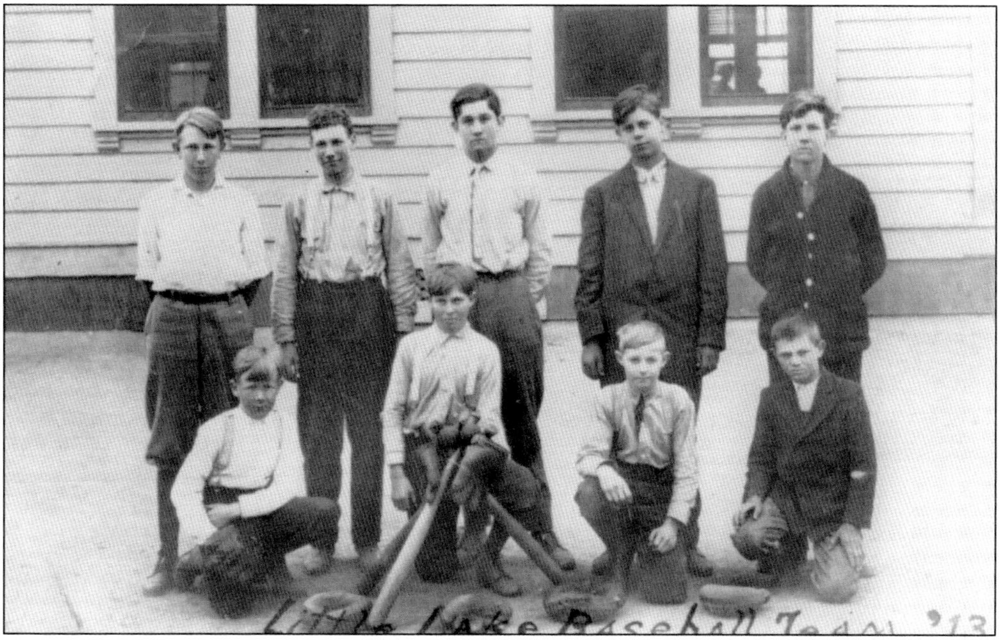

There was no Little League baseball in Santa Fe Springs in 1913, but that did not stop Little Lake School from having a team. The nine-boy team poses for a photograph in front of the schoolhouse. From left to right are (first row) Edgar Nordstrom, Cornelius McKiel, Willie Patterson, and Willie Haddock; (second row) Oswald Nordstrom, Roy Harrison, Roy Walker, R. Ribb, and Albert Ellis.

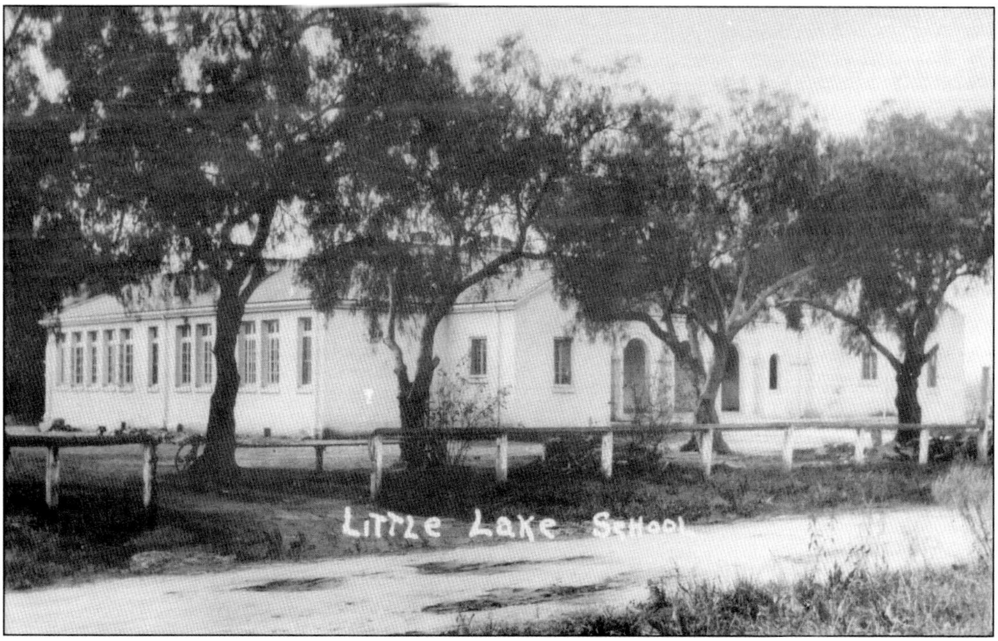

As the population grew, the two-room schoolhouse was replaced by a bigger H-shape concrete building with a hollow tile roof in 1919. The H-shape building was declared unsafe in 1933 after a major earthquake hit Long Beach. The school building was closed for two years during its restoration. Classes were held in tents a safe distance away until the repairs were complete.

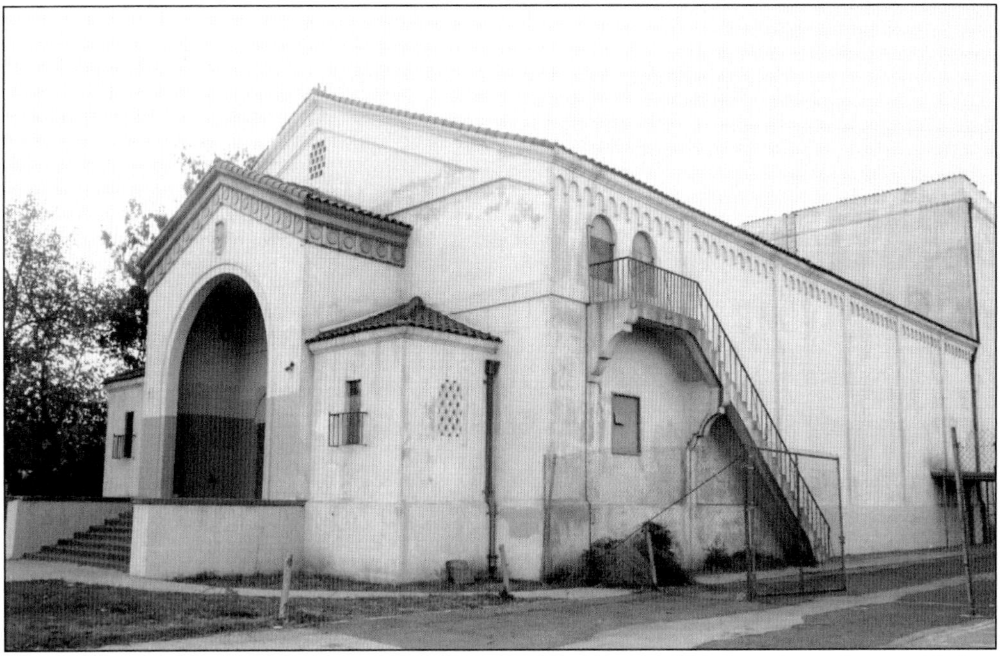

The Little Lake School auditorium, a Spanish-style building with a clay tile roof, was added in 1933. The auditorium was built before the 1933 earthquake and fortunately suffered no damage. The auditorium was a beloved landmark until 1983, when the city tore it down to make the land available for redevelopment, despite tireless efforts by the local historical society to save it.

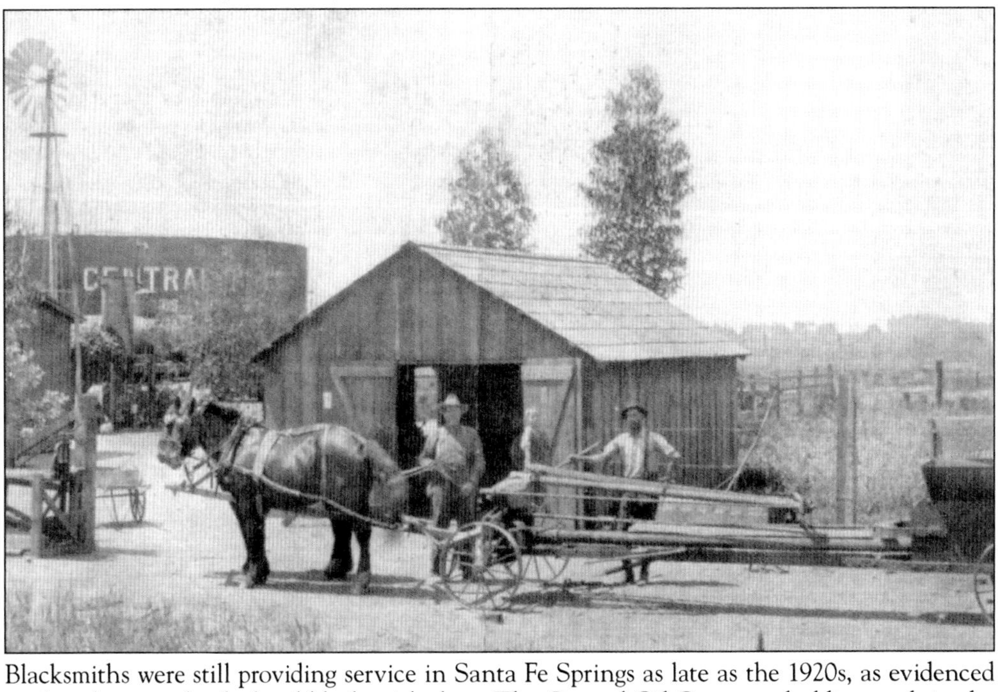

Blacksmiths were still providing service in Santa Fe Springs as late as the 1920s, as evidenced in this photograph of a local blacksmith shop. The Central Oil Company holding tank in the background is a clue as to what time period this photograph was taken. On the left is Sam Wheeler, on the right is Sam Perkins, and Sam's son Charles is between them.

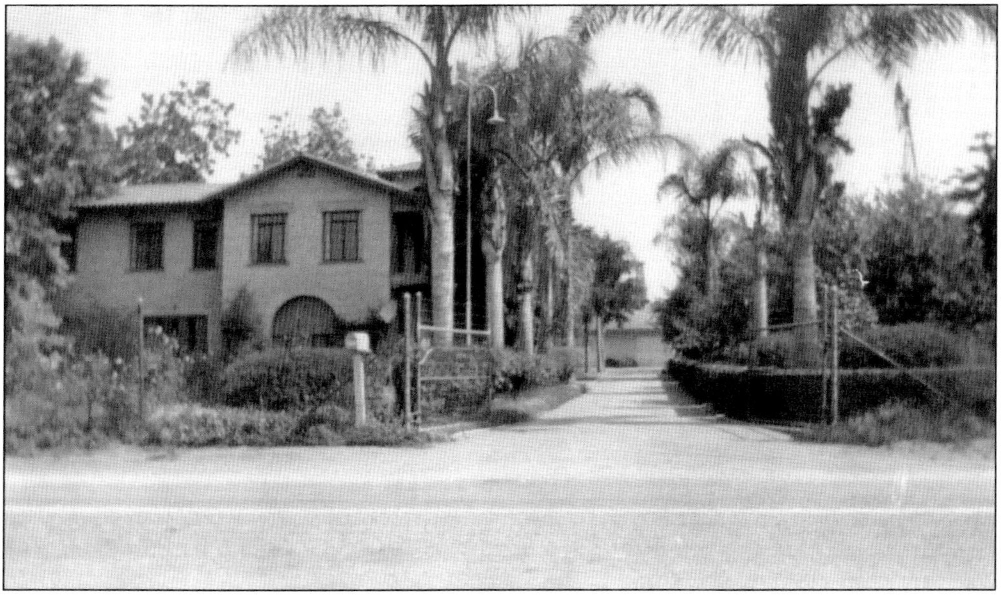

Jesse and Lola Hathaway moved to the Fulton Wells area in 1905 for health reasons. They lived in a three-room shack until they replaced it with this two-story Mediterranean-style house. This new home was under construction with the first floor nearly finished when the Long Beach earthquake of 1933 hit. Because of its sturdy construction, there was no damage to the house, and the work continued.

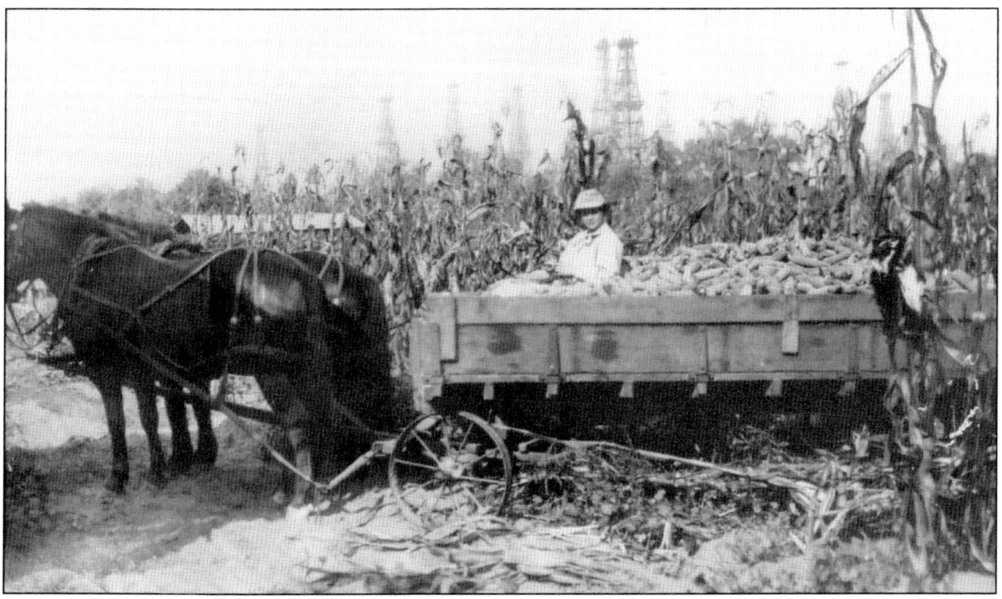

Jesse and Lola, daughter of Franklin McCarric, had three sons, Jesse, Richard, and Julian. In 1935, Richard married Nadine Applegate, seen here driving the wagon during harvest. They moved into a house he built across the driveway from the bigger house. Richard and Nadine moved into the bigger house after the passing of his parents. In later years, Nadine's love for historic preservation led her to turn the estate into a museum of local history.

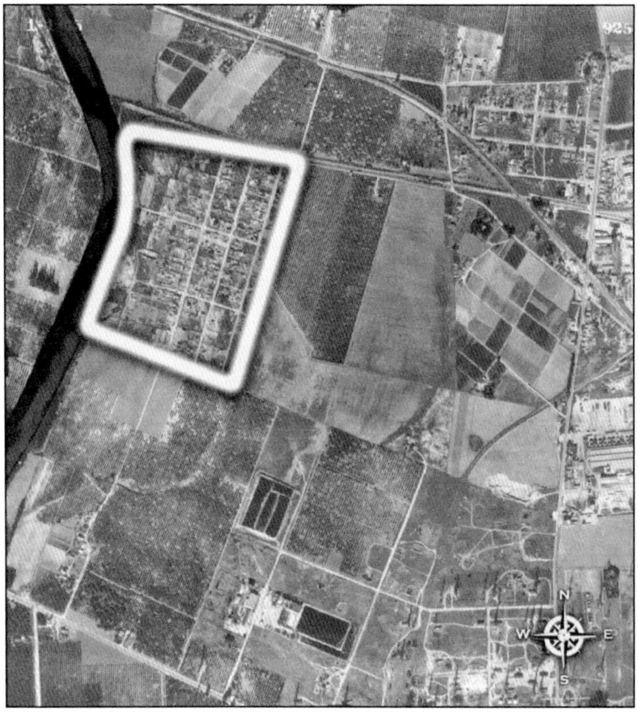

At the time oil was being discovered at Four Corners, a small Mexican American community began to grow in what is now the northwest corner of Santa Fe Springs, as outlined in this 1945 aerial photograph. The area was secluded and hidden by orange groves, the San Gabriel River, and the Santa Fe Railroad tracks. Most of the area's first residents settled there after escaping the violence of the Mexican Revolution. (Courtesy Fairchild Aerial Photograph Collection.)

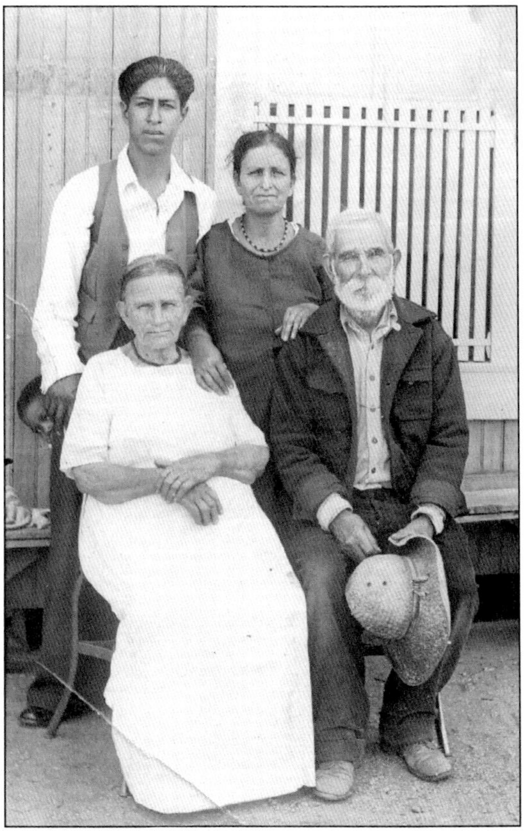

Felipe Rodriguez came from Guanajuato, Mexico, as a single man and met Petra Martinez, who lived and worked at the San Gabriel Mission. They married and had five children, the youngest being Maria Amelia Nabor, who met and married Cruz Estrada Villa. Pictured around 1935 at their Flood Ranch home from left to right are Petra and Felipe Rodriguez, and behind them are Severiano Villa and Nabor Villa. Nabor's youngest child, Makaria, is hiding behind her brother Severiano. (Courtesy Aguilera Collection.)

Pictured around 1935 is Cruz and one of his surviving children, Severiano, at home in Flood Ranch. Nabor and Cruz Villa had seven children. Around 1915, Cruz sent his wife and children to Guanajuato to take care of his ailing father while he stayed to work. After her father-in-law died, Nabor walked back to the United States with all of her children, but the four oldest did not survive the trip. (Courtesy Aguilera Collection.)

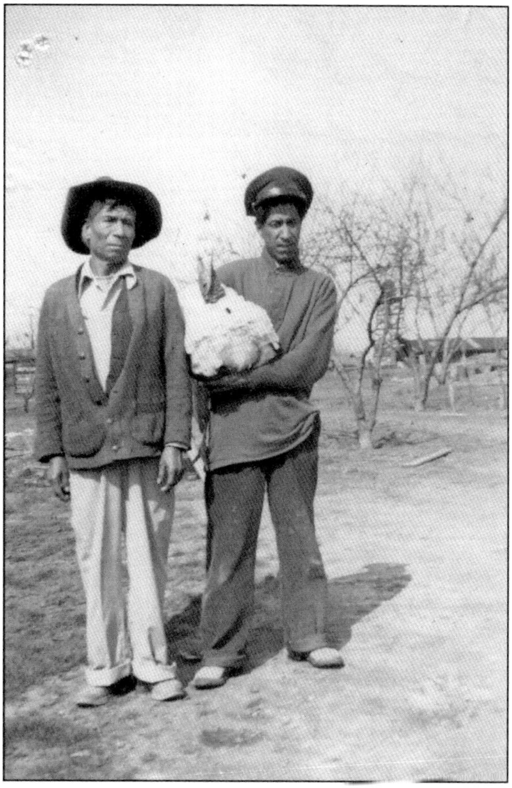

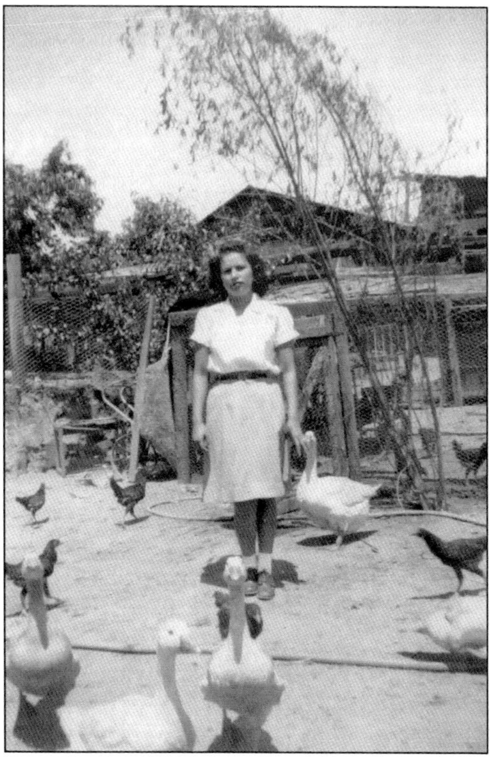

When Nabor returned, she settled in Flood Ranch with Cruz and her parents. Nabor and Cruz had four more children. Pictured around 1945 is their youngest, Makaria Petra Rodriguez Villa, at their Flood Ranch home. Their parcel of land was west of Alabama Street (now Pioneer Boulevard) between Virginia Avenue (now Blue Jay Lane) and the railroad tracks. The property ran from Alabama to the river. (Courtesy Aguilera Collection.)

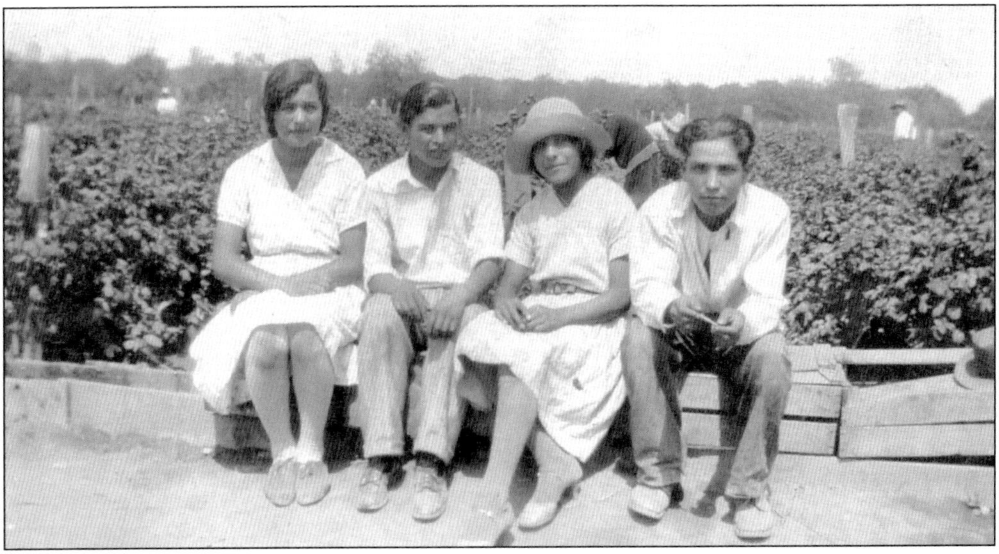

Candelario Orozco Aguilera, second from the left in this 1920 photograph, came to Flood Ranch around 1915 with his grandparents. Luz Cruz, third from left, came to Flood Ranch with her father and two brothers around 1910. Both Candelario and Luz had family living in the area before they moved to Flood Ranch. Here Luz and Candelario are at the Montana Ranch with family. Many Flood Ranch residents worked on the Montana Ranch. (Courtesy Aguilera Collection.)

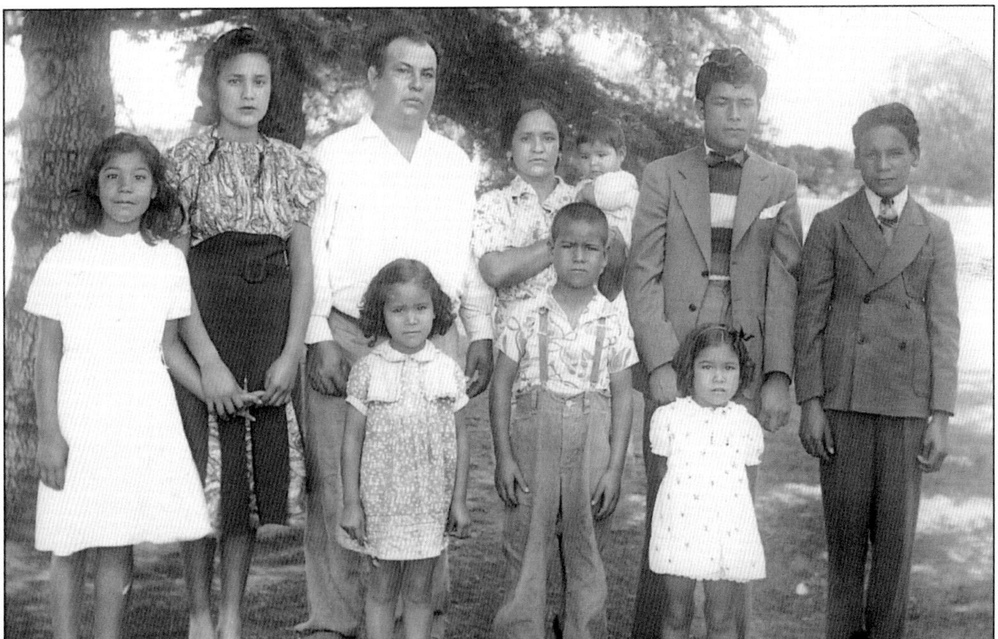

Luz and Candelario married in 1923 when she was 14 years old and he was 12 years old, and they stayed in Flood Ranch. She was said to have slaughtered the cow herself for the wedding feast. Together they had 14 children. This c. 1940 photograph shows, from left to right, (first row) Margaret, Johnny, and Mary Tillie; (second row) Connie, Carmen, father Candelario, mother Luz, infant Lydia, Tony, and Domingo "Mengo." Domingo still lives in Flood Ranch. (Courtesy Aguilera Collection.)

Aurelio Cisneros came to the United States from Michoacan with his wife, Jesusita, and their four young children. Fleeing the violence of the Mexican Revolution, they settled in the Flood Ranch area in the 1920s after purchasing several acres of land. He built his home from several train cars he moved to the site. As his children grew up and married, they added their homes to the property. (Courtesy Cisneros Collection.)

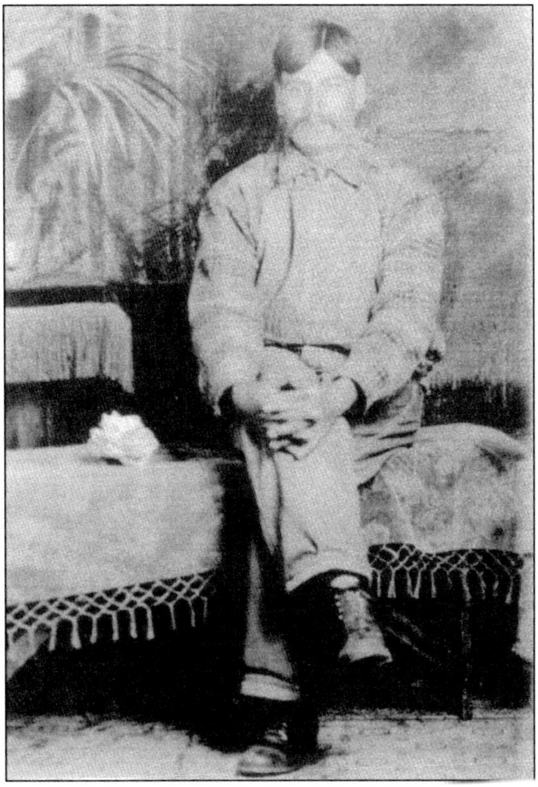

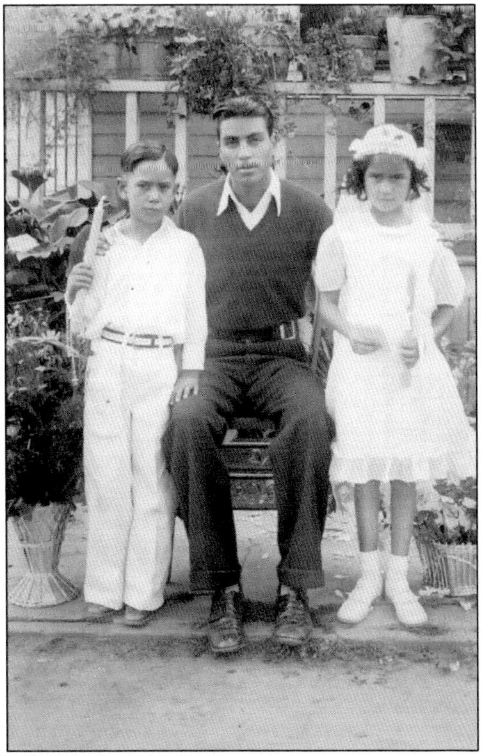

Alberto Baiz Cisneros, in the center of this c. 1930 photograph of a First Holy Communion celebration, came to Flood Ranch with his parents, Aurelio and Jesusita. He was the youngest of the four children that came with them. The family's small ranch was located just to the south of Los Nietos Road and to the west of Garfield Avenue (now Millergrove Avenue). He met and married Guadalupe Cabral in 1945 when he was 29 years old. (Courtesy Cisneros Collection.)

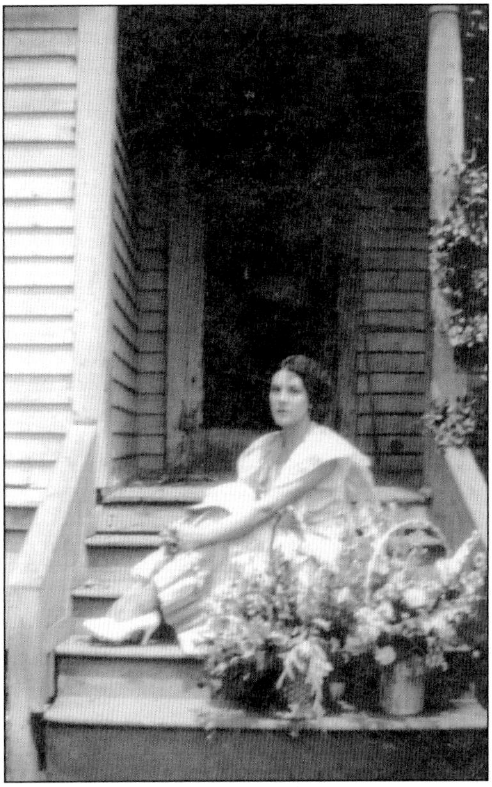

Guadalupe "Lupe" Cabral was born in 1918 and came to Los Nietos with her parents, Gerardo "Jerry" and Luisa Acevedo, in 1926. After marrying Alberto Cisneros, they moved to the Cisneros ranch and into a railroad car that was converted to a small house. Their daughter Rachel still lives in the Flood Ranch area with her family. Many of the Cabral family still live in Santa Fe Springs. (Courtesy Cisneros Collection.)

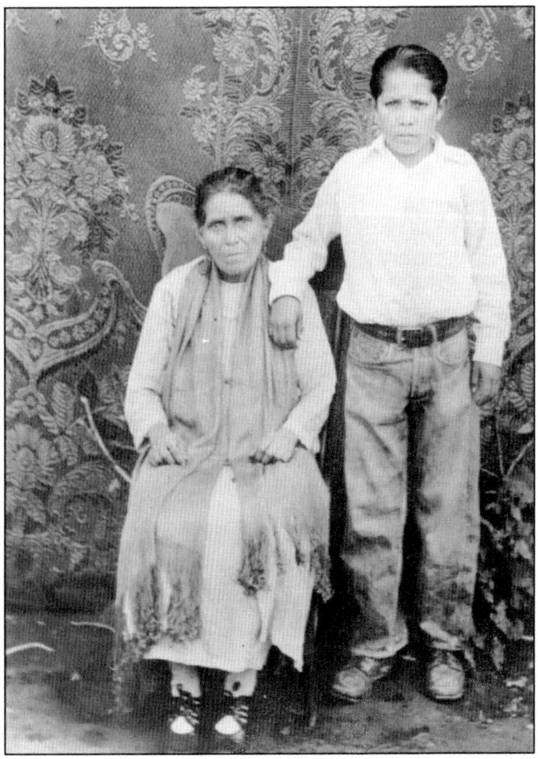

This c. 1925 photograph shows Jacinta and her youngest son, Benjamin. Mauricio Pasillas, wanted by the Mexican government after the revolution, fled with his wife, Jacinta Rodriguez, and their six children. Mauricio died on the journey to Flood Ranch, but Jacinta arrived with all of her children around 1920. She bought a parcel of land on Carpenter Lane (now Los Nietos Road) with the help of her older children. It was just east of Alabama Street (now Pioneer Boulevard). (Courtesy Sanchez Collection.)

Telesforo Pasillas is pictured at his Flood Ranch home around 1930. Telesforo arrived in Flood Ranch with his mother, Jacinta, and siblings in 1920. They first went to Arizona to work in the coal mines and then came to Flood Ranch to join family already living in the area. Telesforo met and married Francisca Zamora and bought property just east of his mother. They had no children. (Courtesy Sanchez Collection.)

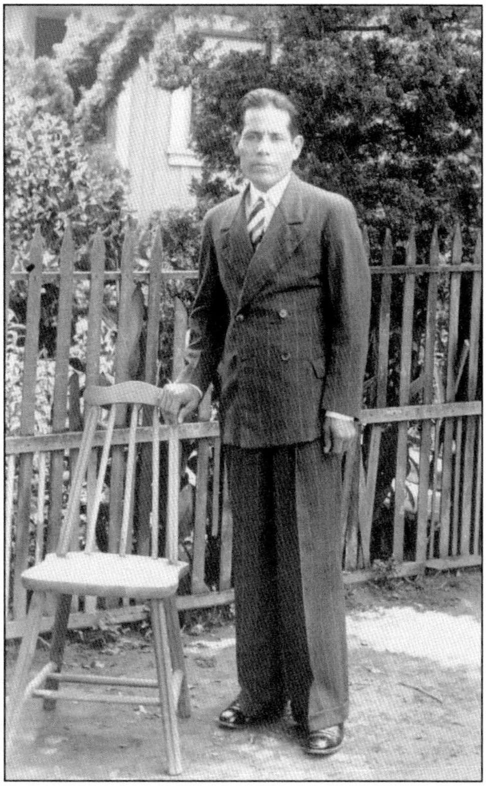

Andrea was the oldest daughter of Mauricio and Jacinta Pasillas. She married Francisco Pasillas, who may have been a distant relative. They lived in Flood Ranch until redevelopment and then relocated to Danby and lived there until they passed away. This 1920s photograph shows Francisco "Frank" and Andrea with four of their five children. Rody, not in the photograph, was born in 1931 and still lives in Santa Fe Springs. (Courtesy Sanchez Collection.)

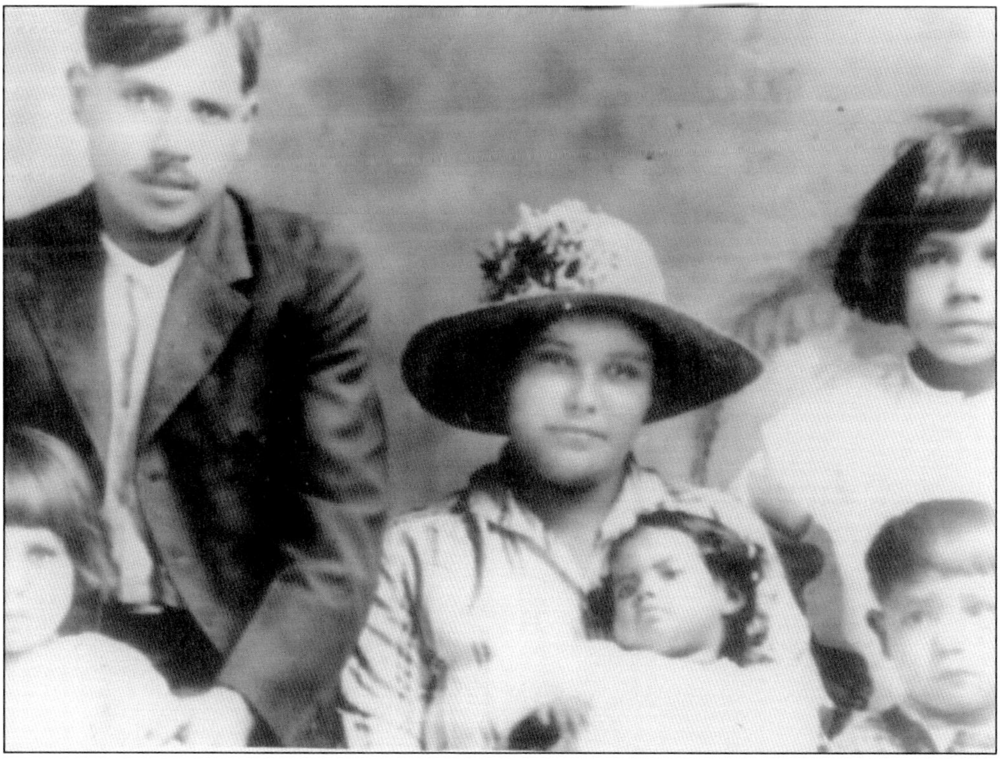

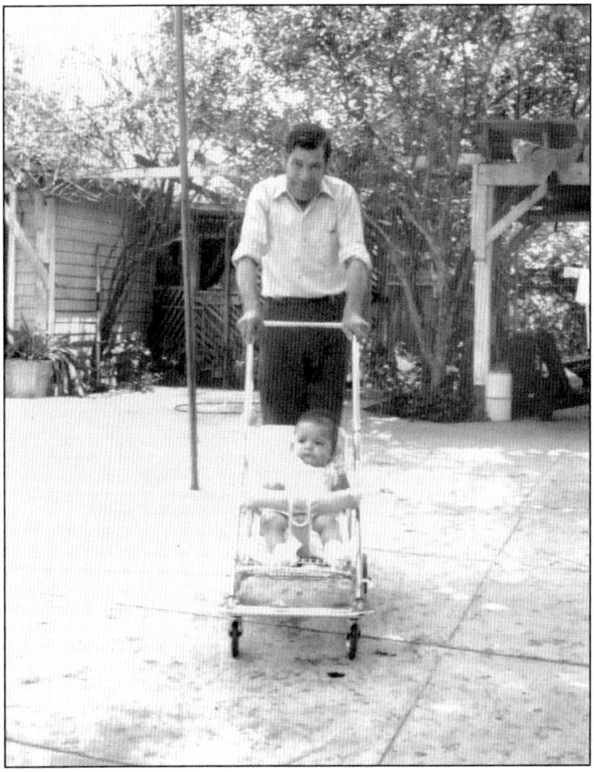

Fidel Pasillas takes his grandson Gilbert Reyes for a stroll in the backyard of his home on Millergrove Drive in the late 1950s. Fidel was the fourth child of Jacinta and Mauricio Pasillas. He met and married Flood Ranch resident Maria Magana Ayala when she was 16 years old, and they moved into a one-room house on Millergrove Drive. Their three children, Gloria, Daniel, and Rosie, still live in Santa Fe Springs. (Courtesy Sanchez Collection.)

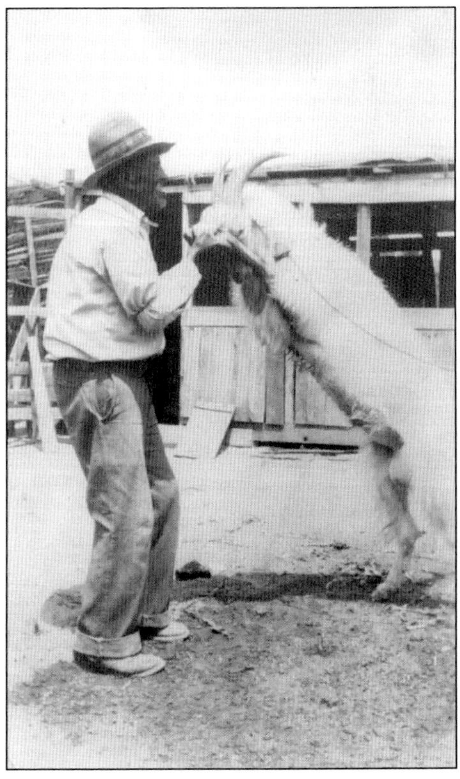

Andres Cerceres is pictured around 1935 dancing with his goat. Andres came to Flood Ranch around 1930. Maria Luisa, his wife, visited but refused to live in his small house because he insisted on bringing the animals in at night. Andres died in 1938 when a Pacific Red Line car struck him. Andres's granddaughter Emilia and her husband, Blandin Bustos, moved into the house in 1947. Emilia's daughter Margaret still lives on the property. (Courtesy Bustos Collection.)

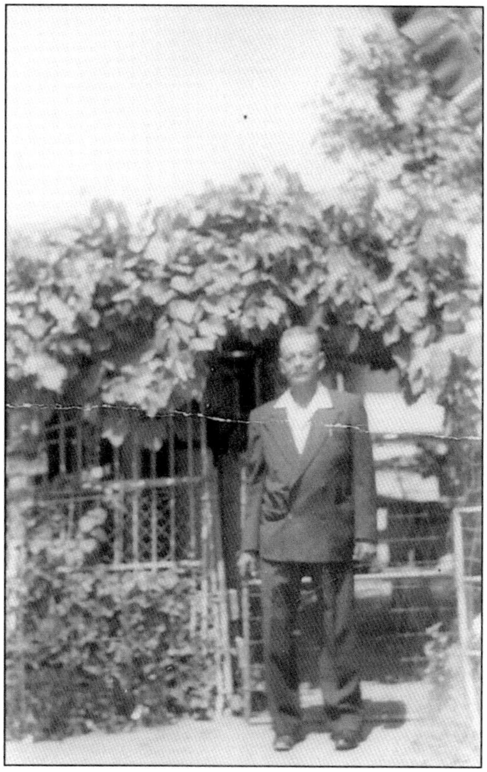

Daniel Mendoza is pictured around 1950 in front of his home. He and his wife, Hilaria, purchased six acres of land in Flood Ranch in 1927. Mendoza worked during the week and built a home on his property on the weekends. He finished his home in the early 1930s, moved in, and started his family. The home was on Virginia Avenue near the river. Daniel and Hilaria had eight children. (Courtesy Mendoza Collection.)

Daniel Mendoza's two sons Jimmy (left) and Daniel Jr. (right) are seen in this c. 1950 photograph on the driveway of their home on Virginia Avenue. The small boy is unidentified. Daniel Sr. started a trash disposal business out of his ranch. In the late 1940s, he sold three acres of land to three men. He sold one acre each to Jack Chocolate, Ferman Nunez, and Art Cadana. Jimmy once commented that his father always wore a suit. (Courtesy Mendoza Collection.)

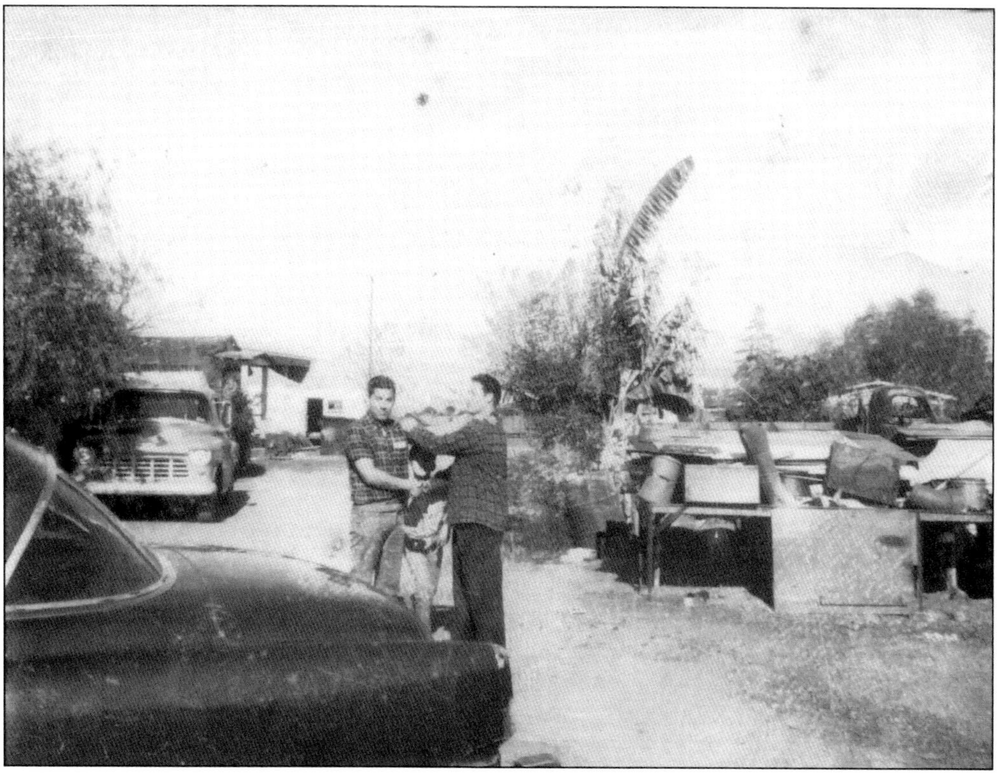

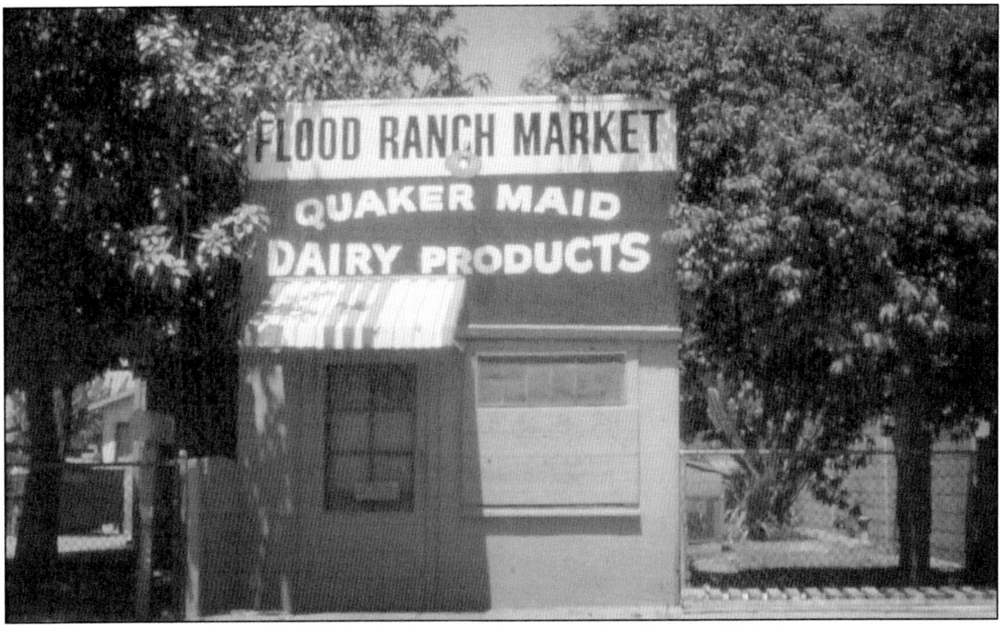

By the 1940s, there were five small markets in Flood Ranch: Ashman's Store on Carpenter Lane; Lincoln Market on Lincoln Avenue; River Market on Virginia Avenue near the San Gabriel River; and Velasco's Market on Garfield Avenue north of Virginia, which opened in 1942. Flood Ranch Market, on Garfield south of Virginia, is pictured here in the early 1960s and was also known as Fina's Market when it opened in the late 1940s. (Courtesy SFS Archives.)

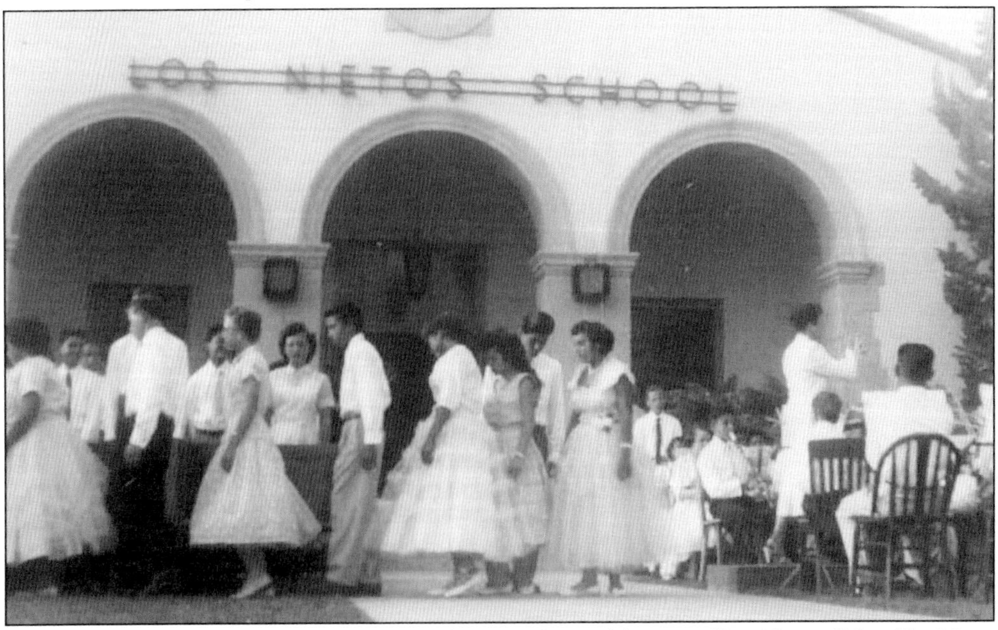

An eighth-grade graduation is pictured around 1950 in front of the second Los Nietos School building. All the children of Flood Ranch attended school in the Los Nietos School District for elementary and junior high school. Those who continued on to high school attended Whittier High School. Before 1962, Los Nietos School taught elementary and junior high classes. The first schoolhouse was located on Norwalk Boulevard north of Carpenter Lane. (Courtesy SFS Archives.)

Three

Black Gold Explosion

Over a decade after the turn of the 20th century, Santa Fe Springs was still a quaint agricultural community where everyone knew each other. Citrus groves covered the landscape, making oranges the dominant commodity in the area. Besides the San Gabriel River, which flowed about a mile west of town, were several small ponds and creeks that crisscrossed the countryside. There was plenty of water for the crops, but for decades, one of the biggest inconveniences when digging a well was discovering smelly water contaminated by sulfur. Unaware to most of those digging the wells, this foul water was evidence of a great oil pool lying dormant beneath their feet. Eugene Sanford had complained for years to his friends and neighbors of the oil that seeped up through the ground in the middle of his fields and ruined his crops, but nobody listened. Seepage of oil from the ground occurred as far back as the time when the Tongva inhabited the area. Even in 1865, the Los Angeles Pioneer Oil Company had a 25-year lease on land in Santa Fe Springs, but when no oil was found, it let the lease expire.

In 1907, Marius Meyer, a local resident and sheep farmer, was drilling a well for water and became excited when a "rotten egg-smelling" gas shot high into the air and was followed by hot water. Meyer tried convincing the Standard Oil Company to take interest, but without success. Alphonso Bell, Meyer's neighbor, contacted an acquaintance of his at the Union Oil Company and told him of their situation. With the demand for oil increasing, he agreed to take a look and began a preliminary investigation. After the study was complete and he was satisfied with the results, Union Oil entered into a lease agreement with both Bell and Meyer in 1907. It took several years before the Meyer No. 1 well was sunk, but with disappointing results. The second well, Meyer No. 2, started a few months later with a newly imported Texas rotary tip, but this, too, had less than favorable results.

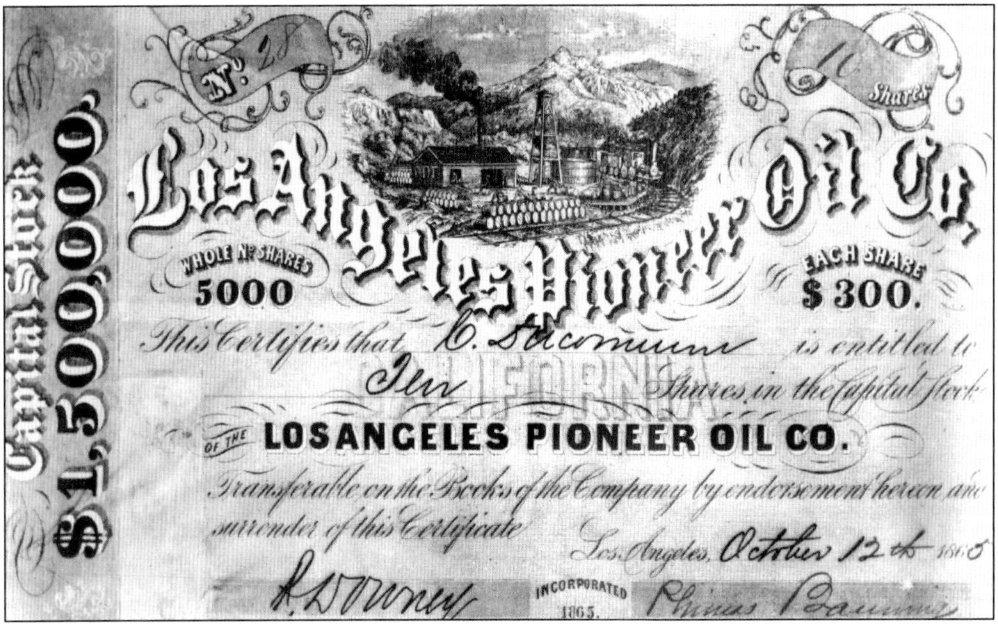

No. 28

10 Shares

Capital Stock $1,500,000

Los Angeles Pioneer Oil Co.

Whole No. Shares 5000

Each Share $300.

This Certifies that [illegible] is entitled to Ten Shares in the Capital Stock of the LOSANGELES PIONEER OIL CO. Transferable on the Books of the Company by endorsement hereon and surrender of this Certificate

Los Angeles, October 12th 1865

Incorporated 1865.

As far back as the 1860s, while digging wells for water, residents would often experience a sudden rumbling and a blast of natural gas followed by a foul smell like rotten eggs. In 1865, the Los Angeles Pioneer Oil Company signed a 25-year lease with the Little Lake School to do exploratory drilling on its land. After years of unsuccessful drilling, the company abandoned its efforts and let the lease run out. (Courtesy SFS collection.)

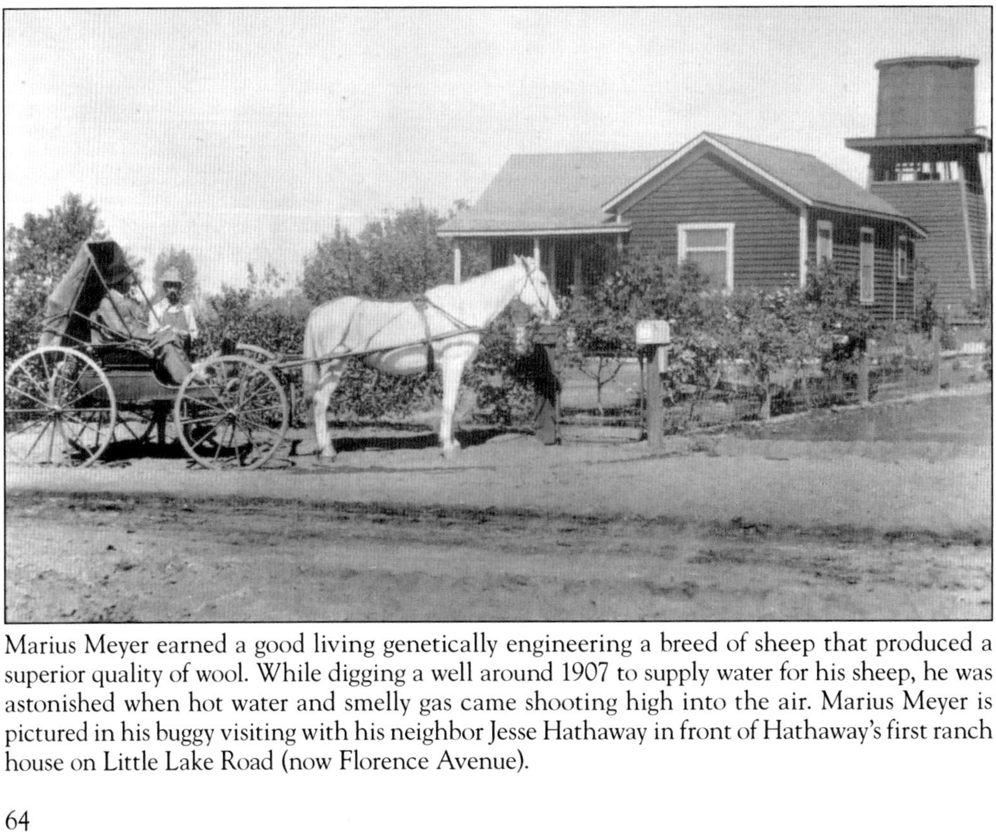

Marius Meyer earned a good living genetically engineering a breed of sheep that produced a superior quality of wool. While digging a well around 1907 to supply water for his sheep, he was astonished when hot water and smelly gas came shooting high into the air. Marius Meyer is pictured in his buggy visiting with his neighbor Jesse Hathaway in front of Hathaway's first ranch house on Little Lake Road (now Florence Avenue).

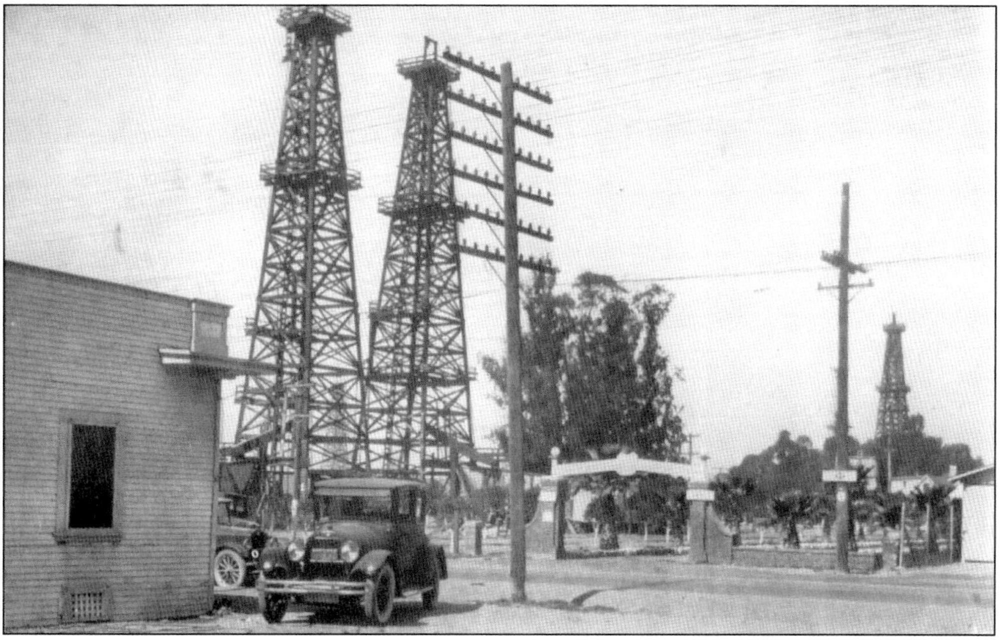

After much convincing on their part, Marius Meyer and his neighbor Alphonso Bell signed an agreement with the Union Oil Company to drill on their land. Here is the entrance to the Bell Ranch, which was located on the north side of Telegraph Road and west of Santa Fe Springs Road. The building on the left is the Spud Inn restaurant. (Courtesy Chas. A. Waer.)

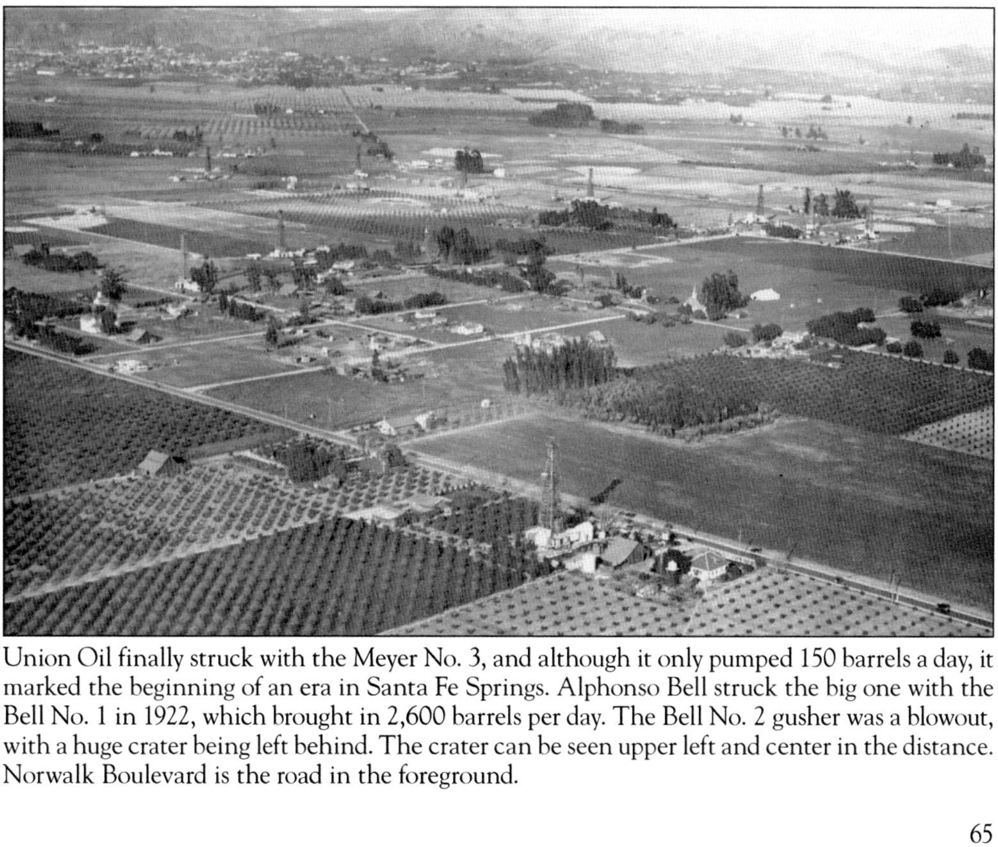

Union Oil finally struck with the Meyer No. 3, and although it only pumped 150 barrels a day, it marked the beginning of an era in Santa Fe Springs. Alphonso Bell struck the big one with the Bell No. 1 in 1922, which brought in 2,600 barrels per day. The Bell No. 2 gusher was a blowout, with a huge crater being left behind. The crater can be seen upper left and center in the distance. Norwalk Boulevard is the road in the foreground.

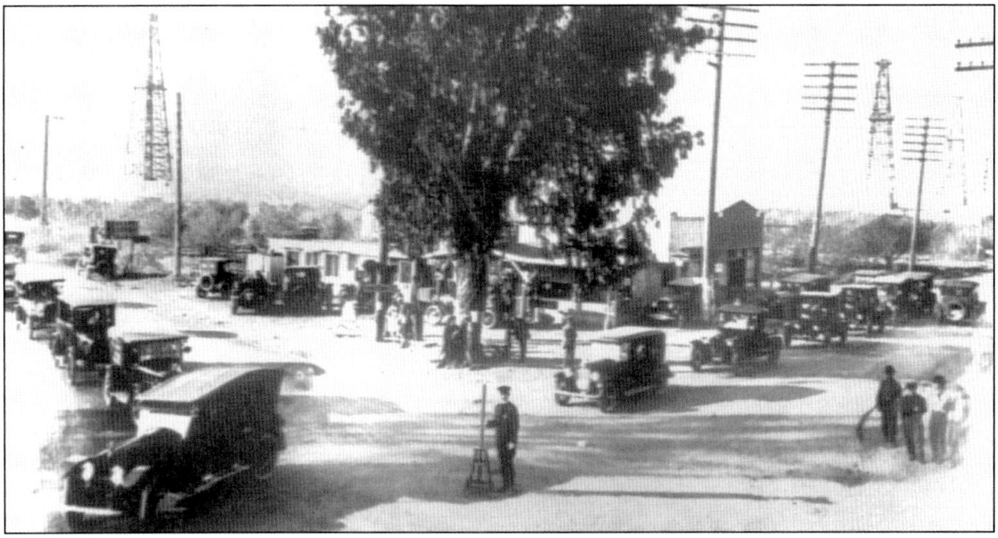

The word was out that there was an oil boom in Santa Fe Springs. Men came from all over looking for jobs with good pay, and some came looking for a chance to get rich quick. The Four Corners community changed almost overnight, and there was not enough room to house the growing population. Many built shacks where they could. The c. 1925 photograph above shows the intersection of Norwalk Boulevard and Telegraph Road looking northwest.

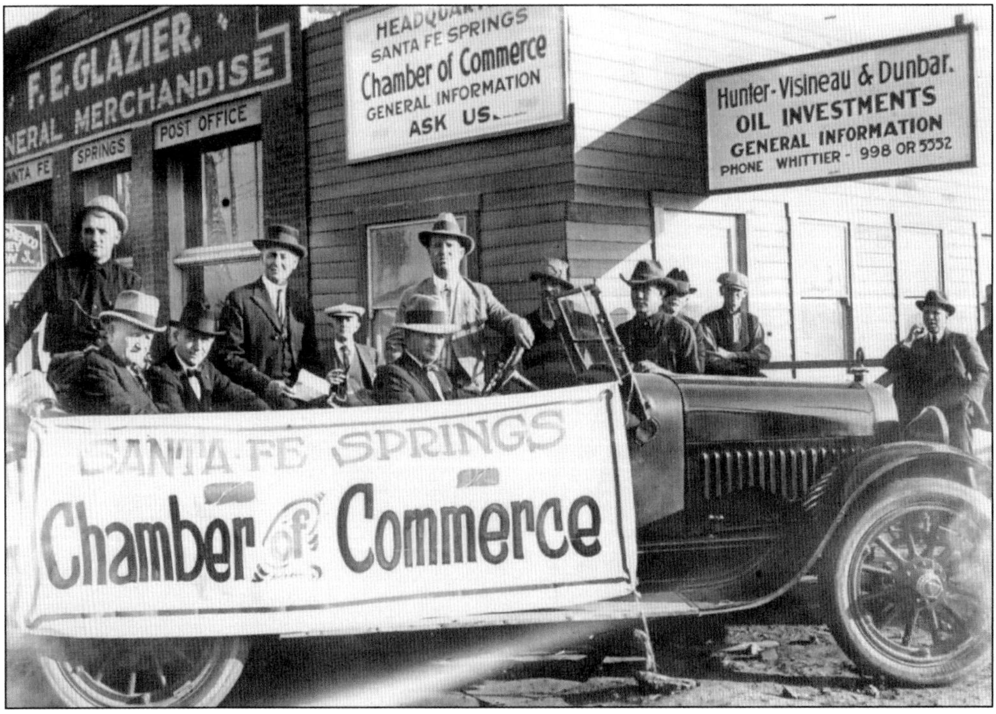

Four Corners was the center of business during the oil boom. In this 1922 photograph, some members of the newly formed Santa Fe Springs Chamber of Commerce—previously known as the Petroleum Club—are seen posing in a Hudson touring car. At the far left is Henry Gross; seated in front of him is W.E. Hawley, Ed Jounigan is behind the steering wheel, and sitting shotgun is Phil Gross.

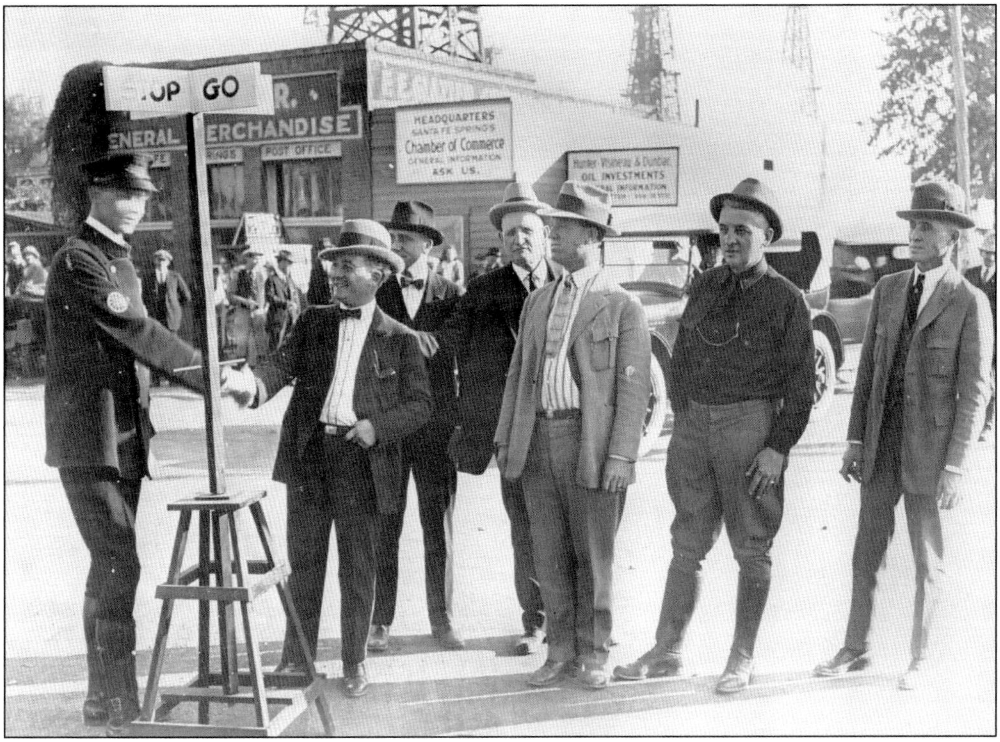

The allure of wealth brought out investors, such as J. Paul Getty, Harry S. Rothschild, C.C. Julian, Charlie Chaplin, Sid Grauman, and William Gibbs McAdoo, Pres. Woodrow Wilson's son-in-law. Standing in the middle of the Four Corners intersection are members of the chamber of commerce ready to welcome any new investors. From left to right are traffic cop S.W. Huntington Jr., Phil Gross, unidentified, Col. W.F. Hawley (the promoter), Ed Jounigan, Henry Gross, and unidentified.

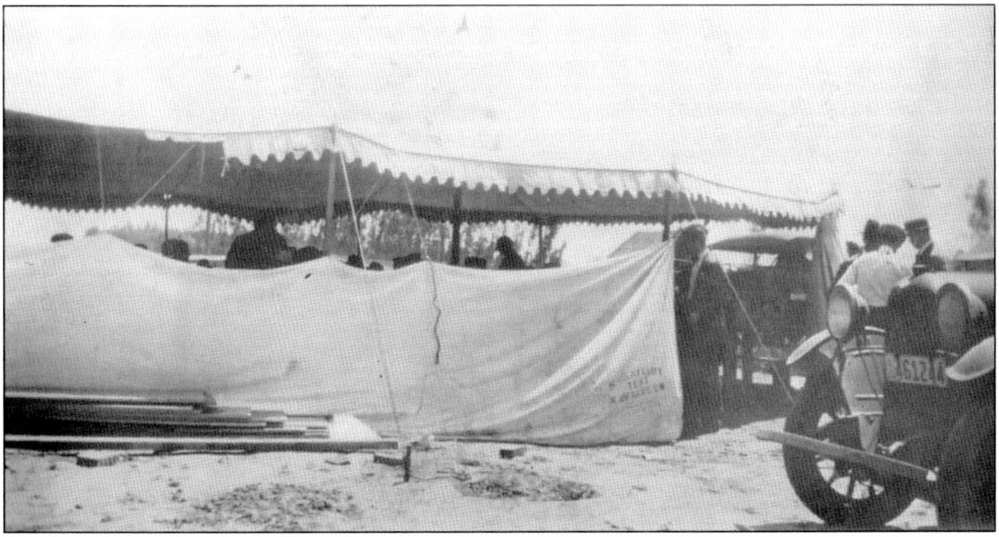

This is William McAdoo's "Sucker Tent," as they were called, similar to many that were erected by promoters to sell shares of oil stock. Unfortunately, not all the promoters were legitimate. Some fast-talking promoters came in and sold shares to unsuspecting investors who did not read the fine print. These shysters would drill one dry well, take all the money, and then skip town.

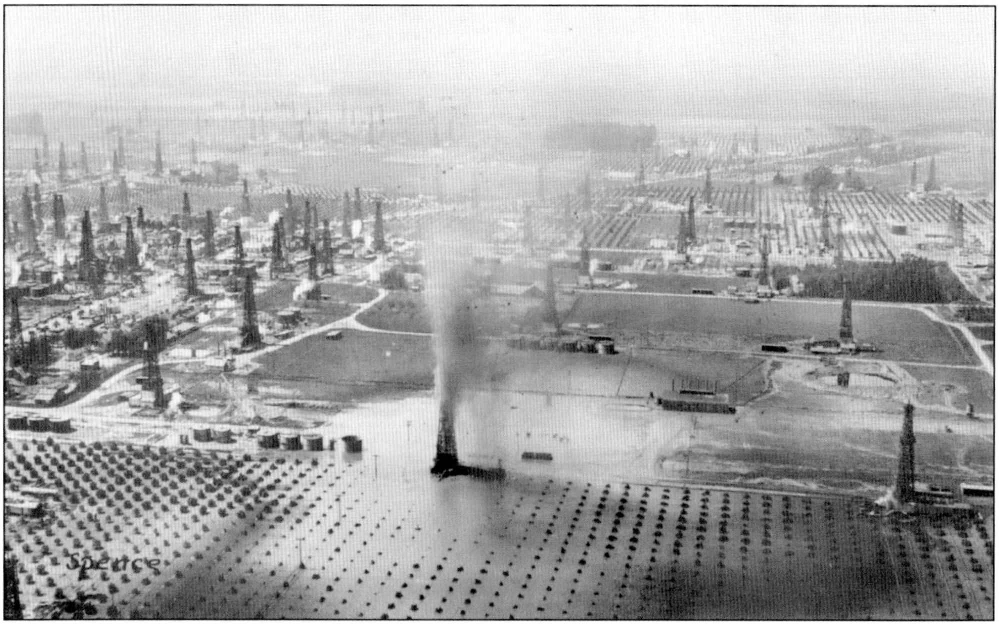

Oil derricks were being built wherever space permitted. Property value skyrocketed, and many people sold their farms at huge profits. Farmers who were barely making a living were suddenly millionaires. The ones who really made their fortunes were those who leased their land and collected royalties. This 1923 aerial view of Santa Fe Springs captures a gusher on the Bell Ranch. Four Corners is visible at center left in the photograph.

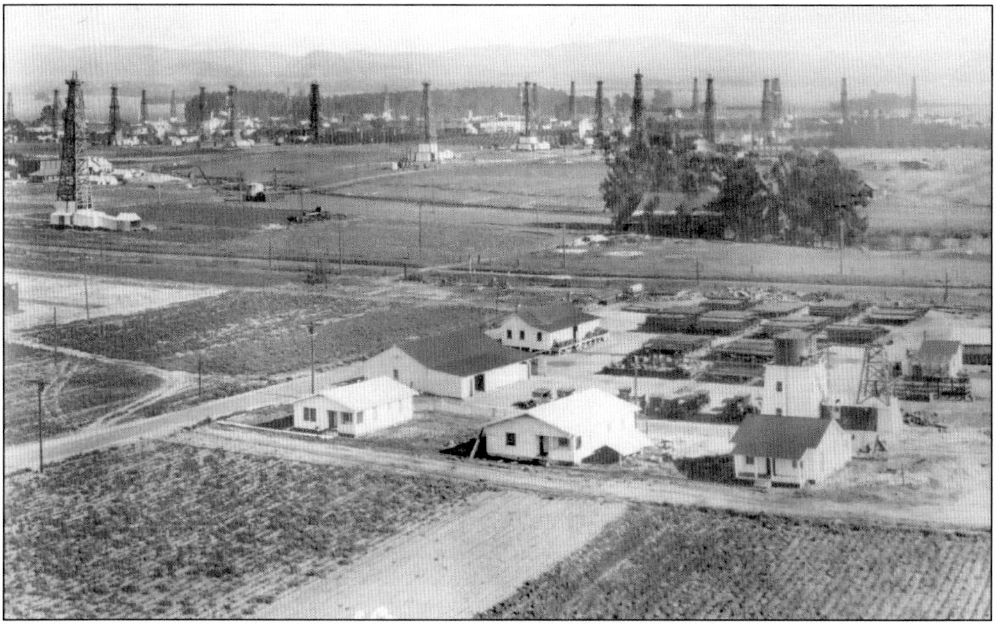

Just a few years after the onset of the oil boom, many families had moved away, like the Bells, the Foixes, and the Alexanders. Their homes became the headquarters for the various oil company crews. Here is the headquarters for the Getty Oil crew, which was the former Baker home. The Getty No. 1 well marked the peak of the oil boom. By 1923, the Santa Fe Springs oil fields had produced 80,671,172 barrels of high-quality oil.

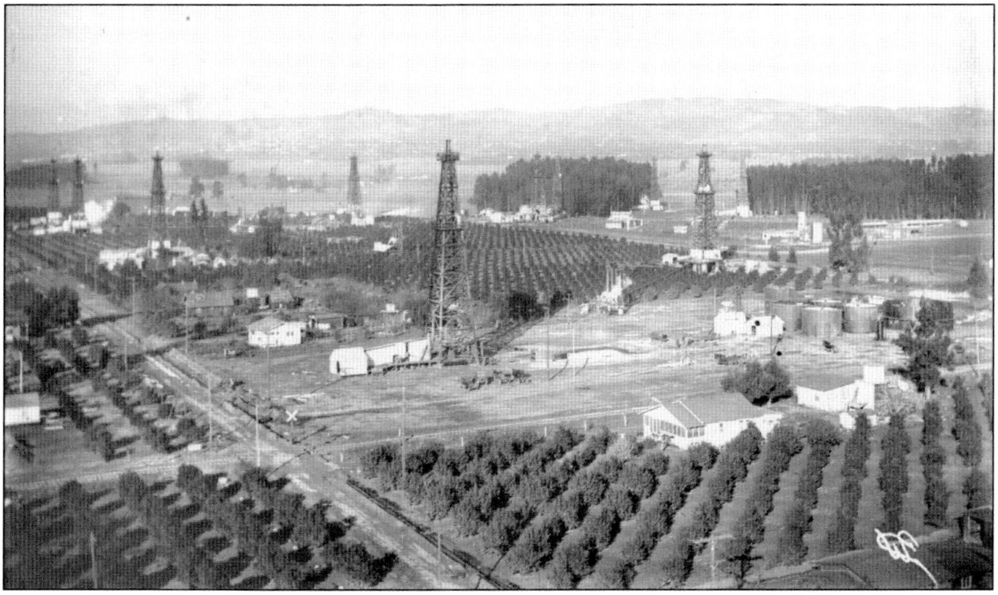

This aerial view shows how oil derricks were built any place they thought there might be oil. Landowners allowed derricks to be built in the middle of their citrus groves and even dangerously close to their homes. Alongside the road on the lower left, it appears that an underground pipeline is being laid, probably for oil production. Also shown is the northern edge of the oil fields with Whittier Hills in the background.

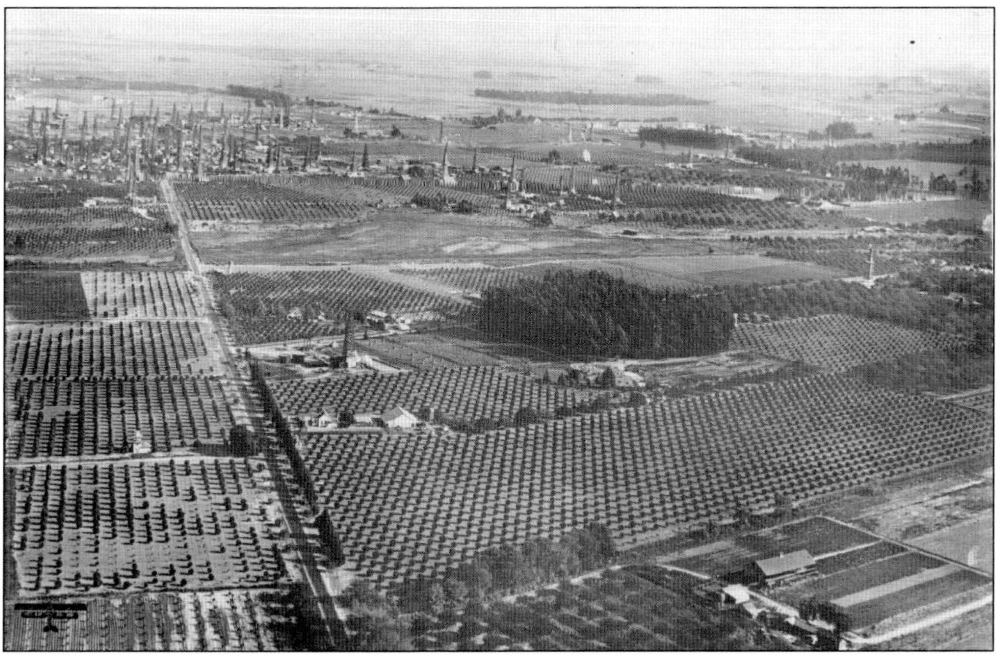

Life on the outside edge of the oil fields continued as usual, except for the constant noise and smell. The Clark Estate, built in 1921, is pictured at center just below the large eucalyptus grove. Trees from the grove were used as fuel before natural gas was available. The road running vertically on the left is Telegraph Road traveling east towards Four Corners (top left), where the major part of the drilling occurred.

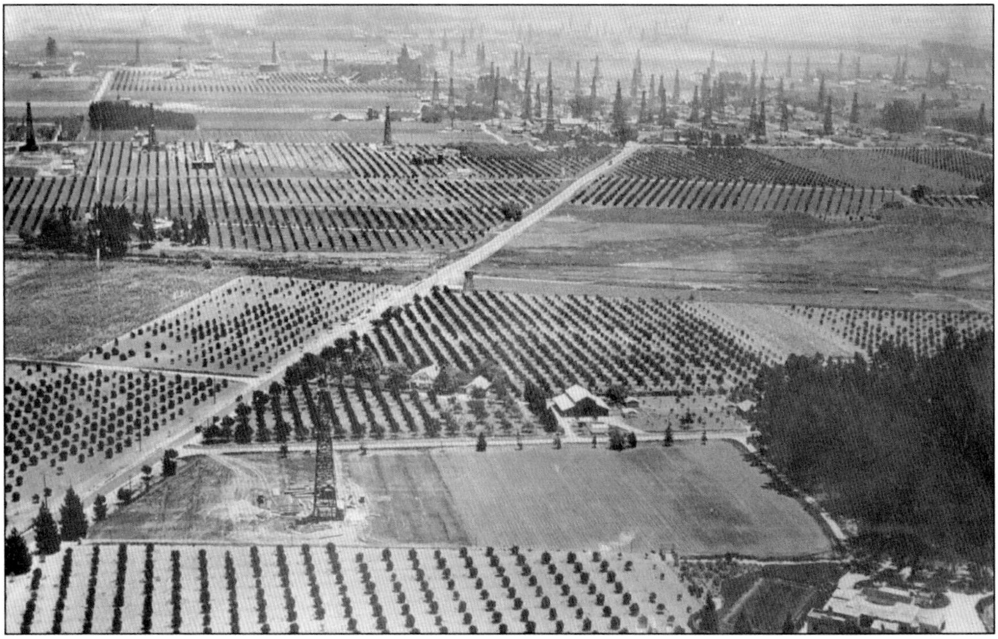

By 1924, the rural beauty of Santa Fe Springs was gone and never to return. The agricultural industry in the heart of the town was being abandoned for the more lucrative oil industry. Many of the citrus fields were no longer being worked but were left to survive on their own. On the bottom right are the Clark estate and Telegraph Road running diagonally across the photograph.

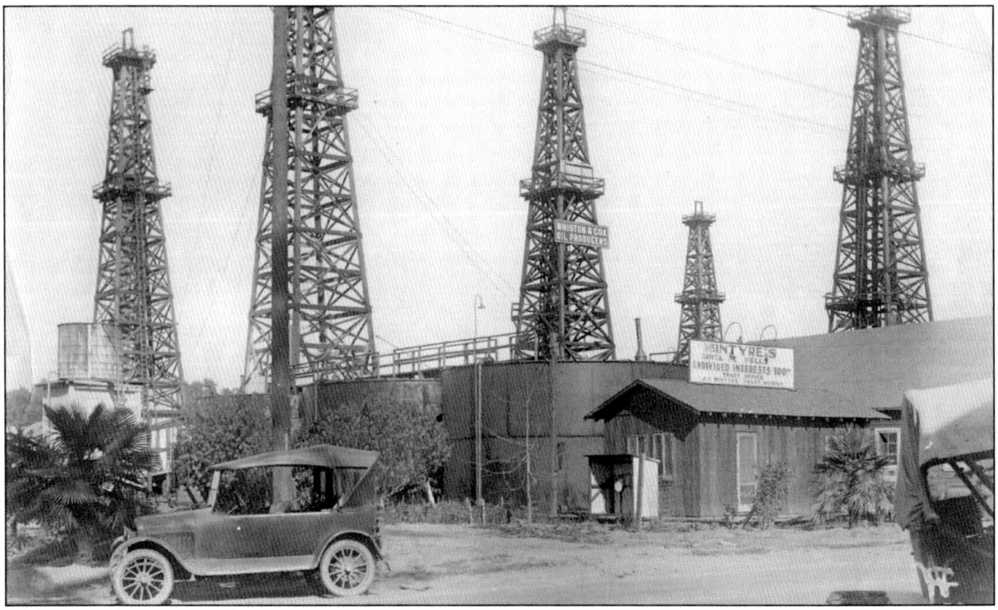

In this c. 1924 photograph, the wooden derrick in the center displays the sign "Whiston & Cox Oil Producers," which stands in what was once the driveway of the Alexander Home and Dairy, located north of Telegraph Road and east of Four Corners next to Bell View. Very likely, this is a well drilled by Wilbur Cox, just east of Frank McCarric's property. McCarric was Lola M. Hathaway's father, and his property became the Hathaway Company's Springs Lease. (Courtesy Chas. A. Waer.)

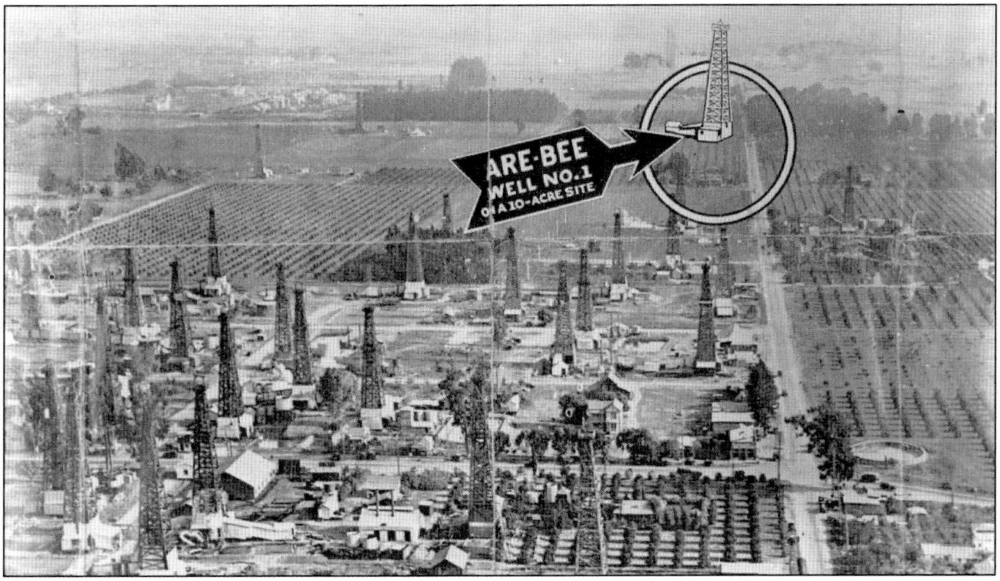

This south-facing 1922 aerial postcard of the oil fields was probably sent to investors. A closer look reveals remnants of the residential community amidst the oil derricks. Note the oil industry supporting businesses that infiltrated the area. Norwalk Boulevard is running up and down the right side of the photograph, the Koontz store is still visible at the lower right, and the Koontz home is to its left.

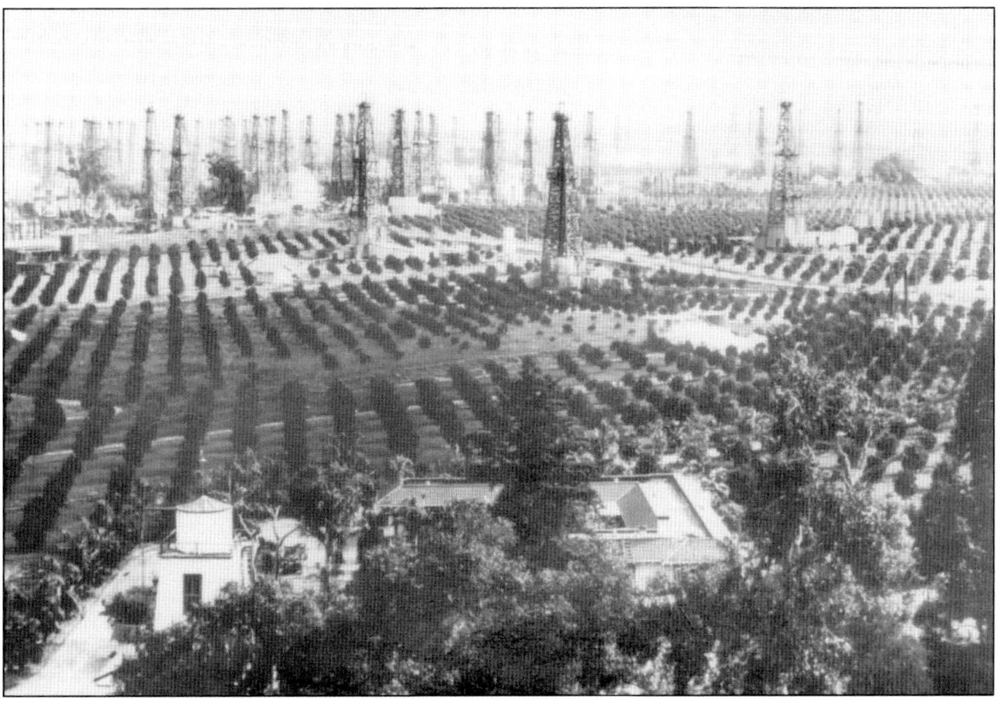

The Materns stayed in the area as long as they could, until 1926, when they decided to move. They allowed Carl Besser and his wife to occupy the home and left him in charge of the oil and agriculture business. After two years of noise, dirt, and fumes, they also left. The house was rented to oil field workers until it was sold in 1931.

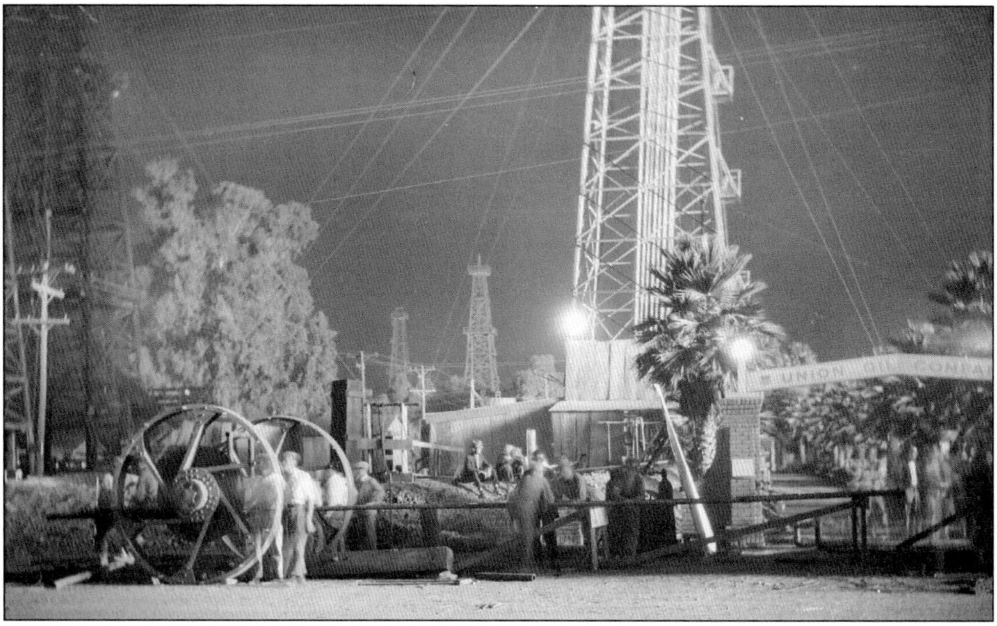

Oil crews worked day and night, and the noise and smell never stopped. This is one of the main reasons residents moved away from Santa Fe Springs. Here, a Union Oil crew is pictured working feverishly through the night. The former entrance to the Bell Ranch is seen on the right. With the proceeds from his oil royalties, Alphonso Bell went on to develop the community of Bel-Air.

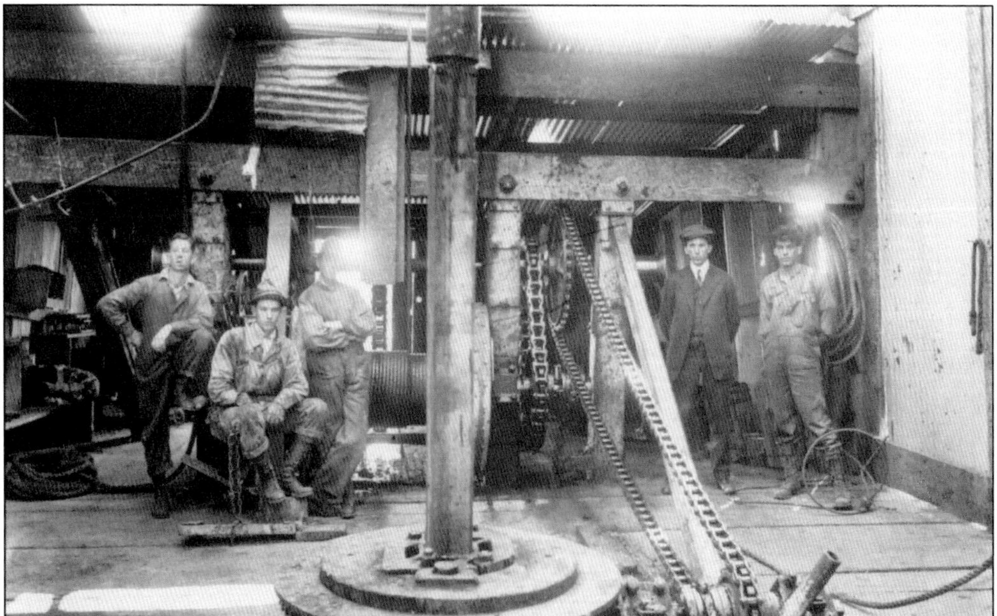

The location of this Santa Fe Springs rig and the names of its crew are unidentified. The early and primitive-style rotary draw-works suggests that either they bought the cheapest equipment they could find or that was all they could get their hands on. Probably a steam-driven engine powered the equipment. Most of the rigs in Santa Fe Springs in the 1920s and 1930s were combination rigs, with both cable tool and rotary drilling operation.

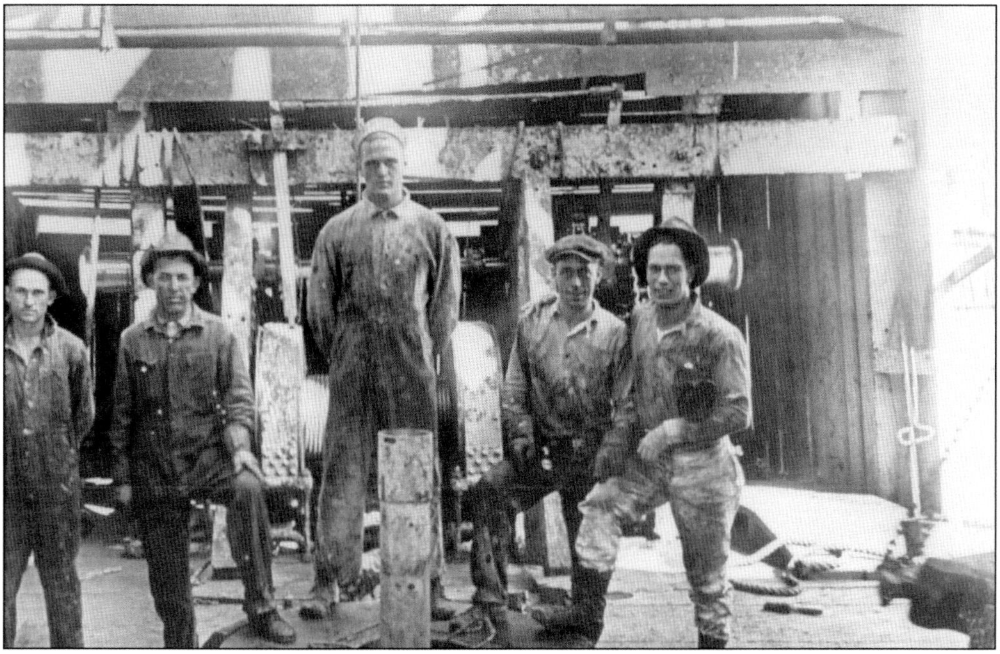

The location of this Santa Fe Springs rig and the names of its crew are unidentified. This rig is a similar style to the rig in the image at the bottom left. What is really interesting, considering the use of such primitive rotary equipment, is the apparent absence of the typical calf and bull wheels found in a combination rig. This suggests that the rig above might have been rotary only.

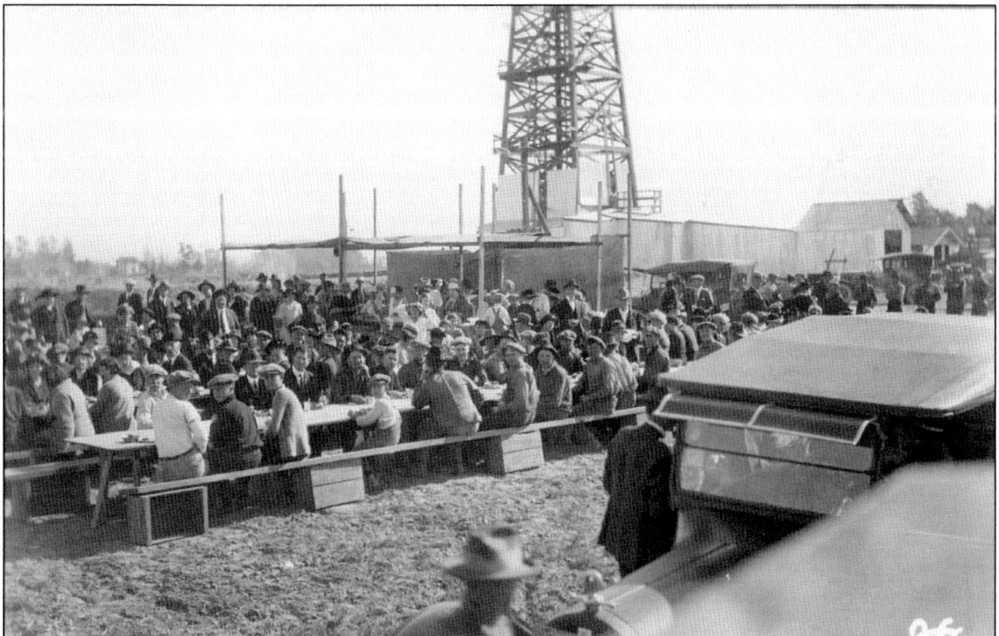

Gathered are prospective investors, or "suckers," who were invited to a free meal by oil company promoters. After dinner, they may have enjoyed drinks and entertainment before entering the "sucker tents" to listen to the sales pitch. Not all transactions were on the up-and-up. This well was located at East Parkford and Lakeland Roads. (Courtesy Chas. A. Waer.)

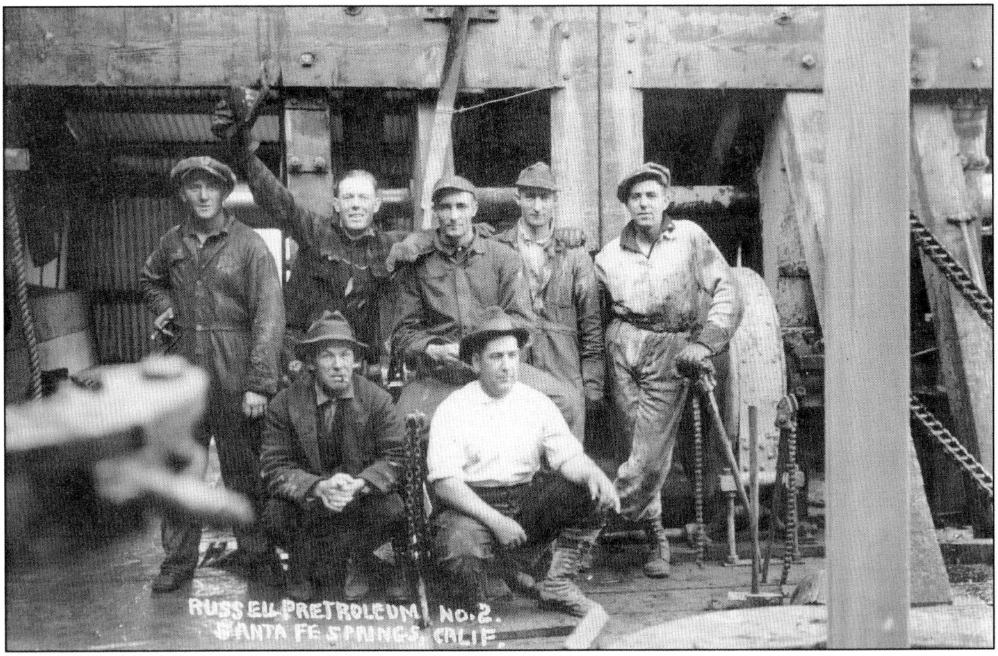

These oil field workers, or "roughnecks," took time to pose for a photograph. Most were seasoned oil workers looking for good pay. They worked hard and at the end of the day were ready for a distraction from their toil. For the accommodation of some, gambling, bootlegging, and prostitution became a part of life in Santa Fe Springs.

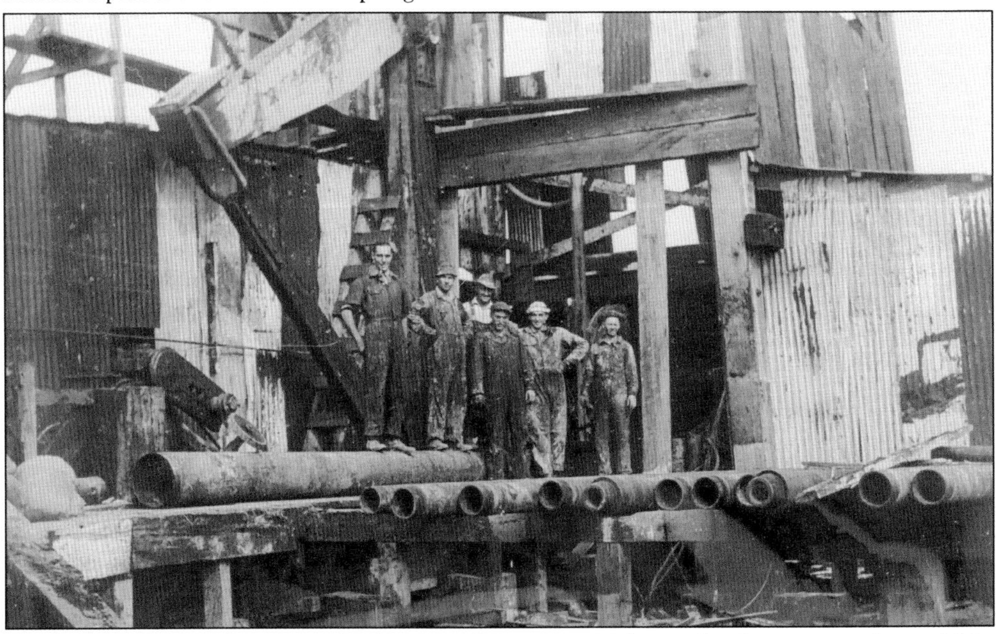
These unnamed roughnecks worked in a rig that appears to be made of any materials available. After work, many of them visited places like Mary's Place, a gambling hall near Little Lake Road (now Florence Avenue) and Bloomfield Road. There was also the Baker barn, now a gambling hall, and Kings Camp in the gum tree grove on Norwalk Boulevard near Little Lake Road, where they could find "ladies of the night."

Not every business in Santa Fe Springs was disreputable. There was the Four Corners Café, which was run by Louise "Mom" Johnson and her sister, Helen Billings, or "Aunt Helen." Here, one could find a home-cooked meal and friendly conversation. Pictured around 1942 at the counter are, from left to right, a bookkeeper from Eagle Oil Company, John, who worked at the Clarke Ranch, Thom Bloomfield, and an unidentified pumper.

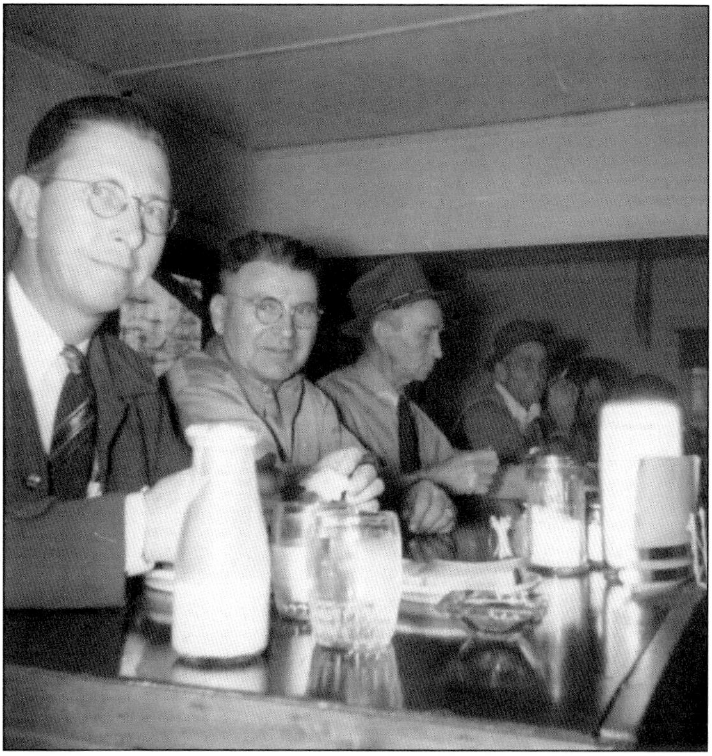

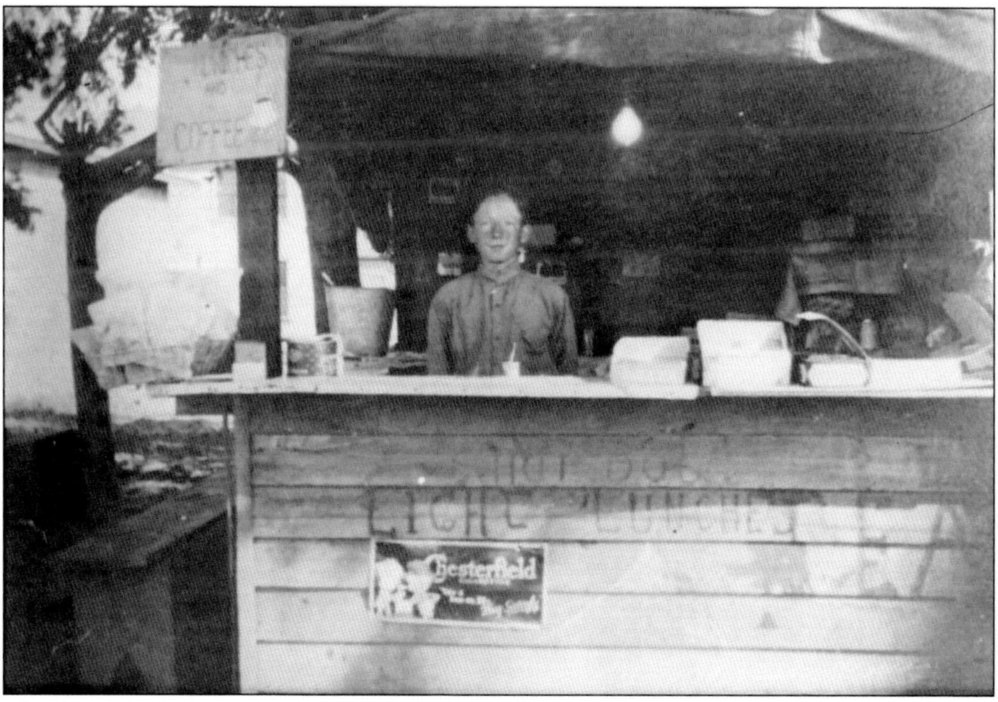

The first fast food place in Santa Fe Springs was Red's hot dog stand. He provided hot dogs, sandwiches, and coffee as a quick lunch for the oil workers. "Old Red," as he was known, put his stand just east of Four Corners on the south side of Telegraph Road.

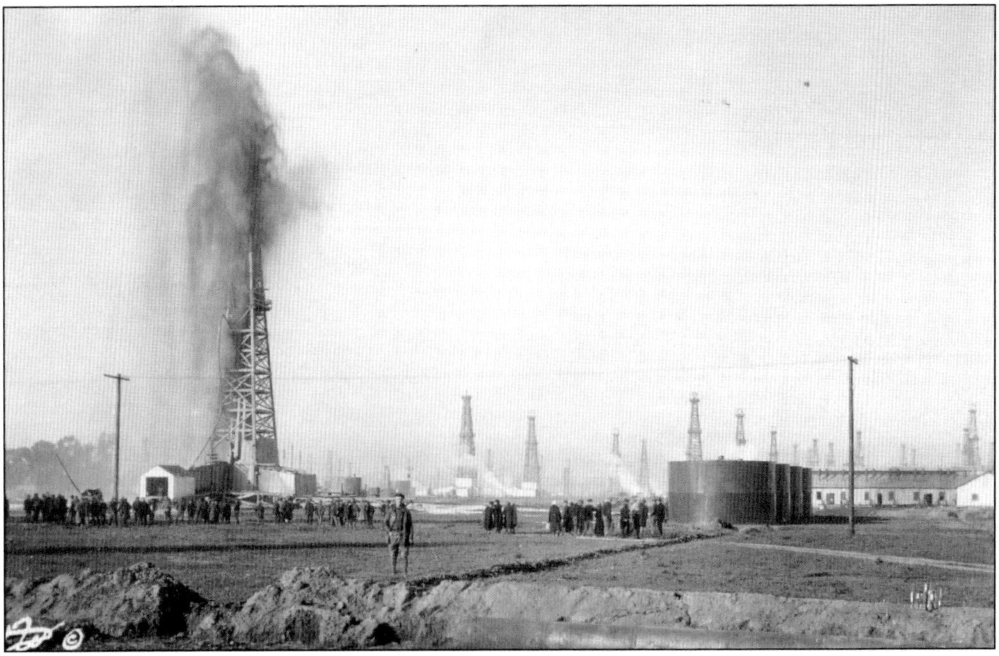

Pictured is the Old Kirkwood blowout of 1923. During the first years of the oil boom, these kinds of blowouts were a common occurrence. First, the ground would begin to rumble, then oil, mud, and rock would come shooting out of the well, covering everything. At first, people gathered to see the phenomenon, but later they became too common.

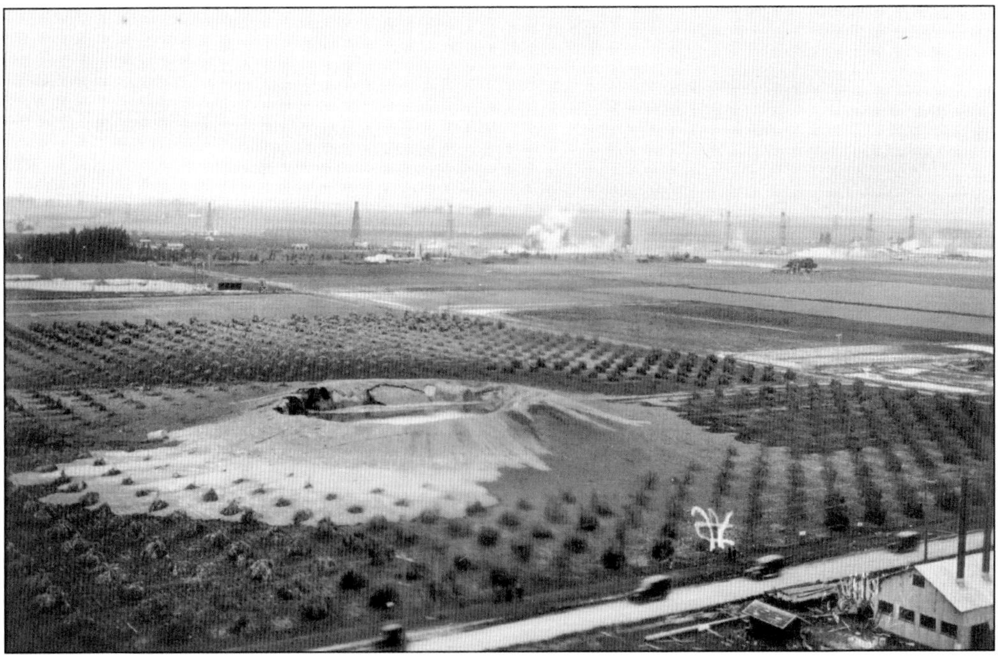

The Bell No. 2 blowout was one of the biggest during the boom. When it was all over, it had swallowed up the entire rig and derrick. Note the size of the crater compared to the size of the cars driving by on Santa Fe Springs Road. The orange trees closest to the crater were covered to the tops in mud.

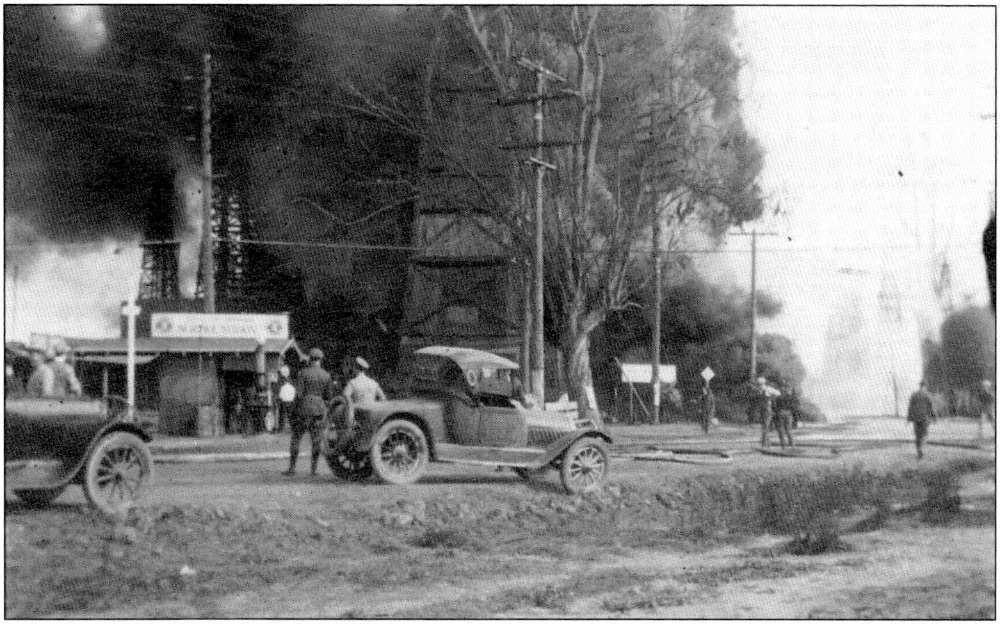

Another frequent occurrence of the oil boom was oil well fires. Fires were intentionally and routinely set to burn off unwanted gas fumes. These fumes never burned off completely and continually collected in pockets around the wells. These pockets easily ignited with a spark from machinery or a passing car, which resulted in firestorms. The Mohawk Petroleum well at Four Corners was one of the most dramatic fires of the boom.

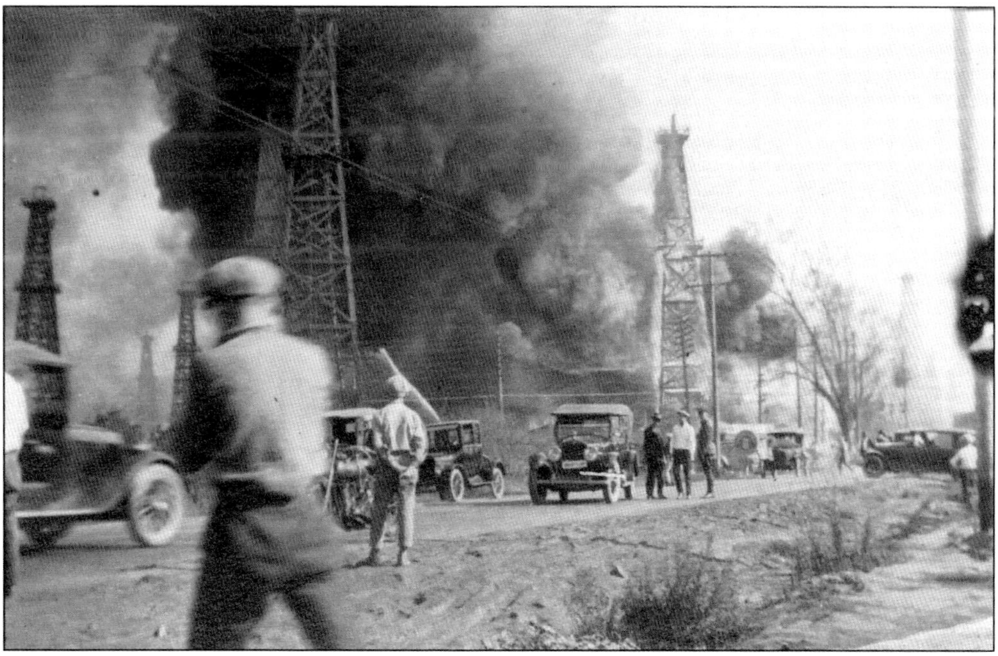

The Mohawk Petroleum fire of 1924 burned for weeks. The close proximity to the Four Corners businesses caused a frenzied effort to keep it from spreading. The plume of smoke could be seen for miles. Spectators came from all over the nearby area to see the fire and the firefighting efforts. Because of the primitive firefighting equipment, it took nearly a month to turn it off.

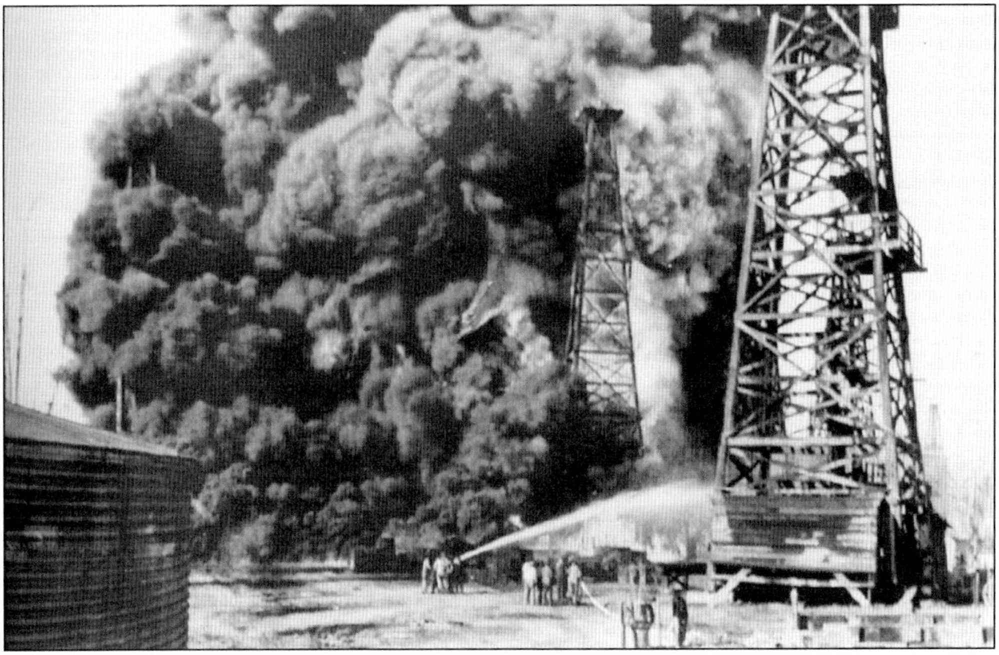

Here is a rear view of the Mohawk Petroleum fire. The wide plume of smoke is the result of the center derrick collapsing just as the photographer took the picture. Despite all the efforts to contain the fire, it still spread to neighboring derricks and buildings. This one would not be the last. In 1930, there was another fire at the Mohawk site that burned for 30 days.

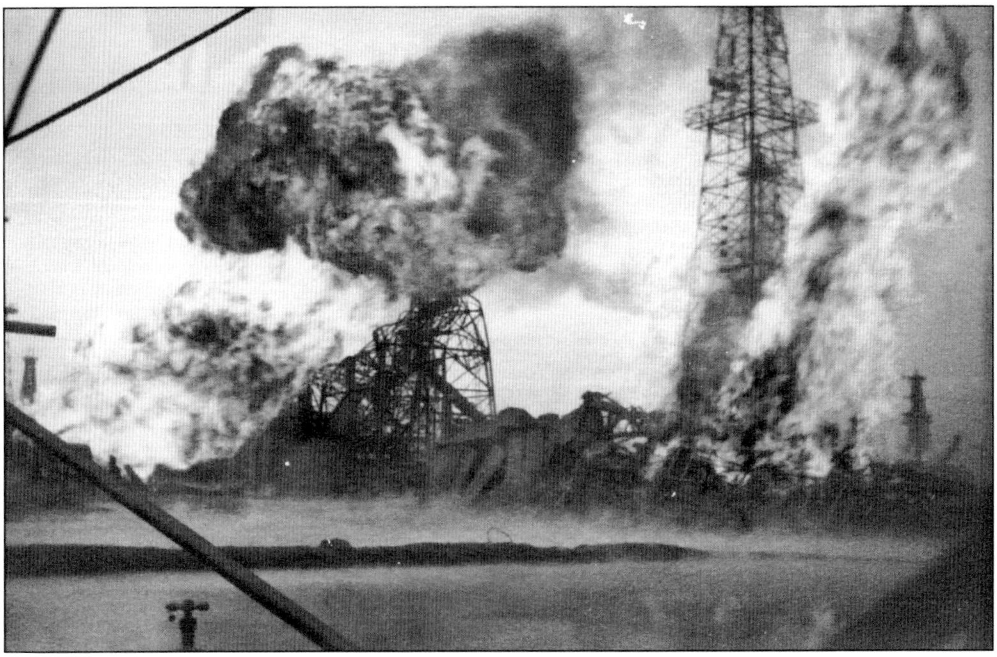

Fires occurred so frequently in one area of the oil fields that it was dubbed "Hell's Half Acre." The intense heat of the fires burned or melted everything in the vicinity. Among the worst fires in the Santa Fe Springs oil fields, besides the ones already mentioned, were the Bellview No. 22, also at Four Corners, and the Hathaway No. 3.

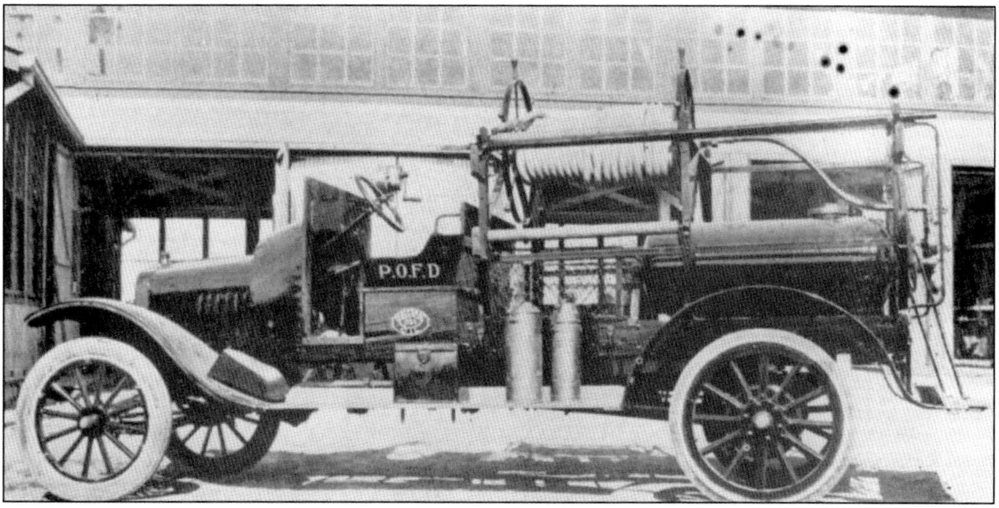

The fire equipment of the time was inadequate to fight the oil fires. The Los Angeles County Fire Department was forced to develop better equipment. The fires burned with such intense heat that only ash and melted metal remained after the fires were out. Light from the fires was so bright that some old timers claimed they were able to read a newspaper at night from the glow of a fire burning a mile away.

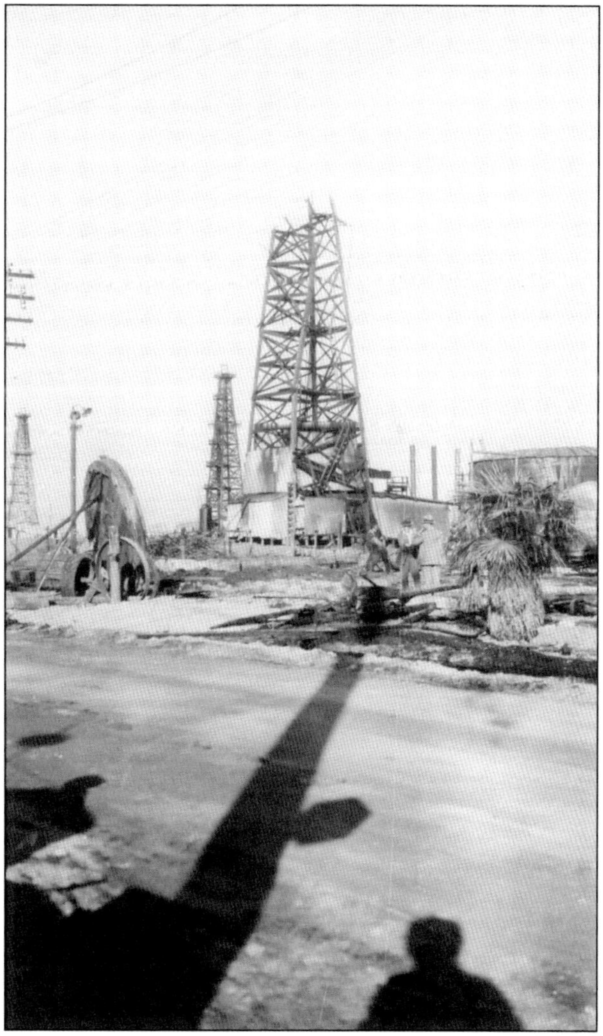

The 1924 Mohawk Petroleum fire destroyed everything on the northeast side of Four Corners. This photograph was taken from across Norwalk Boulevard, adjacent from the ruins, minutes before sunset. Only twisted remains of what was once a productive oil rig are left. The top of a nearby derrick had melted and collapsed from the extreme heat of the fire.

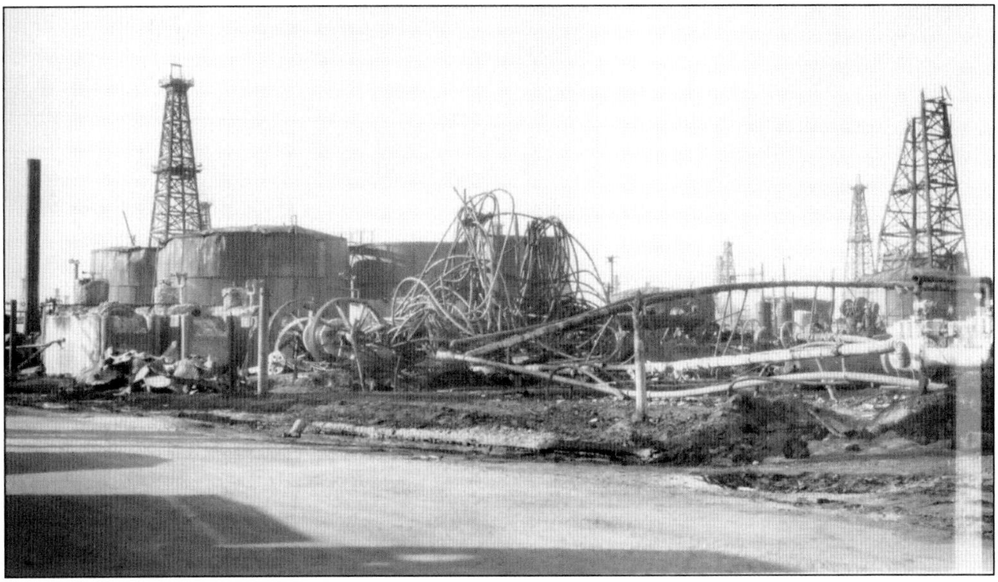

Notice the storage tanks that survived the fire, which appear to be bloated from the pressure that had built up during the Mohawk Petroleum fire of 1924. For years to come, oil well fires would be the biggest show in town. When the alarms sounded, people would come out to view the excitement. During the day, schoolchildren were sometimes bused in to see the fires.

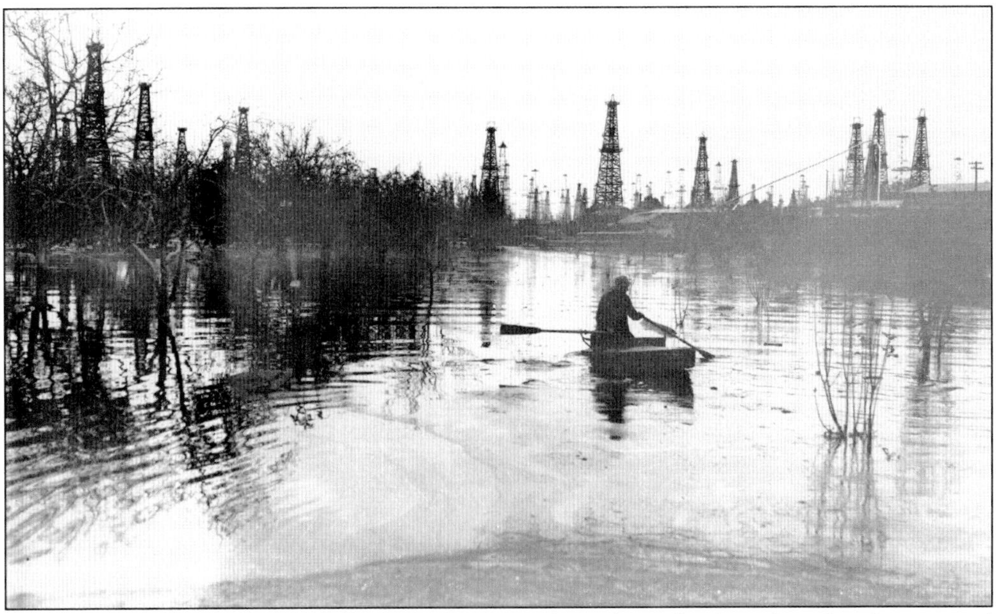

The Los Angeles Flood of 1938 brought devastation through much of Los Angeles, Orange, and Riverside Counties, including along the San Gabriel River. The heavy rains also brought flooding to the Santa Fe Springs oil fields. Julian Hathaway used a small rowboat to inspect the Hathaway Ranch. The Hathaway Ranch headquarters is seen on the right. The photograph was taken from Little Lake Road (now Florence Avenue).

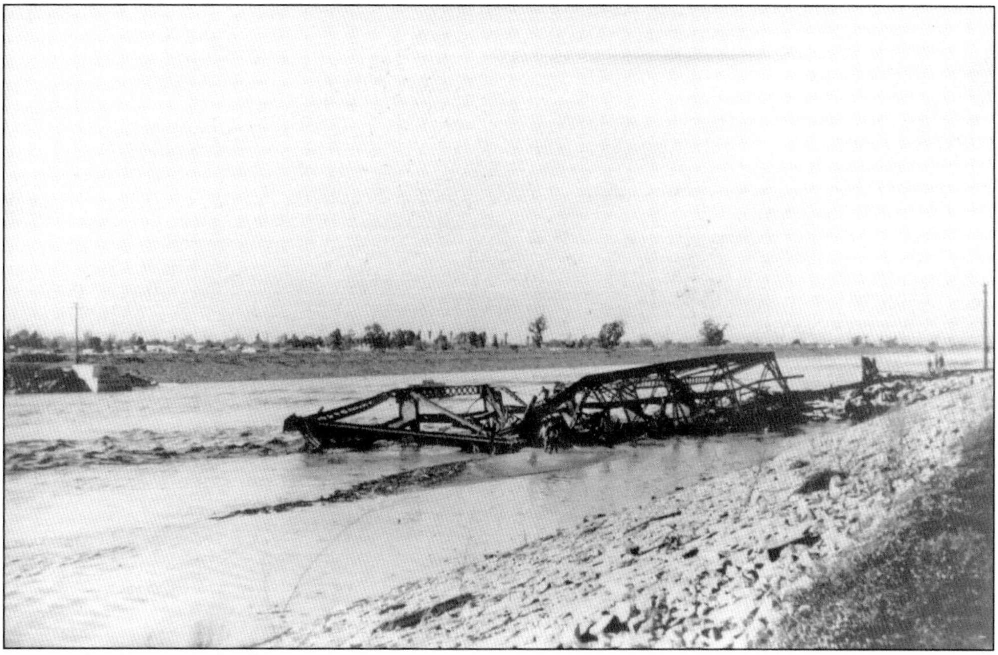

Here, a bridge is washed away at Florence Avenue. The flooding would have been far worse on the San Gabriel River if it were not for the series of flood control dams already in place. This flooding prompted the US Army Corps of Engineers to channelize the river and construct more flood control dams. (Courtesy SFS Archives.)

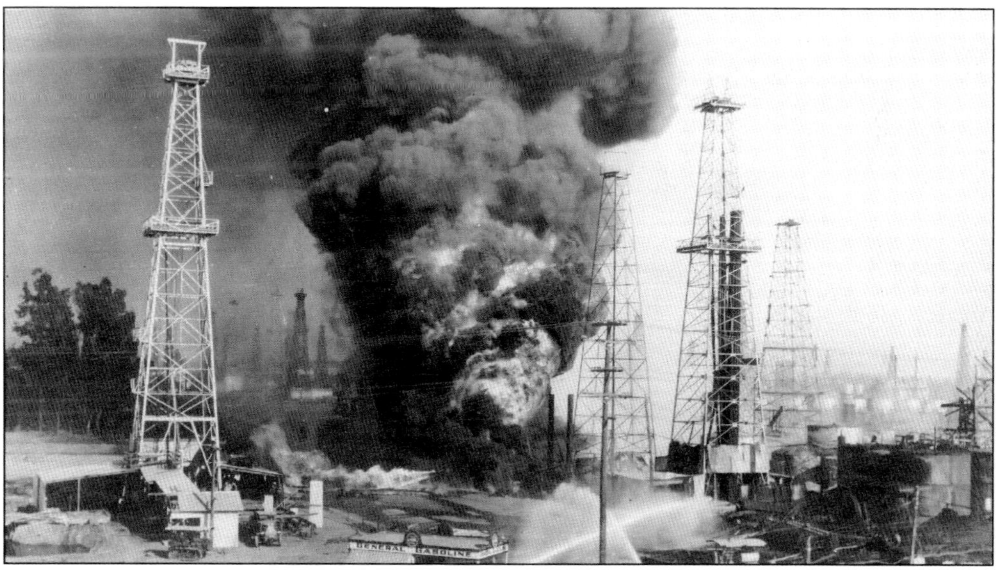

The Getty well, or Nordstrom No. 17 on the Nordstrom property, caught fire in 1928. This fire was located on the corner of Anaheim Telegraph Road (now Telegraph Road) and Butler Road (now Bloomfield Road). The General gas station is in the foreground, and what appears to be the remains of a previous fire are on the right.

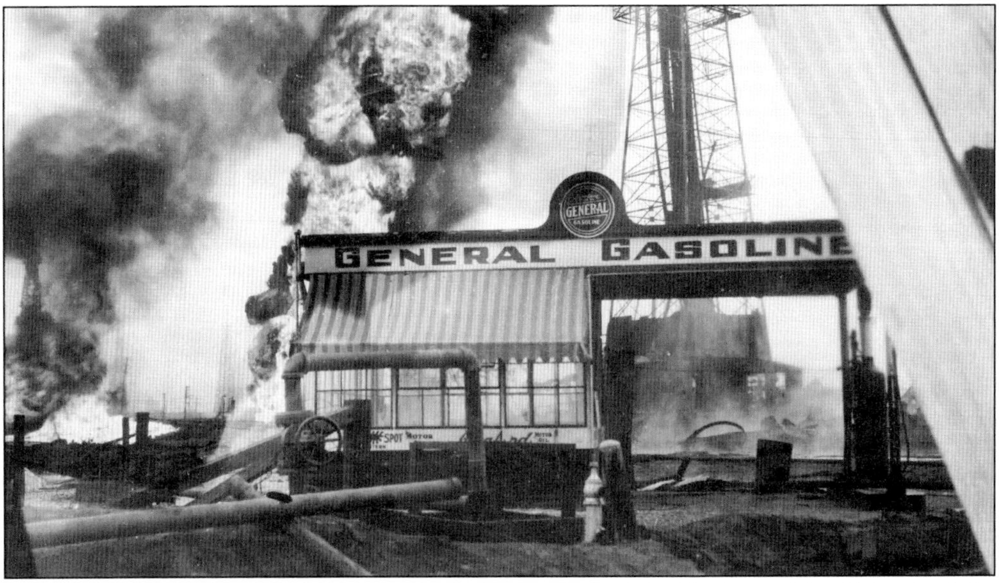

The gas station appears to be burning in this close-up shot of the Nordstrom No. 17 fire. Luckily, this is just a photographic illusion. This fire was one of the worst of the oil boom, burning for 60 days. The fire burned with such heat that all attempts to extinguish it failed. It burned until the firefighters came up with a plan to tunnel underground to the well and snuff it out.

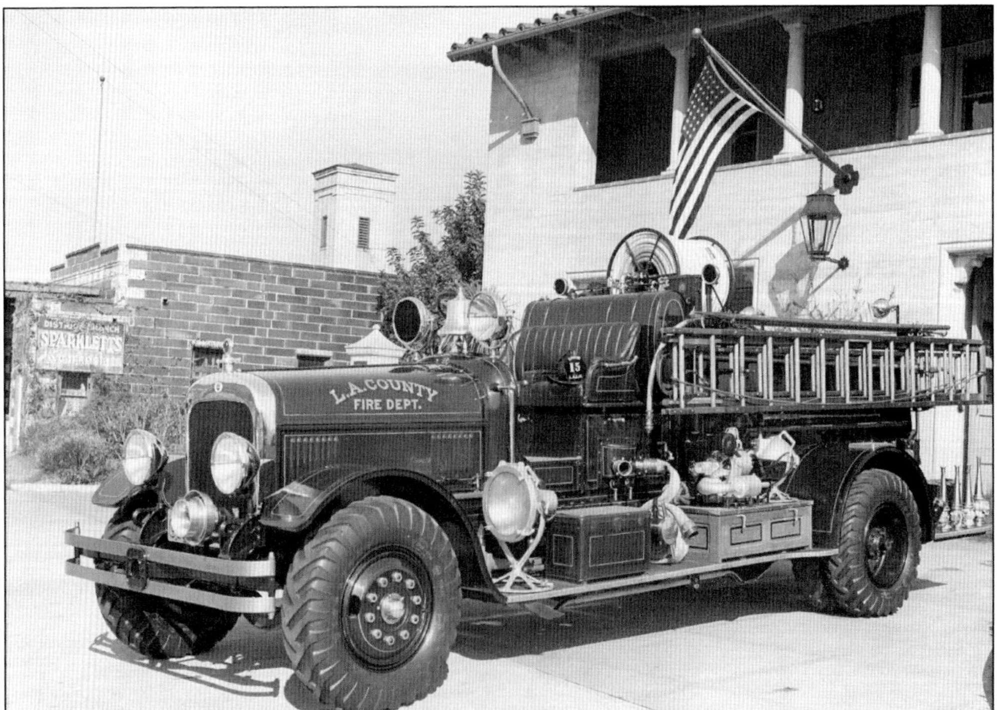

In the 1930s, firefighting technology improved, and the local fire department was able to acquire better equipment to fight the frequent oil well fires. This 1939 state-of-the-art fire truck was one of the Los Angeles County Fire Department's latest acquisitions for the fire station in Santa Fe Springs. The building in the background on the left was the Sparkletts Sparkeeta distribution branch.

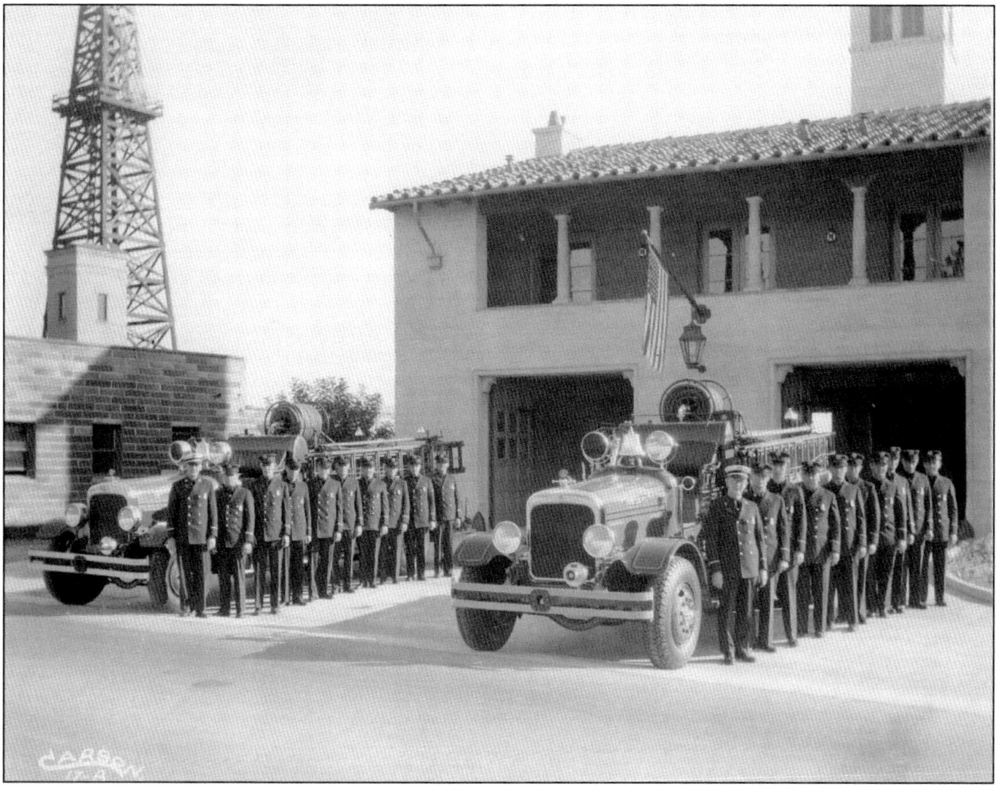

In 1927, Los Angeles County felt it necessary to build a county fire station near the Santa Fe Springs oil fields. The new station was built on the east side of Norwalk Boulevard between Telegraph Road and Los Nietos Road. Engine Company 17 stands proudly in front of their station. Chief Griswold stands in front on the left and Captain Collins heads the line on the right. (Courtesy SFS Archives.)

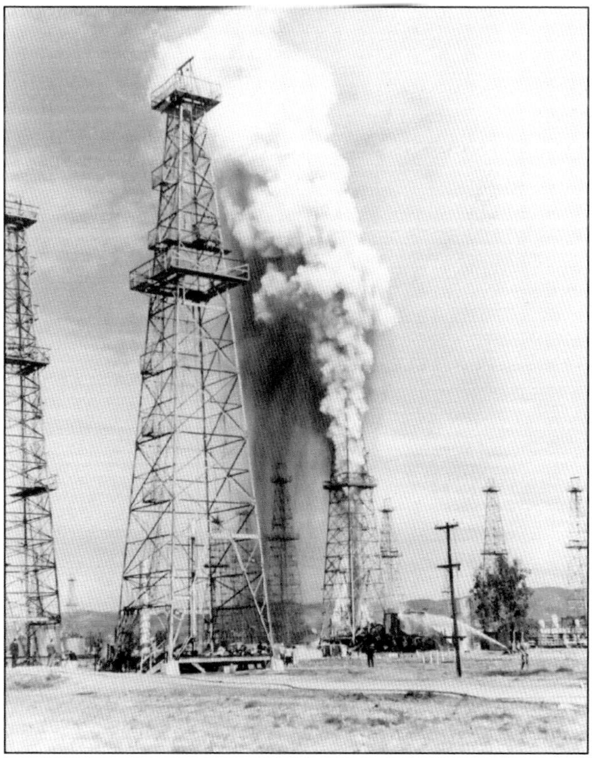

Terry Hathaway remembers the January 1949 blowout of this Union Oil well, which was located on the east side of Santa Fe Springs Road and north of Telegraph Road. Hathaway was in class at Little Lake School when the well blew, and the black column of smoke was visible from there. When school let out, a teacher took those who wanted to go to the blowout in a school bus.

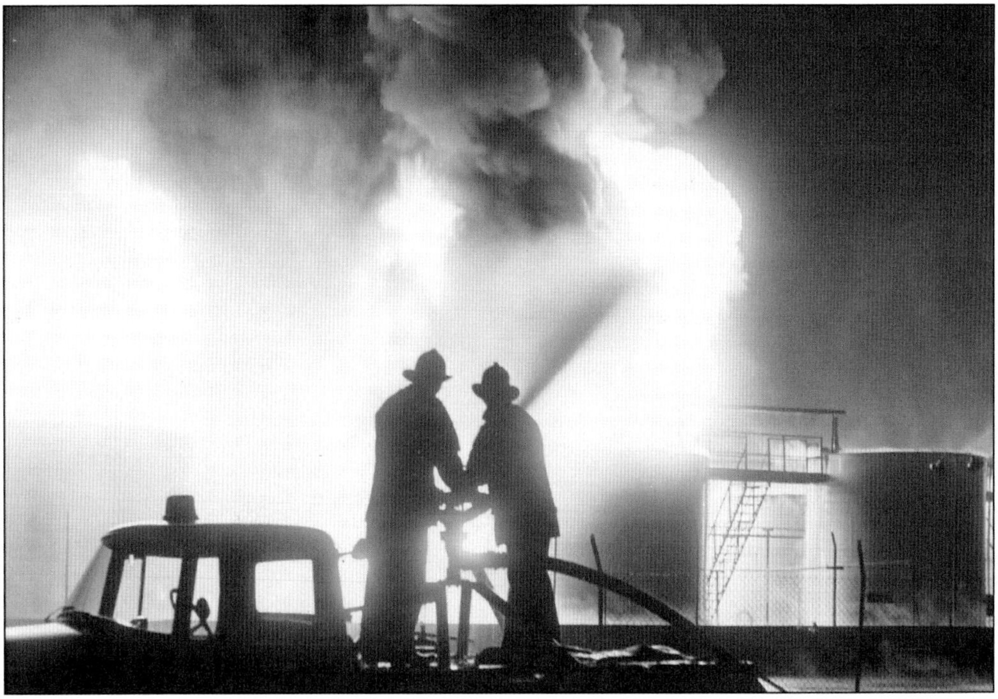

One of the later fires was at Rothschild Oil (Powerine's predecessor) in December 1960 and was believed to have been started by lightning or static electricity. It was the first real test of the young Santa Fe Springs Fire Department. The fire was so large that it brought fire companies from eight neighboring cities, including a Los Angeles County company. Two Santa Fe Springs firefighters are seen fighting the blaze with a truck-mounted water cannon. (Courtesy SFS Archives.)

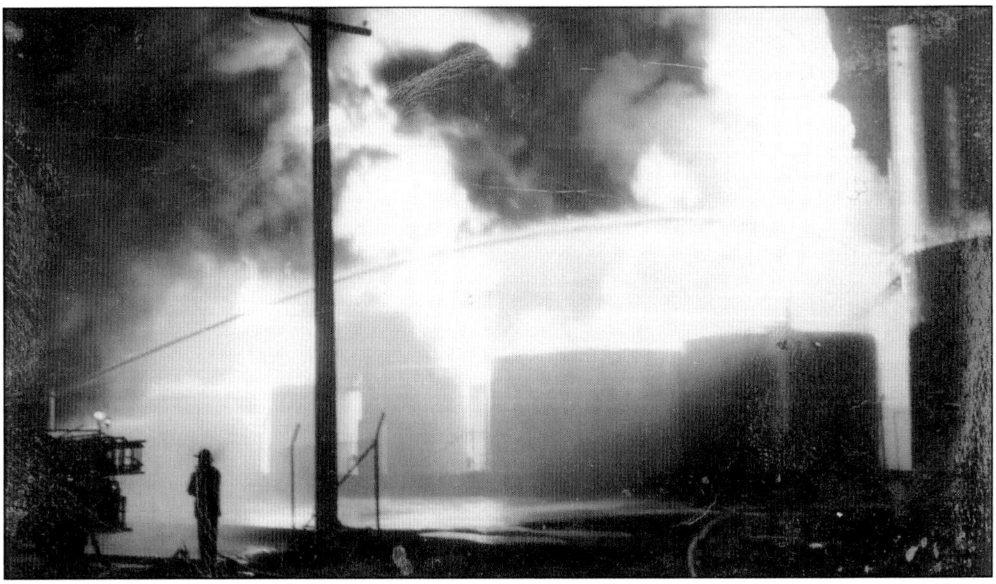

Oil storage tanks were fully engulfed in 100-foot flames that shot into the night sky. It would have taken more than a month to snuff these flames out had it been 30 years prior; however, firefighters were forced to discover more sophisticated methods of firefighting because of the many early oil well fires. Firefighters controlled this blaze in less than a day. (Courtesy SFS Archives.)

Four

Postwar Boom

By the end of the 1930s, Santa Fe Springs had changed drastically from its oil boom days. Gone were the sucker tents, the prostitutes, and gambling halls. Still there were the oil derricks, but they no longer pumped out the volume of oil they once did. Oil production was down from the early 1940s until the mid-1940s, when 30 new wells brought a temporary increase, only to decrease by the end of the decade. By the 1950s, oil production was below 13,000 barrels a day, and it was apparent that the boom was over. With the decline, unproductive wells were being shut down. The acres of land required for oil production in the 1920s were no longer necessary, and large parcels of land began to lie unused. Though the oil boom was over, many positive effects continued in Santa Fe Springs.

The advent of the oil boom produced industries in Santa Fe Springs that otherwise would not have chosen to locate there. Dozens of oil-related businesses sprouted, such as pipe manufacturers, machinists, toolmakers, and pump manufacturers. In 1924, John Reilly, an oil field worker, established the Fluid Packed Pump with just a few workers at the northeast corner of Norwalk Boulevard and Los Nietos Road. The location was the former site of the Los Nietos School, which had been relocated earlier to Rivera Road.

The 1940s also brought World War II, which sent a large number of men off to fight. When the war ended in 1945, soldiers who had left home as boys returned as men who were hoping to start a new life. Many had new families and were searching for a place to live. New homes were needed to accommodate the increasing demand, and developers were in search of land that could be easily acquired. The citrus groves that survived the oil boom but by then were past their prime were ideal for developers. By the late 1940s, new homes began springing up in the area between the western edge of the oil fields and the San Gabriel River. Much of the soil had been contaminated by oil production, and the unused oil fields were deemed undesirable for tract home development.

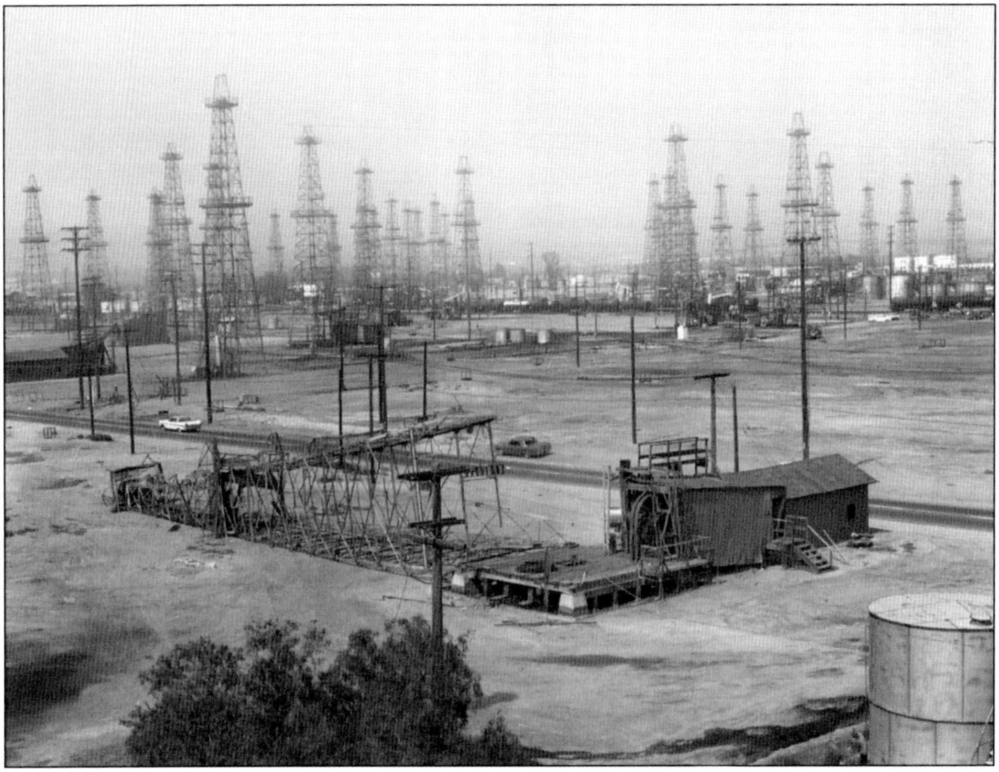

By the end of World War II, oil production in Santa Fe Springs' oil fields was down considerably. By the 1960s, production fell to as low as 15 barrels a day. The oil companies began shutting down wells at a rate of at least one per week. In this c. 1950 photograph, a well that had been shut down is in the process of being dismantled.

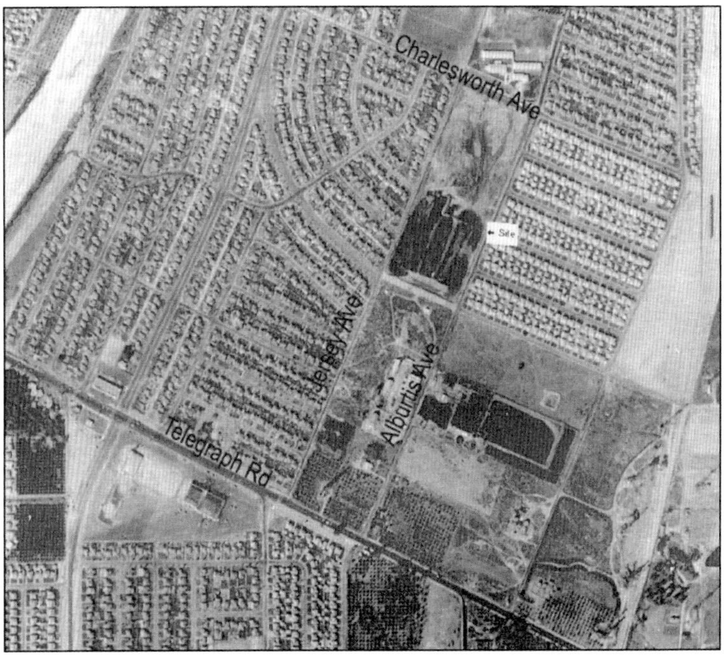

Seeing the need to supply homes for returning soldiers, developers were quick to acquire as much land as they could. By the early 1950s, the orchards were gone and the land was covered with new homes. In this aerial photograph, neat rows of new homes can be seen where orange groves once thrived. The intersection of Telegraph Road and Orr & Day Road is pictured around 1955 in the lower left corner. (Courtesy SFS Archives.)

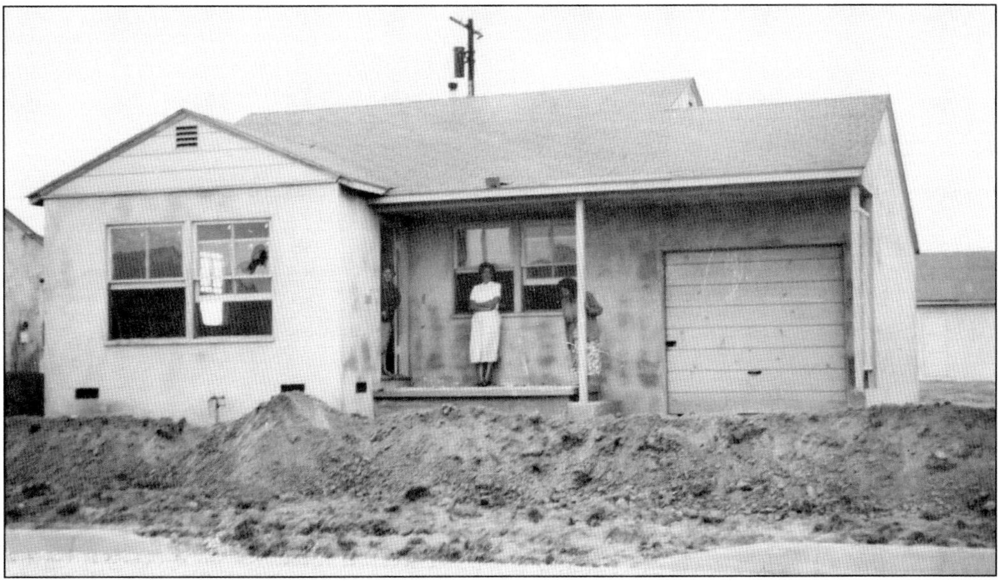

The houses being built were modest bungalow tract homes. Veronica Oblea is pictured in 1951 standing on the porch of a newly constructed home she and her husband, Manuel Oblea, were in the process of buying. Manuel's sisters Annie (at the door) and Mary (standing on the steps) came with them to see the progress of their home on Fredson Street. (Courtesy Oblea Collection.)

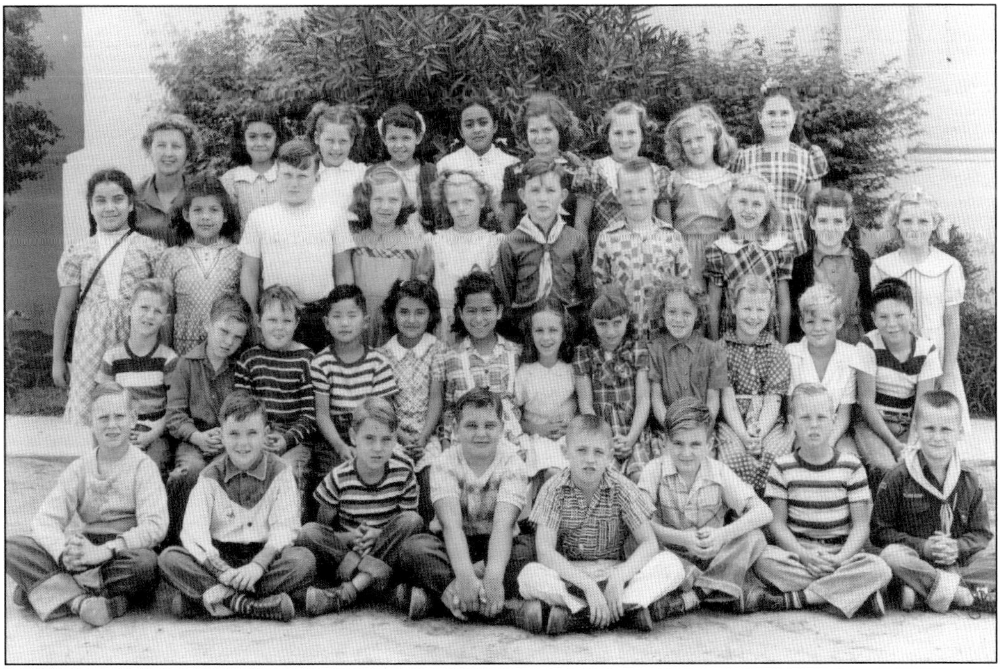

This c. 1950 photograph shows Juanita Bush and her class at Little Lake School. With the influx of new residents to the area, the two existing schools became overcrowded. Kindergarten was offered for the first time in 1949, and enrollment grew to 210 students from kindergarten through eighth grade. By 1950, enrollment doubled and eight more classes were added. Due to the population growth, Lakeview School opened in 1952 with double sessions for its students. (Courtesy SFS Archives.)

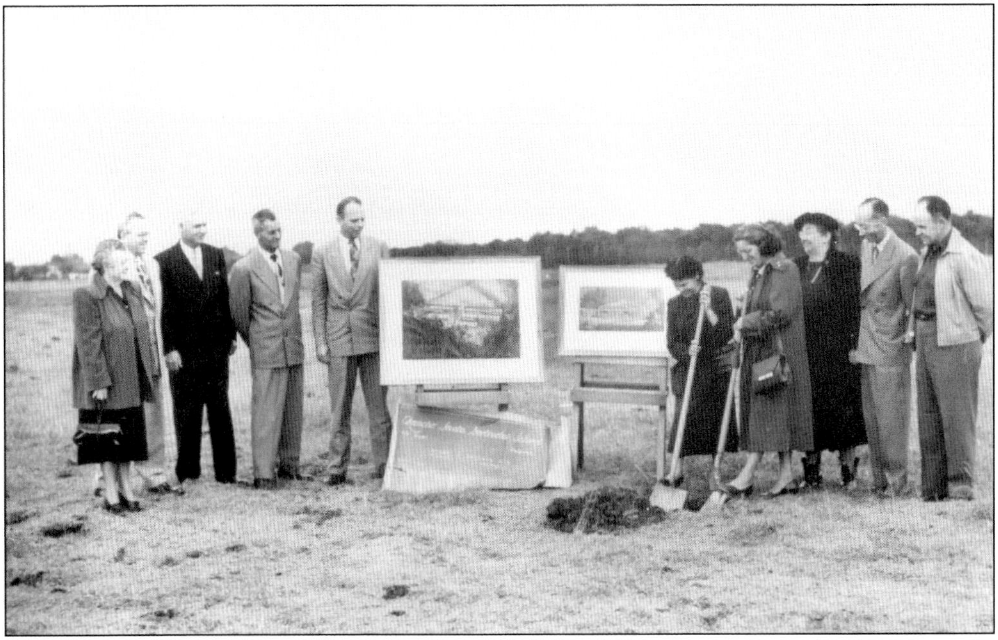

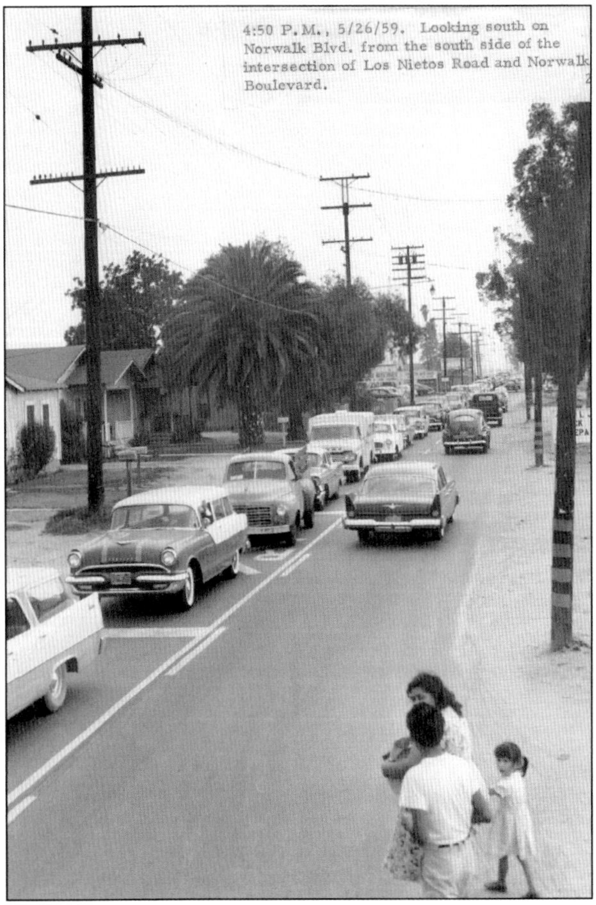

The Los Nietos School District (LNSD) experienced the same sudden overcrowding as Little Lake School. To help relieve this problem, the district opened Rancho Santa Gertrudes Elementary School, north of Telegraph Road, in 1952. The 1951 ground breaking was attended by, from left to right, Miss Cryon, teacher; four school board members or administrators; Margaret Vicuña, PTA president; Mrs. Aguaya, parent; Ada Nelson, LNSD superintendent; Wallace Wiggins, school board member; and Mr. Nelson. (Courtesy Vicuña Collection.)

Overcrowding in its schools was not the only problem the Santa Fe Springs area was facing. The local infrastructure was deficient for the number of people now in the region. The streets were too few and too narrow to handle all the cars on the road. This late-1950s photograph of Norwalk Boulevard looking south from Los Nietos Road shows the traffic problem in the area. (Courtesy SFS Archives.)

The new homeowners quickly realized that there were almost no stores to buy their weekly groceries and to take care of other household needs, so they were forced to travel to Whittier or Los Angeles. The groundbreaking ceremony for the Bank of America branch and W.T. Grants Department Store was a welcome event. Pictured around 1955 from left to right are Ann Bartunek, SFS Homeowners Association; Bank of America manager; W.T. Grants manager; and Earleen Pearson, SFS Homeowners Association. (Courtesy SFS Archives.)

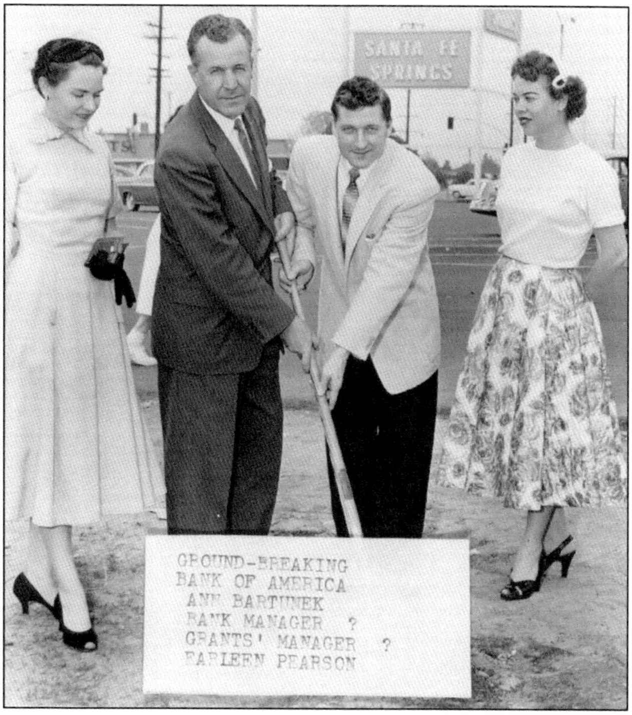

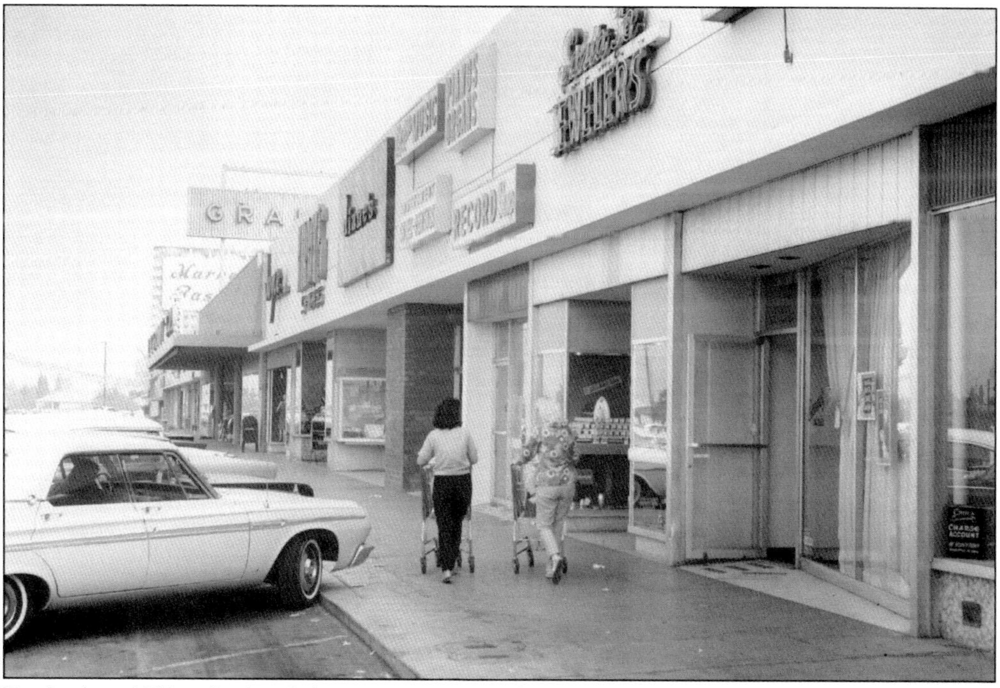

By the late 1950s, the local shopping center at the corner of Telegraph Road and Orr & Day Road had a good variety of shops. In this c. 1957 photograph, some of the earliest vendors at the Promenade Shopping Center are pictured, including Paul's Coffee Shop, Market Basket, Robert's Department Store, W.T. Grants Department Store, Brownies Toy Store, Santa Fe Furniture, and Vincent Drug Store, to name a few. (Courtesy SFS Archives.)

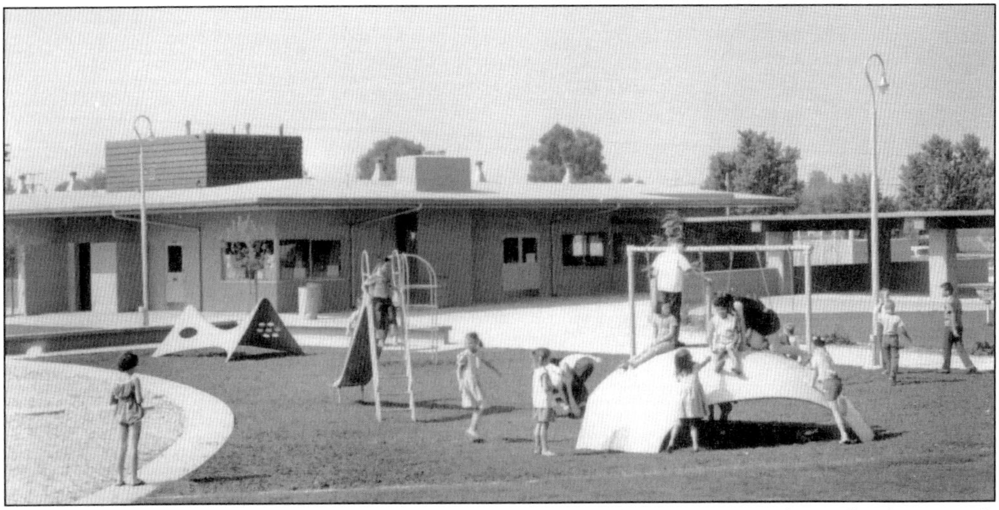

In the early 1950s, the County of Los Angeles saw the need for a recreational area for the region's children. A nine-acre parcel of land north of Telegraph Road and next to the proposed site of the Rancho Santa Gertrudes Elementary School was chosen. Los Nietos Park was developed and designed as a community park. The building and grounds represented the most modern concept of sound park planning of the time. (Courtesy SFS Archives.)

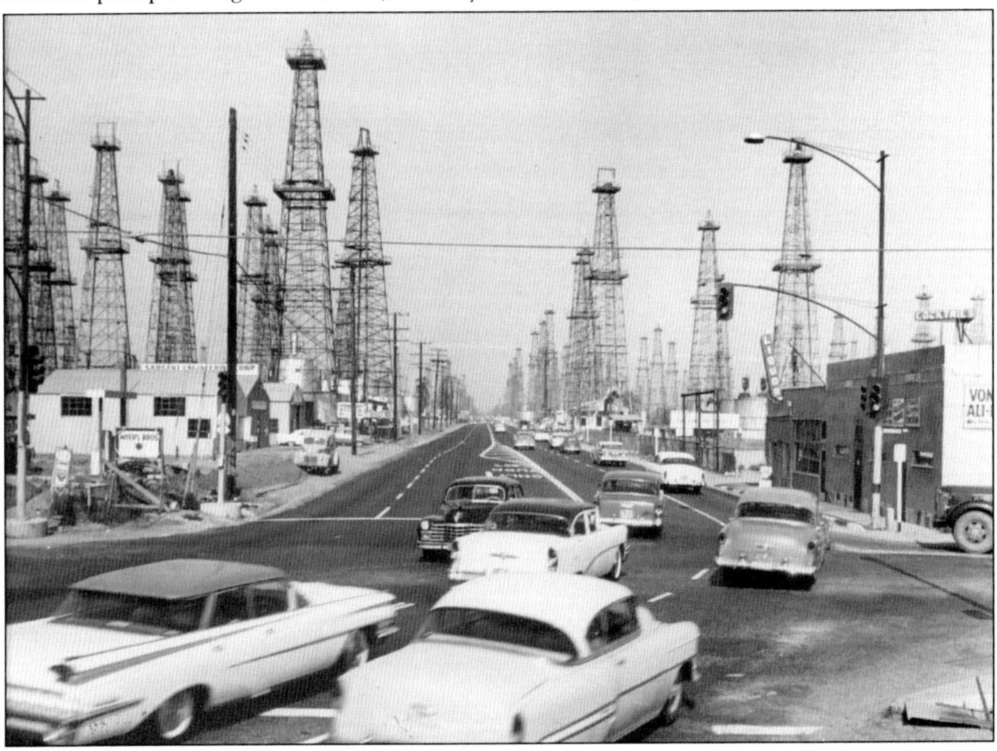

As a result of the oil boom, many businesses sprang up or moved into the area. By the early 1950s, most of the oil wells in Santa Fe Springs had passed their peak of production, and many were being dismantled. Even with the drop in production, the familiar forest of derricks would remain in the city for at least two more decades. Pictured around 1950 is Telegraph Road looking east at Norwalk Boulevard. (Courtesy SFS Archives.)

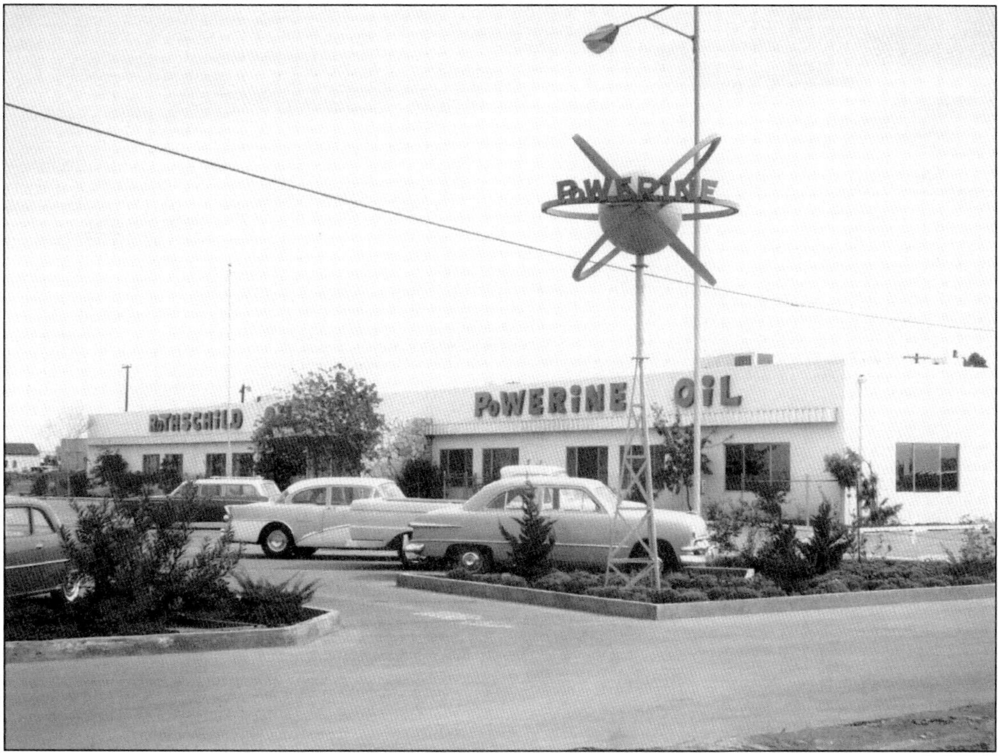

Clearly, the principal types of businesses brought on by the oil boom were oil companies. One of the largest was Powerine Oil Company, which continued to operate in the city for over 60 years. Harry S. Rothschild purchased two acres of land in the early 1930s and founded Rothschild Oil Company, a partnership between him and his wife, Josephine. Powerine Oil Company was the name by which their oil products were marketed. (Courtesy SFS Archives.)

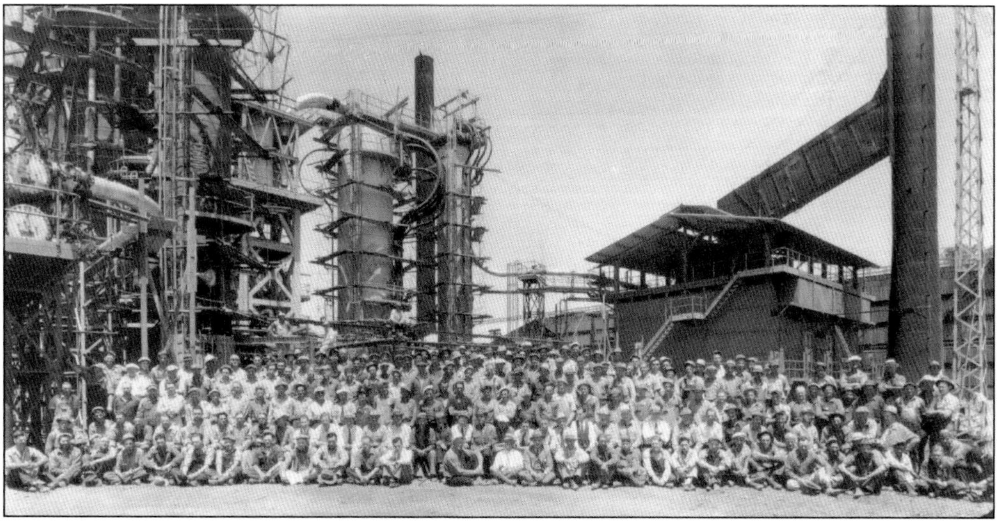

Powerine Oil grew steadily, and by 1940, it had 20 employees. In this c. 1945 photograph, its employees number almost 200. In the 1950s, 1960s, and 1980s, Powerine made upgrades to its Santa Fe Springs refinery. It also opened retail service stations throughout the Los Angeles area. Powerine Oil Company was a pioneer in the self-service gas station. (Courtesy SFS Archives.)

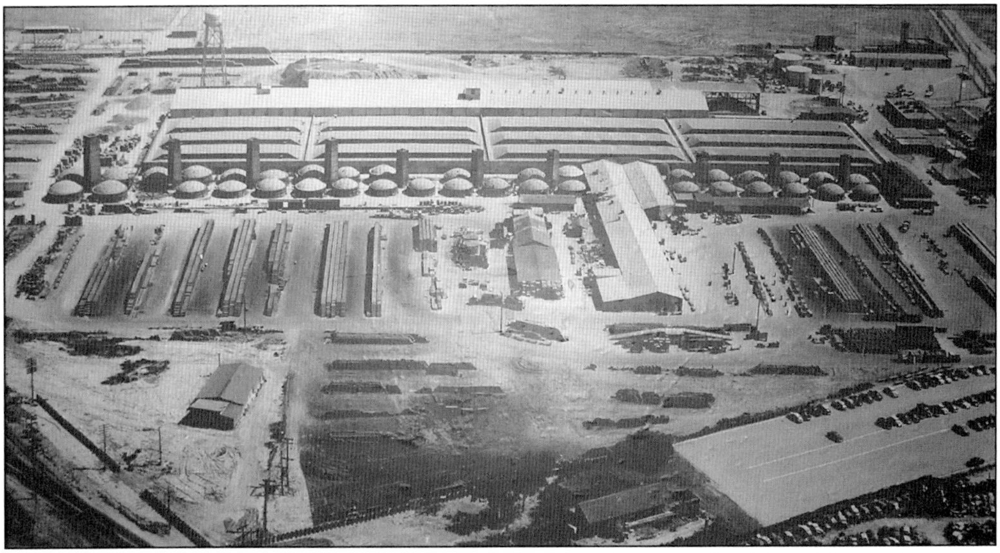

Pacific Clay Products was another company that was an indirect result of the oil boom. It opened its plant on the east side of Norwalk Boulevard just south of Los Nietos Road in 1916. It originally opened as the Pacific Sewer Pipe Company, but when the company went public, the name was changed to Pacific Clay Products. The company operated at this location until 1980, when the plant was moved to Corona.

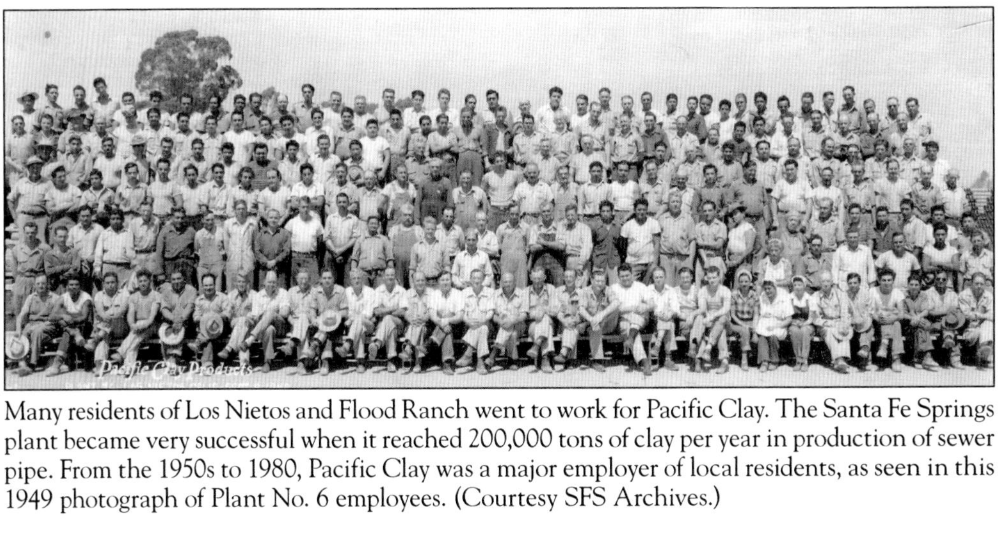

Many residents of Los Nietos and Flood Ranch went to work for Pacific Clay. The Santa Fe Springs plant became very successful when it reached 200,000 tons of clay per year in production of sewer pipe. From the 1950s to 1980, Pacific Clay was a major employer of local residents, as seen in this 1949 photograph of Plant No. 6 employees. (Courtesy SFS Archives.)

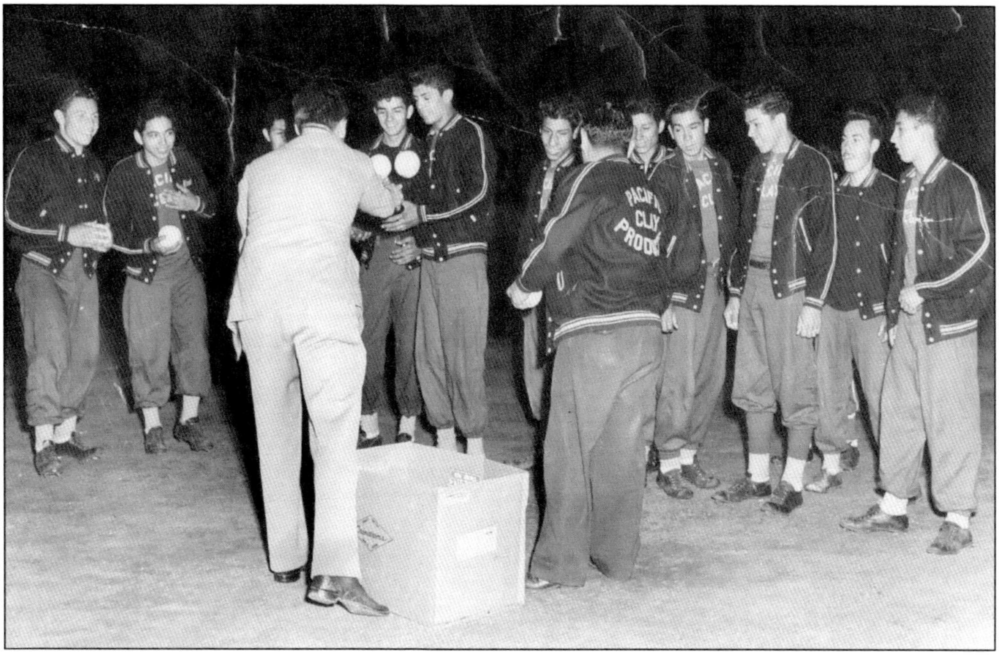

In the mid-1940s, some Flood Ranch residents, all of whom lived within a block of each other, organized a men's softball team. Many worked for Pacific Clay, so the company sponsored the team. Pictured in 1949 at the start of a new season are, from left to right, Jerry Sepulveda, David Vicuña, Napoleon Barajas, an unidentified gentleman distributing baseballs, Gilbert Alvarado, Frank Marquez, Mike Vicario, Manager Steve Vicuna, Dave Guzman, Joe Macias, Richard DeLaRosa, Manuel Villaneda, and Louis Garcia. (Courtesy Vicuña Collection.)

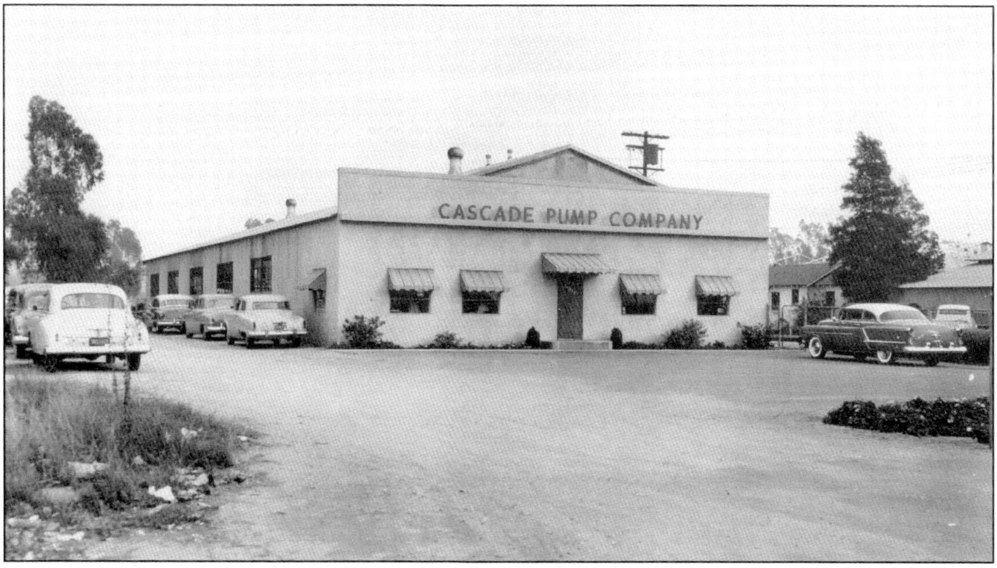

In 1950, the Summerfield family purchased this parcel of land on Norwalk Boulevard south of Lakeland Road from the Water Well Supply Company. In 1951, they built their manufacturing plant and moved in. In 1975, the company moved to its present location on Norwalk Boulevard north of Telegraph Road. The family-owned company was founded in 1948 and is in its third generation of ownership. (Courtesy Tom Summerfield.)

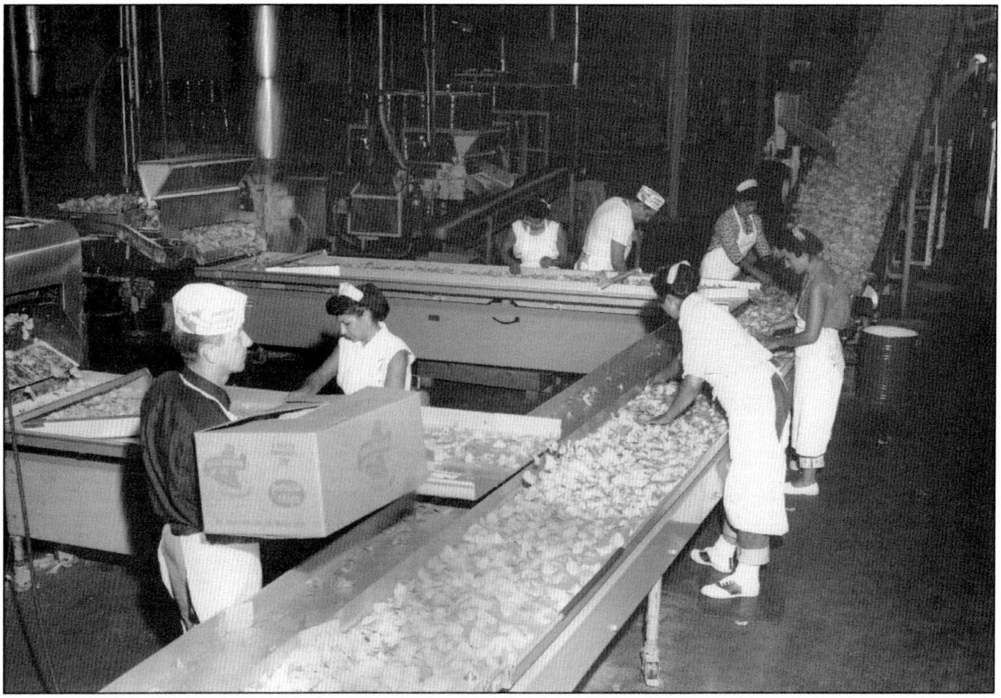

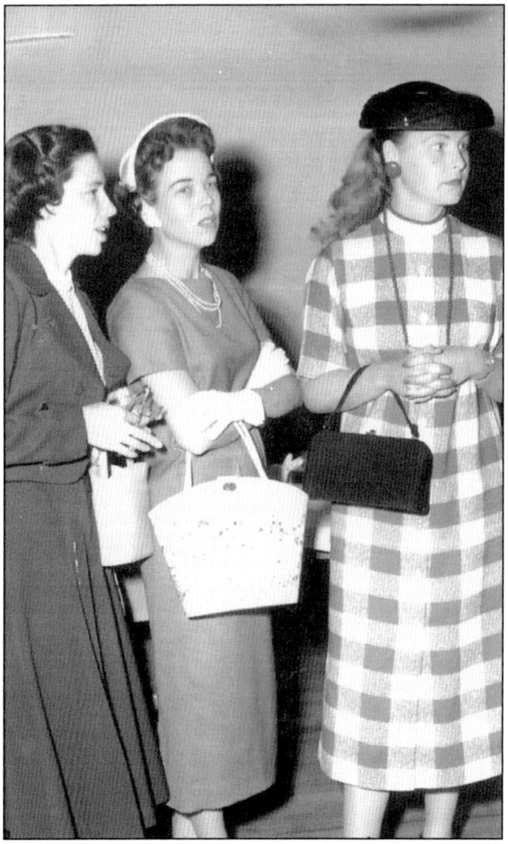

Bell Brand Snack Food, founded in 1925, opened its Santa Fe Springs plant in the early 1950s on the east side of Pioneer Boulevard just north of Los Nietos Road. It provided many jobs for the residents of the city. In this c. 1960 photograph, workers inspect potato chips for quality as they go by. Bell Brand potato chips received national recognition when they appeared in *The Seven Year Itch*, starring Marilyn Monroe. (Courtesy Placencia Collection.)

With the influx of residents to the area in the early 1950s, it quickly became apparent that services for their children were almost nonexistent. The area known as Santa Fe Springs was not yet incorporated, so the County of Los Angeles provided all of its services. Residents organized to create youth programs for their children. Some of these early organizers, pictured in 1957 from left to right, are Margaret Snyder, Earleen Pearson, and Beverly Moreno. (Courtesy Snyder Collection.)

Five

INCORPORATION

"Incorporation!" The word flew through the community on speeding wings in September 1954. Young men, newly equipped with college degrees received on the G.I. Bill of Rights, were establishing their careers while their wives were concentrating on the needs of their children. The schools were on half-day sessions because of the recent overcrowding. They were all working at putting their individual touches on their new tract homes.

The new owners of these homes were puzzled as to where they lived. The names of the tracts caused confusion, as did the fact that three post offices serviced the area: Whittier, Norwalk, and in the eastern section, Santa Fe Springs. The telephones were divided between the Downey and the Whittier exchanges. There were few shopping centers, churches, or parks nearby. In desperation, spirited citizens began to do the best they could with what they had. The parent-teacher association began to sponsor a rudimentary recreation program. To help solve some of these problems, the Little Lake Homeowners Association was formed in August 1952. It later changed its name to the Santa Fe Springs Homeowners Association. A coordinating council and a junior chamber of commerce were also formed during this period of intense civic activity.

A group of landowners, businessmen, and industrialists located to the east of these tract homes, which were between Norwalk Boulevard and the San Gabriel River, had formed the Industrial League to represent their particular needs in the county. One of the league's members, Bill Emmens, was having trouble with the rezoning of his property. C.D. Eib, the league's executive secretary, suggested, "Why not incorporate? A local city government would allow us to maintain a better business climate."

A pivotal point arrived when Gov. Pat Brown initiated a one-percent sales tax to help with the rapid growth of cites all over California after World War II. The next decisive point came when the homeowners league and the Industrial League came together to talk about a joint effort to incorporate Santa Fe Springs.

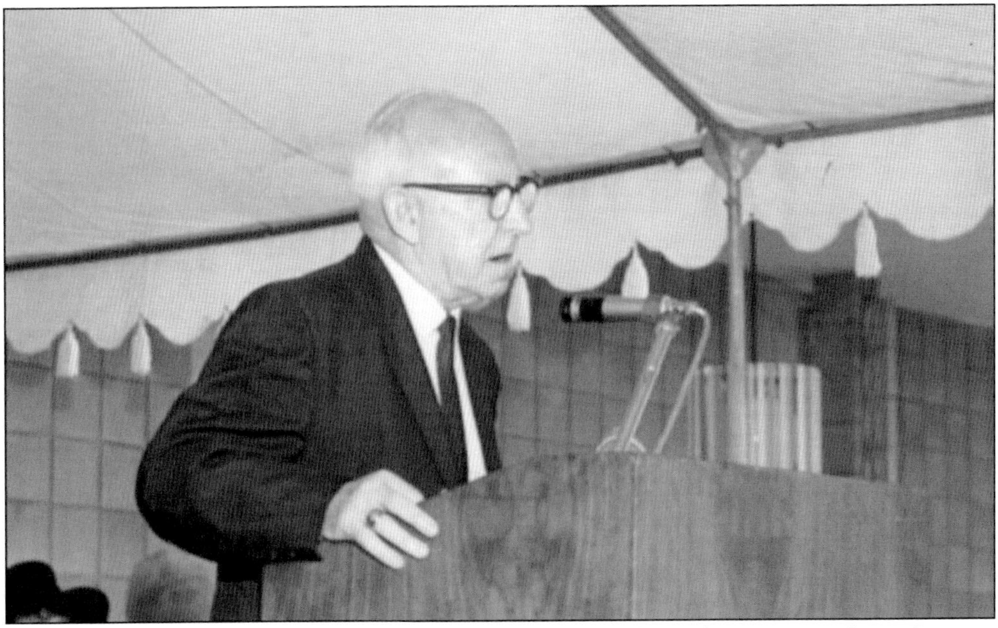

William Emmens (above) and Claude Duval Eib were two Industrial League members who were instrumental in the league's decision to incorporate. Both men represented the league and, on behalf of the Harbor Box Company, approached the South Whittier School District to purchase one of its school site properties. After failing that attempt, the league tried convincing the county to rezone the adjacent property for manufacturing but failed again. (Courtesy SFS Archives.)

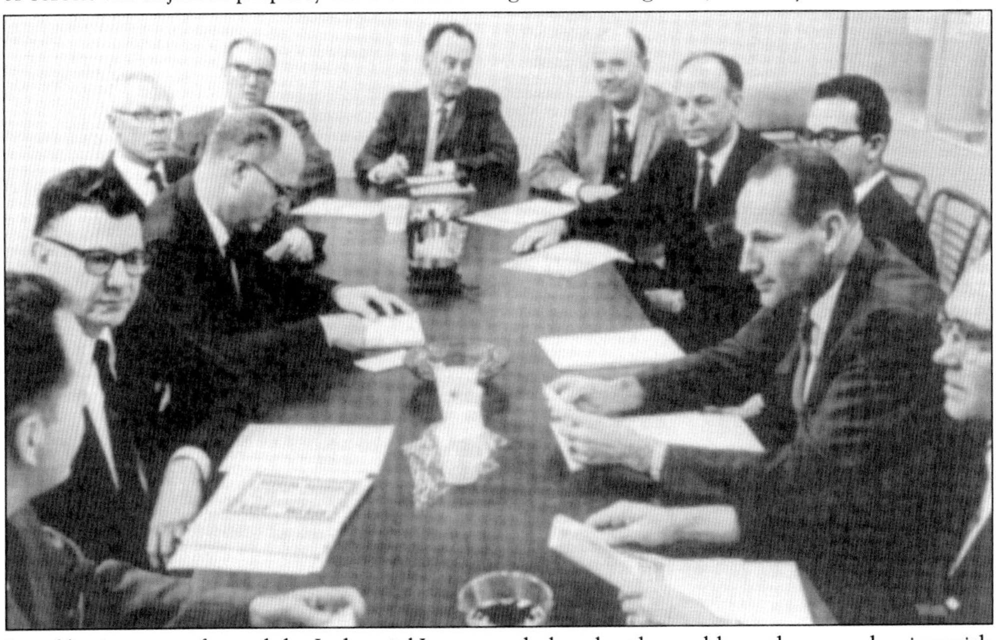

Local businessmen formed the Industrial League to help solve the problems they were having with county government. One of their biggest problems was trying to get their properties rezoned in order to build their companies. Much to their dismay, they had little success in accomplishing this goal. This problem was a driving force for incorporation. Above, the Industrial League discusses the prospect of incorporation. (Courtesy SFS Archives.)

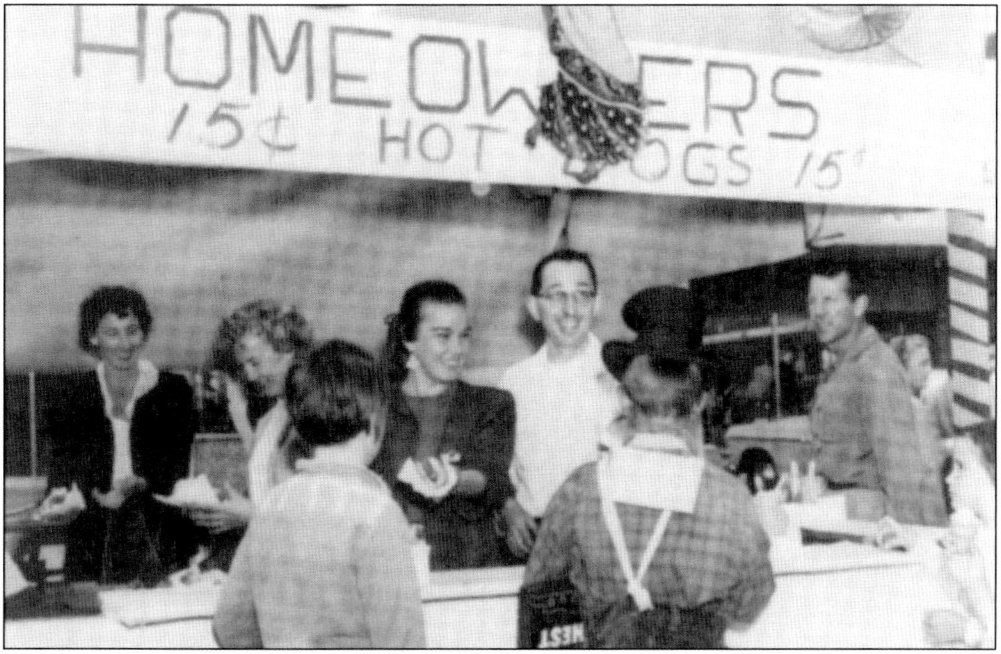

Local homeowners formed a homeowners association to provide activities and social events in the area. They raised funds to pay for baseball leagues, dances, and Boy Scout and Girl Scout troops, along with other activities. Above, the homeowners association sells hot dogs at one of its picnics. Beverly Waller and Bill Camil are pictured (center) waiting on two young customers. (Courtesy of Ann Bartunek Collection and Frank White.)

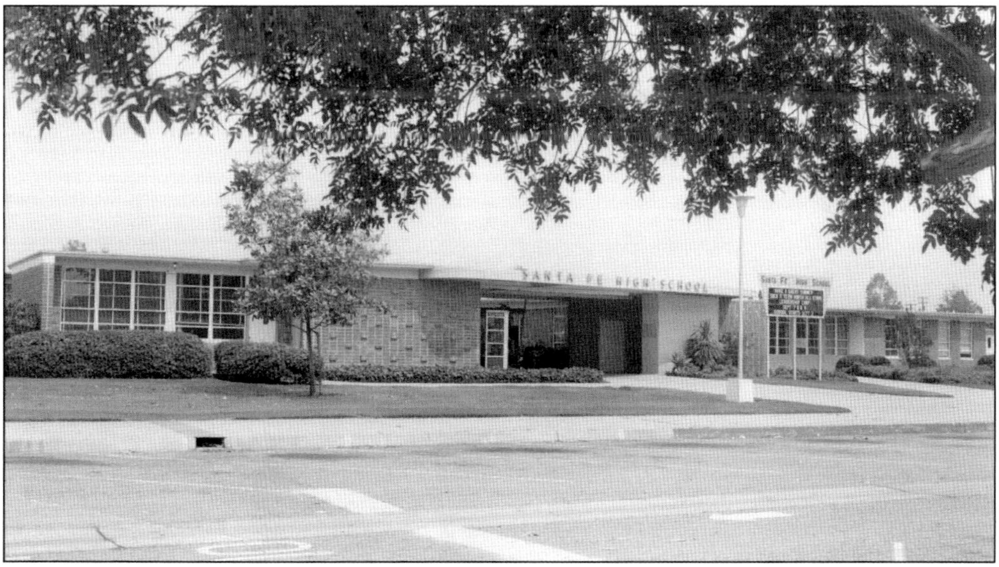

The Santa Fe Springs Recognition League was formed in an effort to get community recognition. Its first objective was to have Little Lake High School's name changed to Santa Fe Springs High School. After confirming that the majority of the community was for the change, the league members packed a Wittier Union High School District school board meeting. The board did not concede completely but renamed the school Santa Fe High School, dropping "Springs." (Courtesy SFS Archives.)

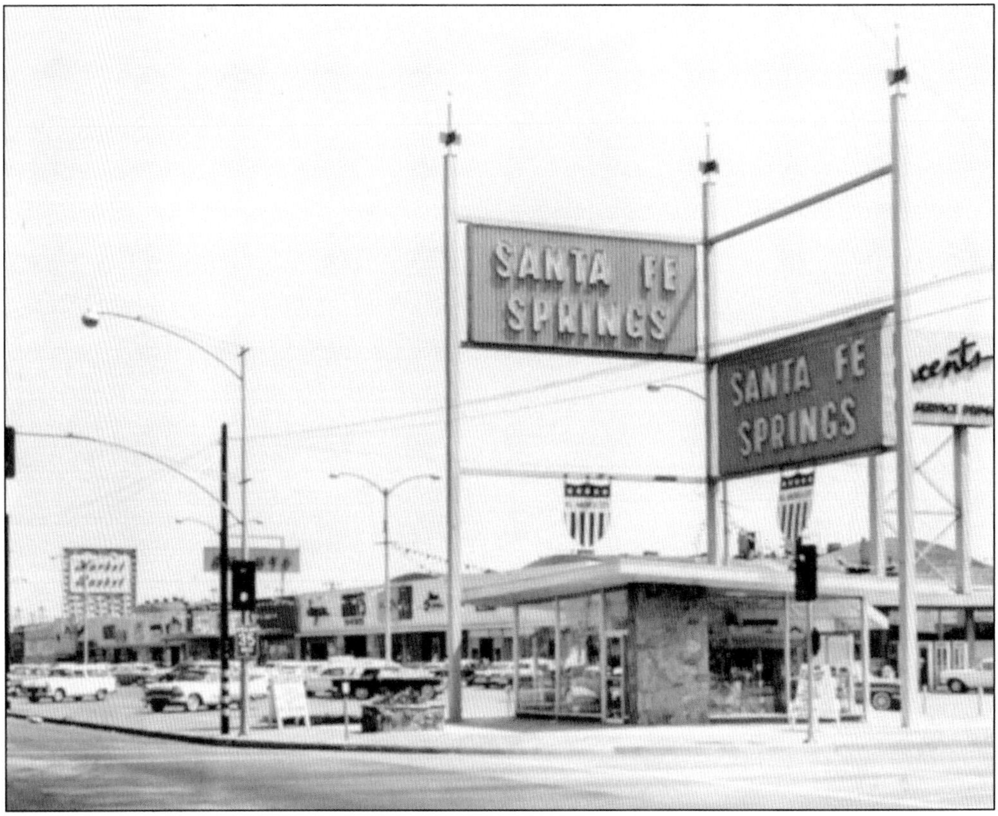

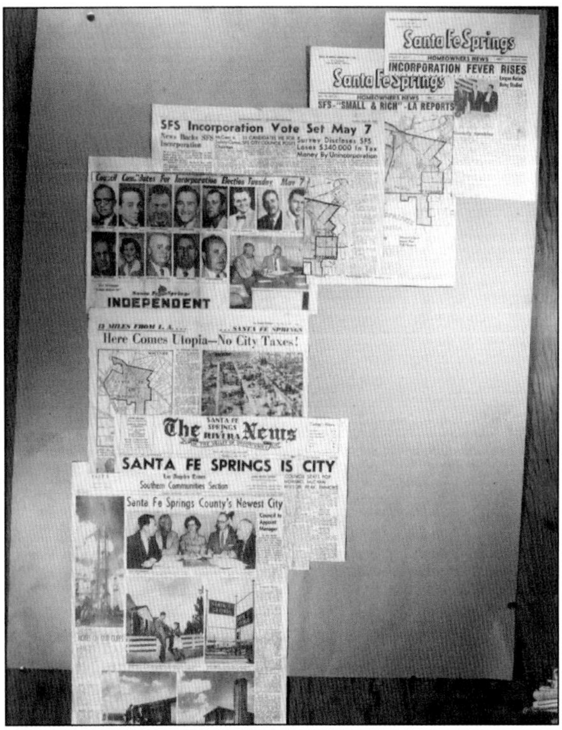

The SFS Recognition League persuaded the shopping center owner to install a big Santa Fe Springs sign on the corner of Telegraph Road and Orr & Day Road even before incorporation. A big party was held for the dedication, with a platform of civic and political dignitaries and a live band. Other significant accomplishments included getting the post office and Bank of America to use the name "Santa Fe Springs." (Courtesy SFS Archives.)

These newspaper headlines boasted the advantages of the incorporation of Santa Fe Springs. Pro-incorporation supporters insisted the new city would have no new taxes. It was predicted that the revenue brought in by the new city would make it one of the wealthiest cities in the county. Articles like this gave momentum to the pro-incorporation movement. (Courtesy SFS Archives.)

Not everybody was for incorporation, with many residents fearing that as a city they would not be able to afford many of the vital services. With funding assistance from the County Firefighter Association, they launched an anti-incorporation campaign. The pro-incorporation camp labeled this group the "Aginners." At right is a letter from the Aginners stating their reasons against incorporation. (Courtesy SFS Archives.)

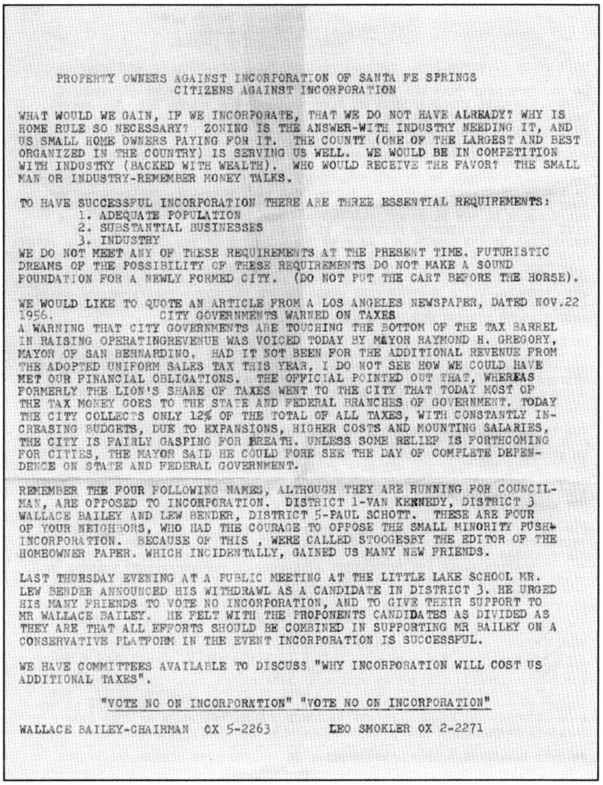

PROPERTY OWNERS AGAINST INCORPORATION OF SANTA FE SPRINGS
CITIZENS AGAINST INCORPORATION

WHAT WOULD WE GAIN, IF WE INCORPORATE, THAT WE DO NOT HAVE ALREADY? WHY IS HOME RULE SO NECESSARY? ZONING IS THE ANSWER-WITH INDUSTRY NEEDING IT, AND US SMALL HOME OWNERS PAYING FOR IT. THE COUNTY (ONE OF THE LARGEST AND BEST ORGANIZED IN THE COUNTRY) IS SERVING US WELL. WE WOULD BE IN COMPETITION WITH INDUSTRY (BACKED WITH WEALTH). WHO WOULD RECEIVE THE FAVOR? THE SMALL MAN OR INDUSTRY-REMEMBER MONEY TALKS.

TO HAVE SUCCESSFUL INCORPORATION THERE ARE THREE ESSENTIAL REQUIREMENTS:
1. ADEQUATE POPULATION
2. SUBSTANTIAL BUSINESSES
3. INDUSTRY

WE DO NOT MEET ANY OF THESE REQUIREMENTS AT THE PRESENT TIME. FUTURISTIC DREAMS OF THE POSSIBILITY OF THESE REQUIREMENTS DO NOT MAKE A SOUND FOUNDATION FOR A NEWLY FORMED CITY. (DO NOT PUT THE CART BEFORE THE HORSE).

WE WOULD LIKE TO QUOTE AN ARTICLE FROM A LOS ANGELES NEWSPAPER, DATED NOV.22 1956. CITY GOVERNMENTS WARNED ON TAXES
A WARNING THAT CITY GOVERNMENTS ARE TOUCHING THE BOTTOM OF THE TAX BARREL IN RAISING OPERATINGREVENUE WAS VOICED TODAY BY MAYOR RAYMOND H. GREGORY, MAYOR OF SAN BERNARDINO. HAD IT NOT BEEN FOR THE ADDITIONAL REVENUE FROM THE ADOPTED UNIFORM SALES TAX THIS YEAR, I DO NOT SEE HOW WE COULD HAVE MET OUR FINANCIAL OBLIGATIONS. THE OFFICIAL POINTED OUT THAT, WHEREAS FORMERLY THE LION'S SHARE OF TAXES WENT TO THE CITY THAT TODAY MOST OF THE TAX MONEY GOES TO THE STATE AND FEDERAL BRANCHES OF GOVERNMENT. TODAY THE CITY COLLECTS ONLY 12% OF THE TOTAL OF ALL TAXES, WITH CONSTANTLY INCREASING BUDGETS, DUE TO EXPANSIONS, HIGHER COSTS AND MOUNTING SALARIES, THE CITY IS FAIRLY GASPING FOR BREATH. UNLESS SOME RELIEF IS FORTHCOMING FOR CITIES, THE MAYOR SAID HE COULD FORE SEE THE DAY OF COMPLETE DEPENDENCE ON STATE AND FEDERAL GOVERNMENT.

REMEMBER THE FOUR FOLLOWING NAMES, ALTHOUGH THEY ARE RUNNING FOR COUNCILMAN, ARE OPPOSED TO INCORPORATION. DISTRICT 1-VAN KENNEDY, DISTRICT 3 WALLACE BAILEY AND LEW BENDER, DISTRICT 5-PAUL SCHOTT. THESE ARE FOUR OF YOUR NEIGHBORS, WHO HAD THE COURAGE TO OPPOSE THE SMALL MINORITY PUSH+ INCORPORATION. BECAUSE OF THIS , WERE CALLED STOOGESBY THE EDITOR OF THE HOMEOWNER PAPER. WHICH INCIDENTALLY, GAINED US MANY NEW FRIENDS.

LAST THURSDAY EVENING AT A PUBLIC MEETING AT THE LITTLE LAKE SCHOOL MR. LEW BENDER ANNOUNCED HIS WITHDRAWL AS A CANDIDATE IN DISTRICT 3. HE URGED HIS MANY FRIENDS TO VOTE NO INCORPORATION, AND TO GIVE THEIR SUPPORT TO MR WALLACE BAILEY. HE FELT WITH THE PROPONENTS CANDIDATES AS DIVIDED AS THEY ARE THAT ALL EFFORTS SHOULD BE COMBINED IN SUPPORTING MR BAILEY ON A CONSERVATIVE PLATFORM IN THE EVENT INCORPORATION IS SUCCESSFUL.

WE HAVE COMMITTEES AVAILABLE TO DISCUSS "WHY INCORPORATION WILL COST US ADDITIONAL TAXES".

"VOTE NO ON INCORPORATION" "VOTE NO ON INCORPORATION"

WALLACE BAILEY-CHAIRMAN OX 5-2263 LEO SMOKLER OX 2-2271

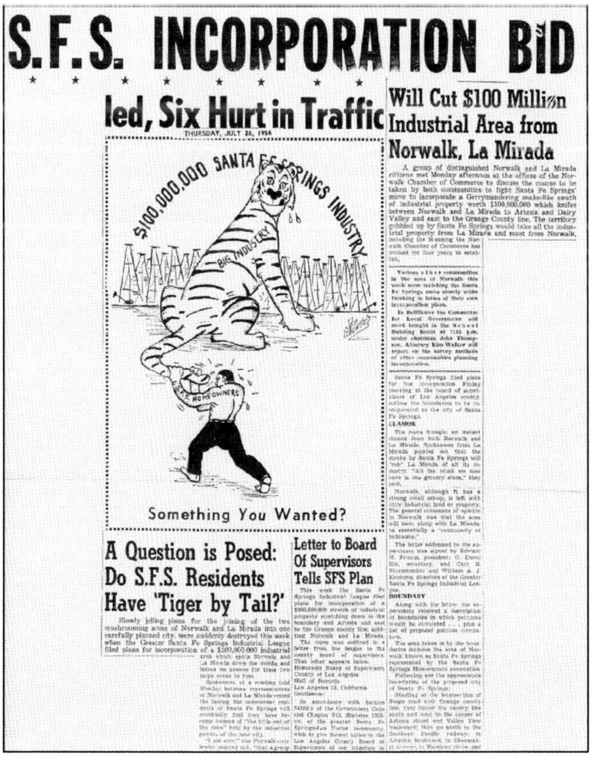

S.F.S. INCORPORATION BID

led, Six Hurt in Traffic

THURSDAY, JULY 26, 1956

Will Cut $100 Million Industrial Area from Norwalk, La Mirada

A group of distinguished Norwalk and La Mirada citizens met Monday afternoon at the offices of the Norwalk Chamber of Commerce to discuss the course to be taken by both communities to fight Santa Fe Springs' move to incorporate a Gerrymandering snake-like swath of industrial property worth $100,000,000 which knifes between Norwalk and La Mirada to Artesia and Dairy Valley and east to the Orange County line. The territory gobbled up by Santa Fe Springs would take all the industrial property from La Mirada and most from Norwalk, ...

A Question is Posed: Do S.F.S. Residents Have 'Tiger by Tail?'

Letter to Board Of Supervisors Tells SFS Plan

Many people did not think incorporating land that was controlled by the oil companies was a good idea. The *Herald Examiner* newspaper article above also talks about the negative effect an incorporation of Santa Fe Springs could have on some of its neighboring communities. According to the article, La Mirada and Norwalk were both concerned about the large portion of industrial land being taken from them. (Courtesy SFS Archives.)

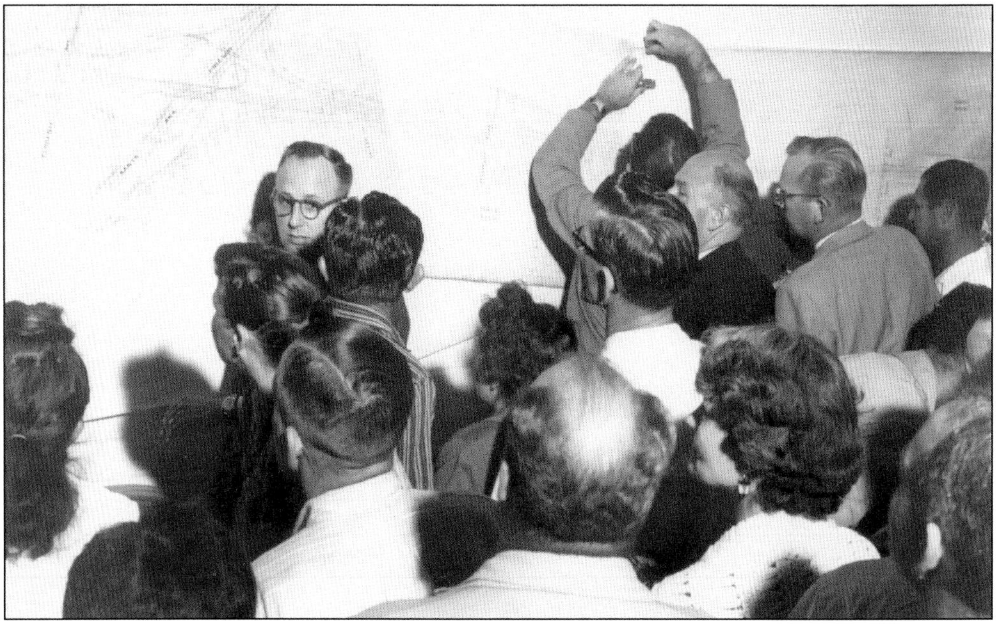

From the beginning, the Industrial League and the homeowners association were in agreement. The league was to decide the industrial boundaries, and the homeowners were responsible for outlining residential boundaries. The homeowners wanted the area of the Little Lake School District to be the boundaries of Santa Fe Springs. Above, Industrial League members and the homeowners meet to decide on the boundaries of their new city. (Courtesy SFS Archives.)

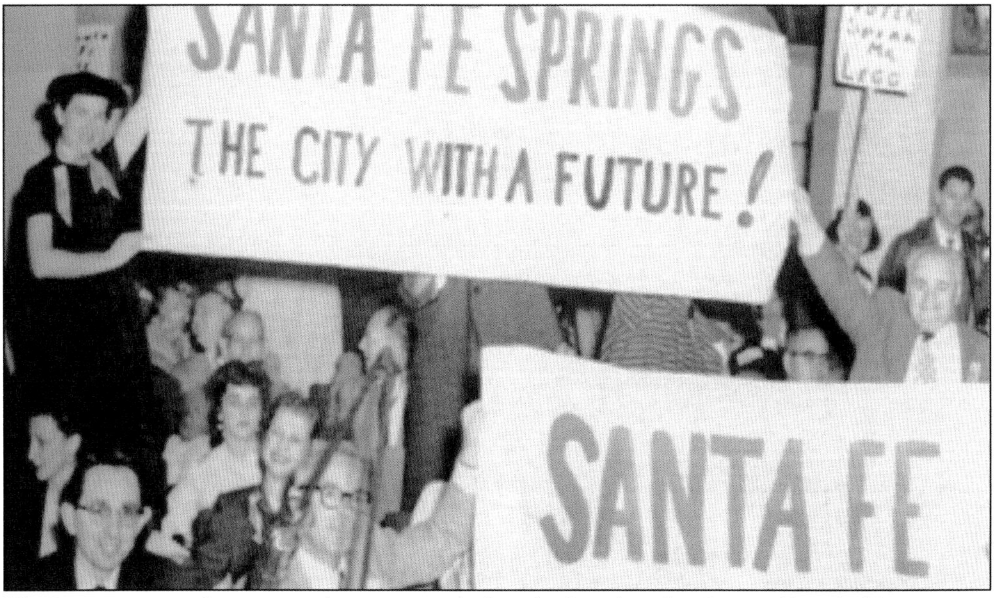

The Incorporation Committee demonstrates before the Los Angeles County Board of Supervisors at the official boundary hearing in January 1957. In this meeting, Supervisor Herbert C. Legg, with one stroke of his pen, eliminated the southern portion of the proposed city boundaries. After the adjustments were made, the boundary lines were approved, allowing the incorporation effort to go forward. Ann Bartunek and Hank Gleeksman are pictured holding the top sign, and Bill Camil is at front left. (Courtesy SFS Archives.)

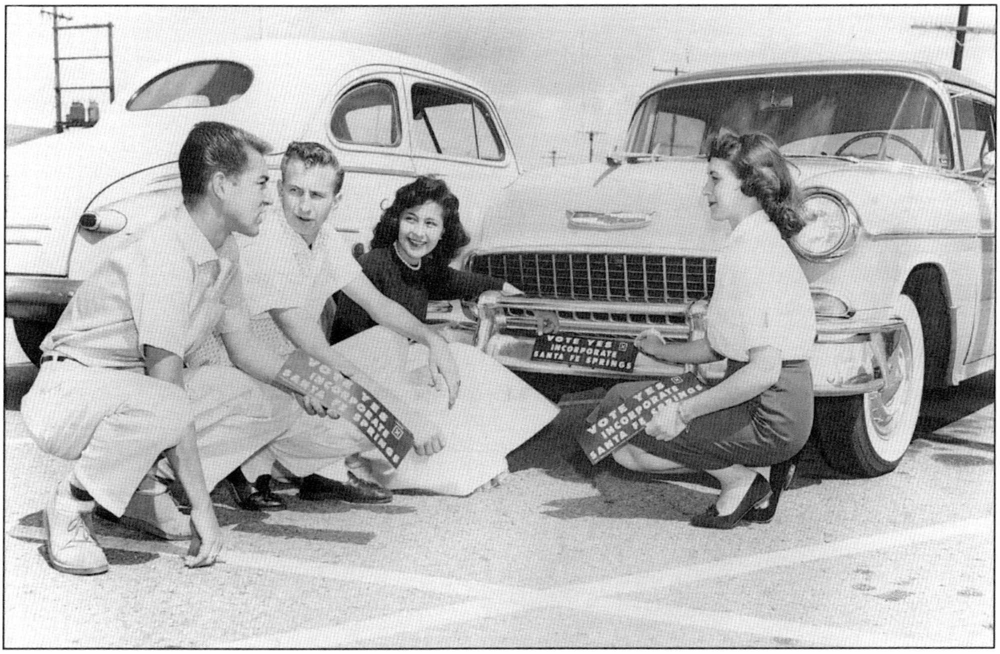

The excitement of incorporation was contagious, with even the young people of the community getting on the bandwagon. Pictured above from left to right are Dick Schawcroft, Don Hickock, Eva Barcelo, and Ann Barrett. Petition coordination was done from Ann Bartunek's home. Petitions were passed out to eager association members who canvassed the neighborhoods collecting signatures for incorporation. Daily, volunteers were constantly coming and going from the Bartunek house. (Courtesy SFS Archives.)

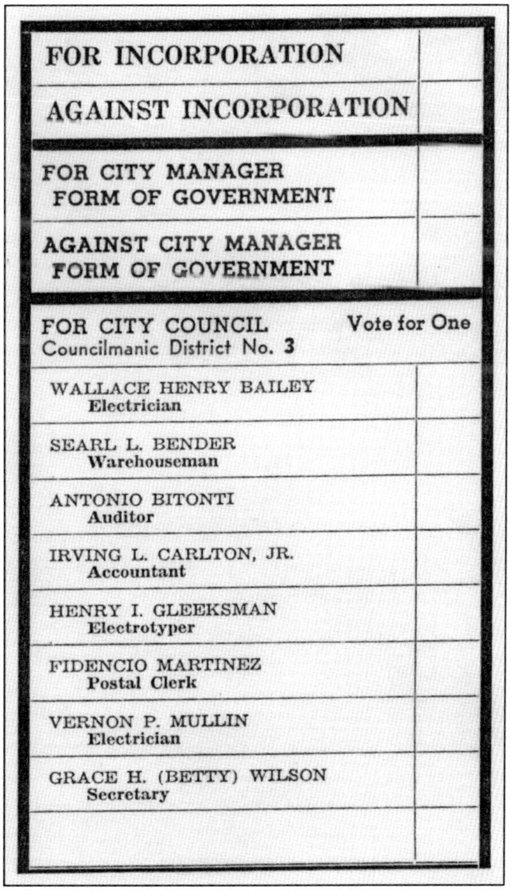

FOR INCORPORATION	
AGAINST INCORPORATION	
FOR CITY MANAGER FORM OF GOVERNMENT	
AGAINST CITY MANAGER FORM OF GOVERNMENT	
FOR CITY COUNCIL Councilmanic District No. 3 — Vote for One	
WALLACE HENRY BAILEY Electrician	
SEARL L. BENDER Warehouseman	
ANTONIO BITONTI Auditor	
IRVING L. CARLTON, JR. Accountant	
HENRY I. GLEEKSMAN Electrotyper	
FIDENCIO MARTINEZ Postal Clerk	
VERNON P. MULLIN Electrician	
GRACE H. (BETTY) WILSON Secretary	

The election for incorporation was held on May 7, 1957. The proposed city was to be divided into five districts, with each district to have one council member. There were three decisions the voters had to make: to incorporate or not; to have a city manager form of government or not; and to elect a council member for their district. By the end of the day, the people had voted to become a city. (Courtesy SFS Archives.)

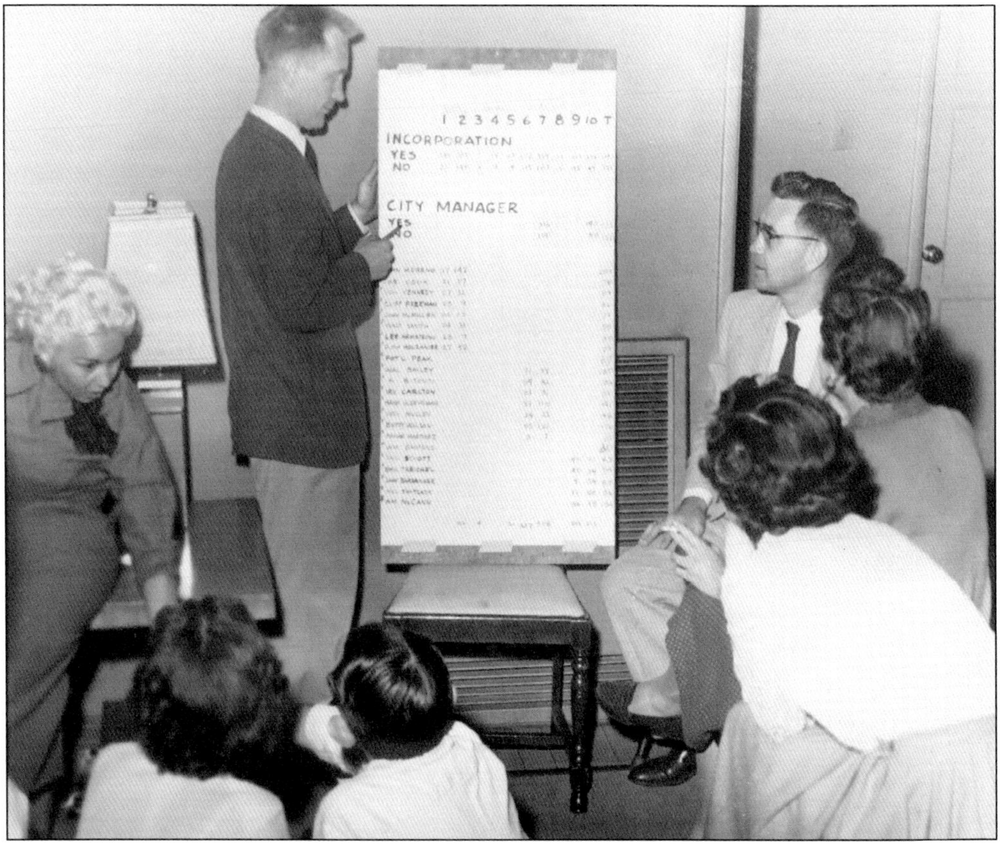

After the election, members of the homeowners association gathered at a member's home to await the results. They were anxious to find out if the years of hard work had paid off. Ted Snyder is pictured going over the results of whether or not to incorporate and the type of city government the people chose. (Courtesy SFS Archives.)

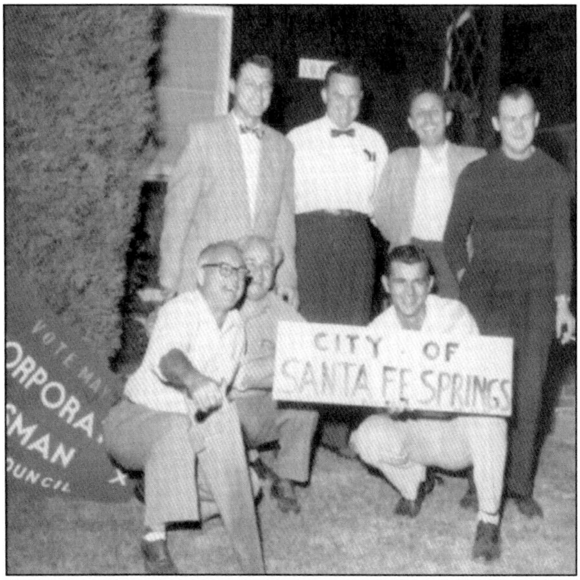

Eight days after the election, the State of California certified the election and declared the City of Santa Fe Springs the 53rd incorporated city in Los Angeles County. It was a time to celebrate in Santa Fe Springs. Members of the homeowners association gathered to celebrate the fruit of their many months of hard work. Hank Gleeksman (center bottom row) was a pro-incorporation supporter who unsuccessfully ran for city council. (Courtesy SFS Archives.)

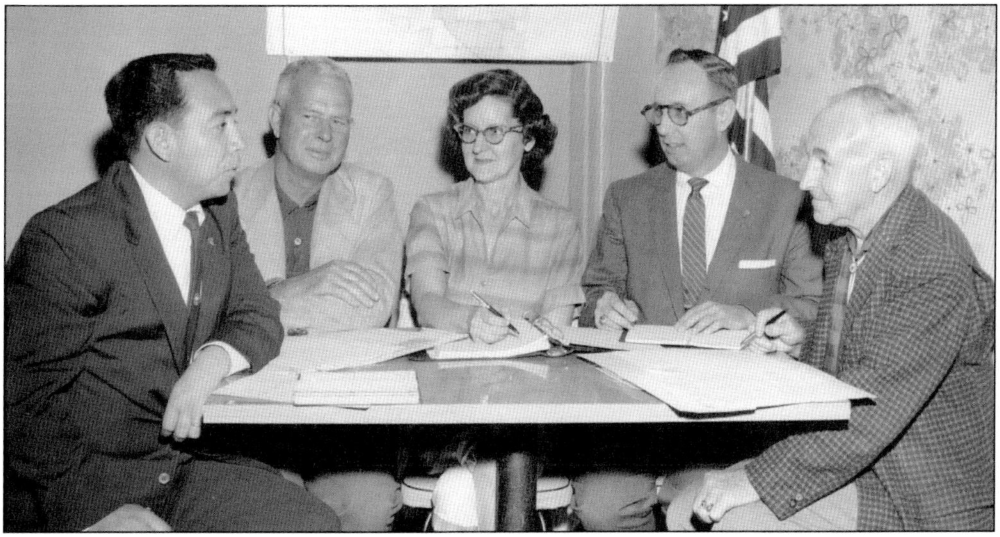

The first official city council meeting with the newly elected city council was to be held on May 15, 1957. The council members elected, pictured from left to right, are John Moreno, Foy Peak, Grace H. "Betty" Wilson, William McCann, and William Emmens. Council members held an informal meeting at Paul's Restaurant in the Santa Fe Springs Shopping Center before the official meeting because they wanted to go over procedural matters in advance. (Courtesy SFS Archives.)

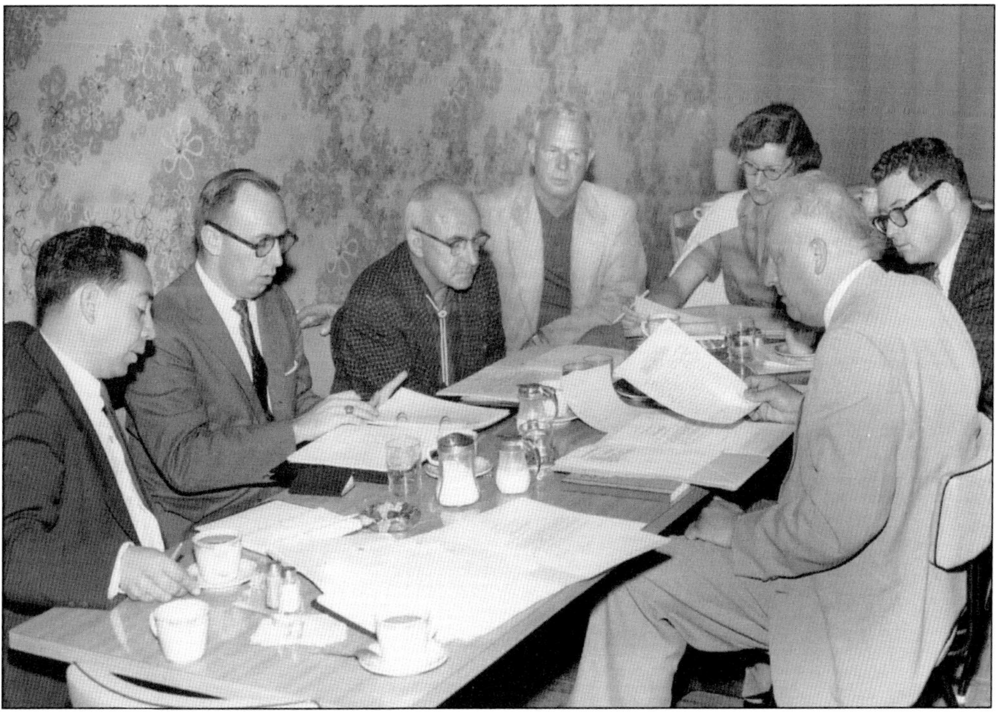

Also discussed was which council member would be the first mayor. John Moreno was chosen, but as a public relations ploy, Ted Snyder, in charge of publicity, suggested electing Betty Wilson as mayor, which would make Santa Fe Springs the first city in the county to have a woman mayor and give the new city some desired publicity. Also pictured are first city manager Meno Wilhelm and the interim city attorney. (Courtesy SFS Archives.)

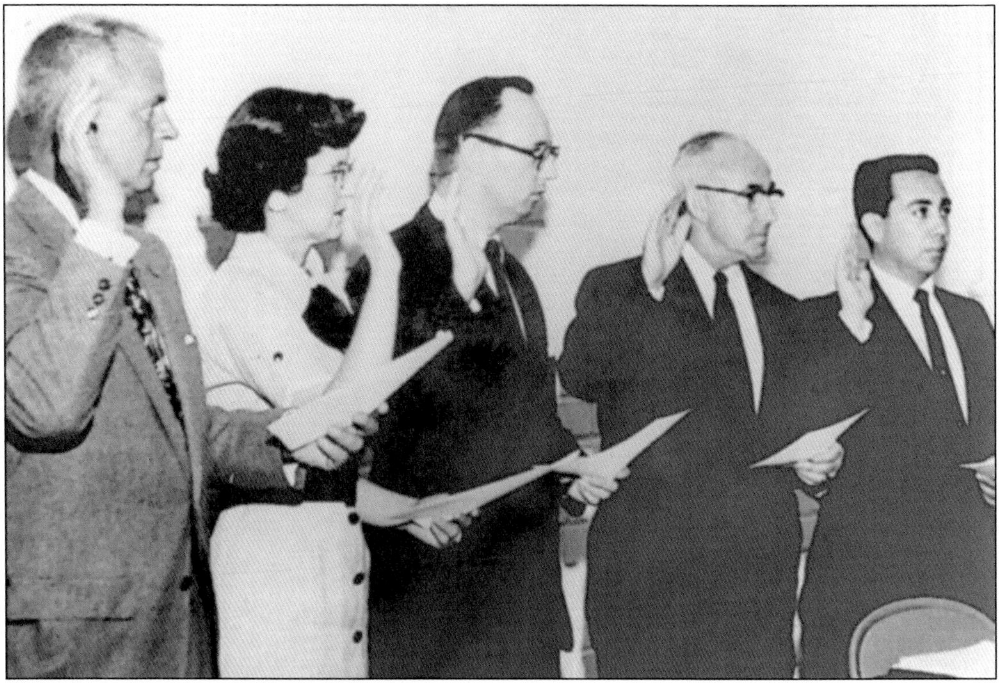

The newly elected council members were sworn in at the first official Santa Fe Springs City Council meeting. The meeting covered many organizational essentials and a number of annexation proposals. Things went smoothly until the agenda got to matters of annexations and zoning. There were some tense moments and angry exchanges between the Industrial League and city council. At one point, the league threatened to incorporate "South Santa Fe Springs." (Courtesy SFS Archives.)

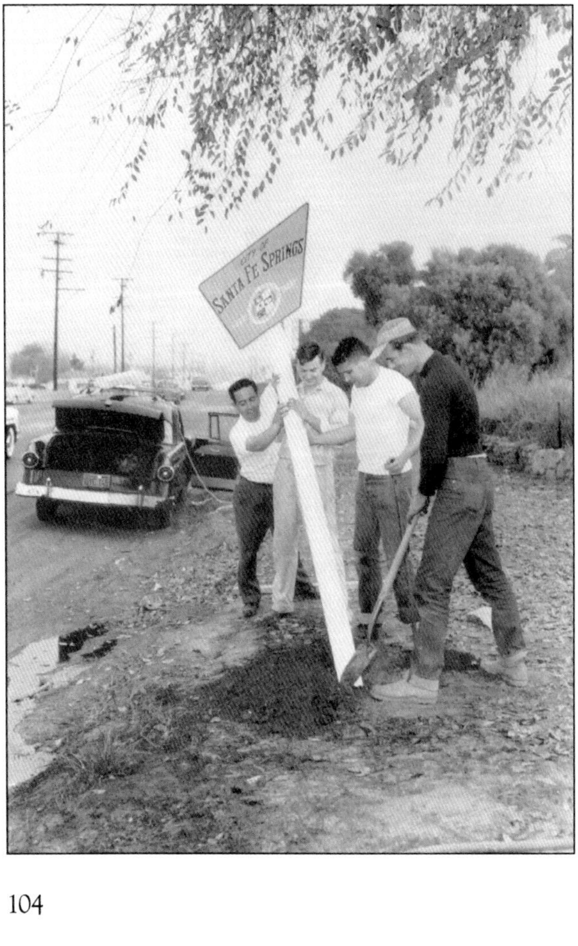

Almost immediately, city limit signs started going up. Council member John Moreno and three residents are pictured installing one of the first city limits signs. John Moreno became mayor of Santa Fe Springs after council member Betty Wilson resigned her post as the first woman mayor in the county. (Courtesy SFS Archives.)

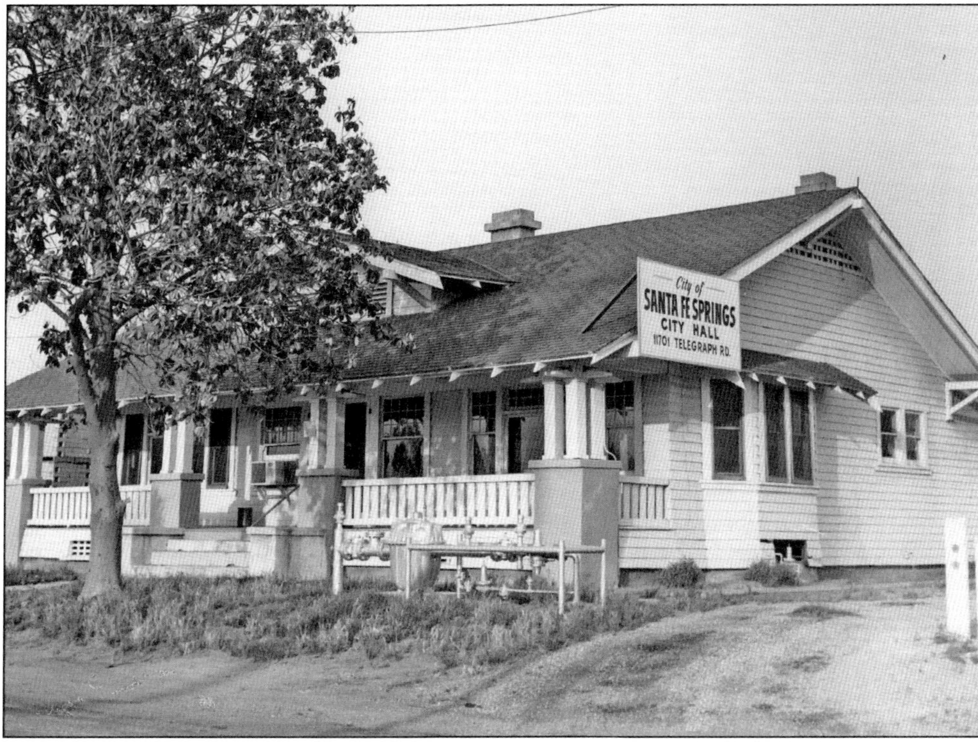

The first city hall was an old converted home made available rent-free by Ira C. Lackey, a generous businessman. The home was intended for use as the city hall for only a few years. Since the home was only large enough to be used for administrative offices, city council meetings were held in the multipurpose room of Santa Fe High School's gymnasium. (Courtesy SFS Archives.)

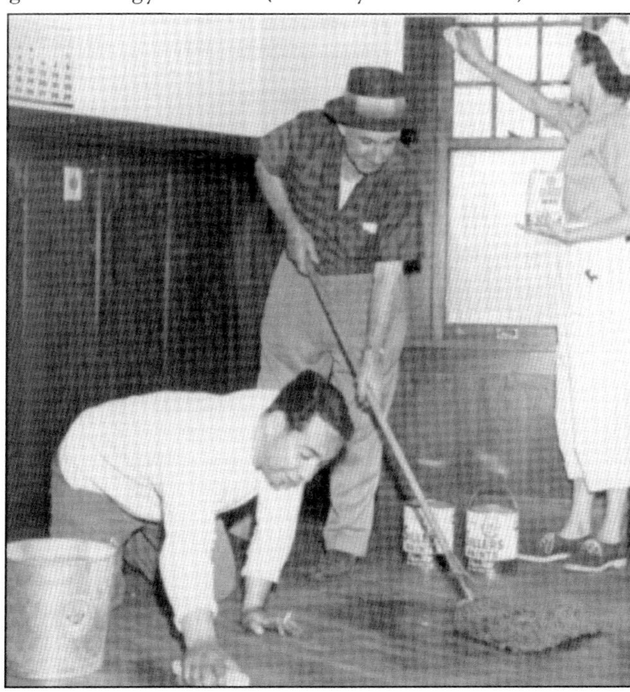

Santa Fe Springs' first city hall needed lots of work and cleanup to get it ready for the business at hand. Council members John Moreno and Bill Emmens are just two of many who helped clean up the old building. In order to align city elections with the rest of the state, the council's first term only lasted a year and a half. At her first reelection bid, Betty Wilson lost to challenger Bill Camil. (Courtesy SFS Archives.)

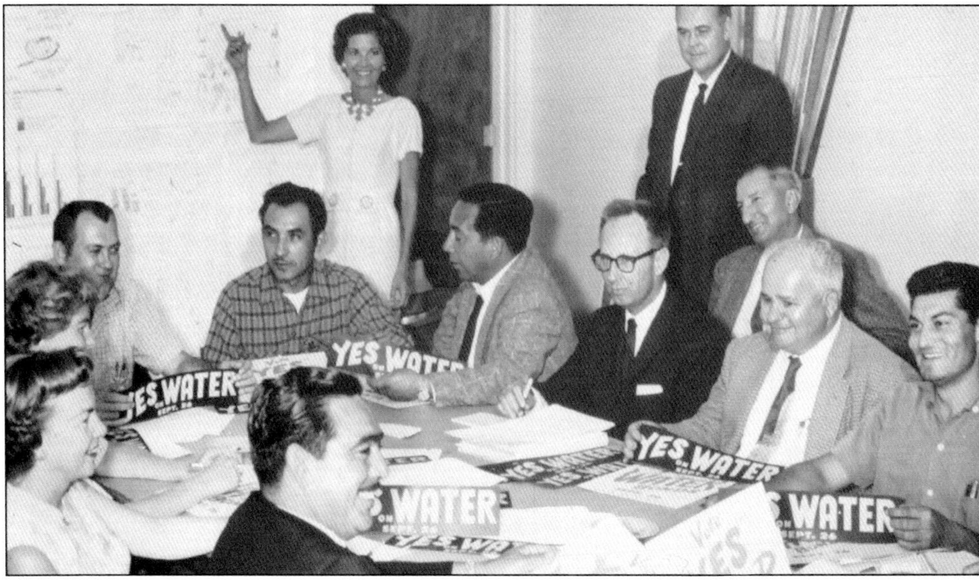

After the city council studied the possibility of improving the water service to city residents, it proposed buying up several local small water companies. A bond measure was placed on the ballot for residents to approve funding. The residents approved the bond measure, and the improvements were made to the Santa Fe Springs Water Company. (Courtesy SFS Archives.)

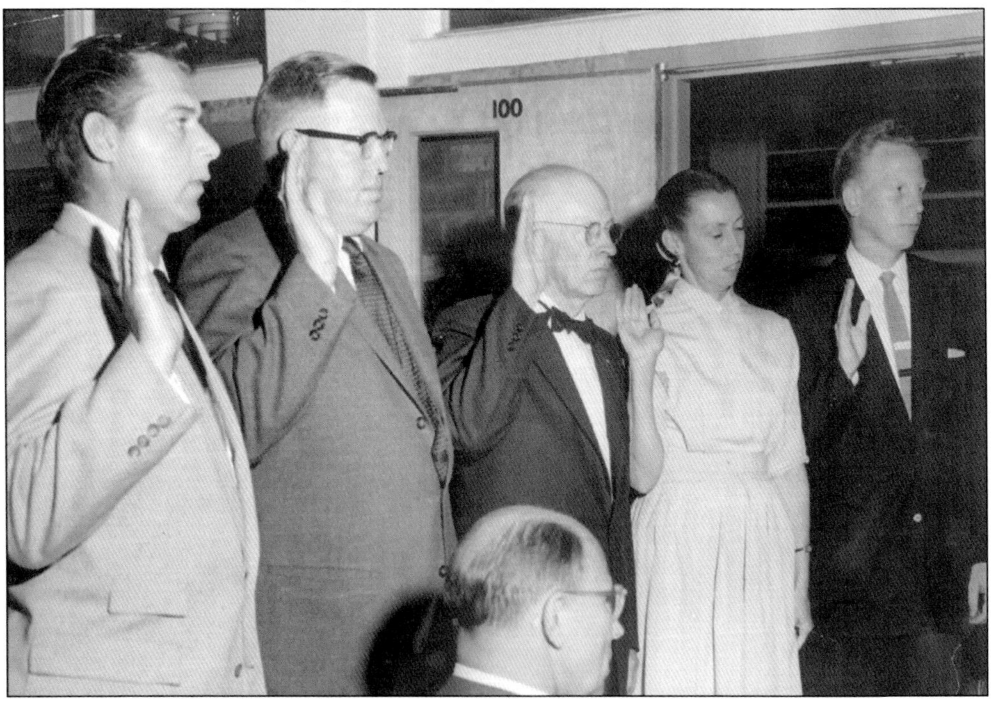

Within months of incorporating, the city council passed ordinance No. 15, which established the Santa Fe Springs Planning Commission. On July 17, 1957, the first planning commissioners were sworn in. They were George Boal, appointed by council member Betty Wilson; Dixie Pollard, by Bill Emmons; Robert Kline, by Foy Peak; Walter C. "Dutch" Holzhauer, by John Moreno; and Malcolm Burton, by Bill McCann. (Courtesy SFS Archives.)

Six

Developing Santa Fe Springs

Santa Fe Springs was now officially a city, and all the time and hard work of the Santa Fe Springs Homeowners Association and the Industrial League paid off. The work, though, was not over; in fact, it had just begun. The city council and residents realized early on that they needed to establish necessary city services. To complicate matters, the freshman city council was facing formidable obstacles.

The vote for incorporation and for the first city council took place in a special election on an off year. As a result, the fledgling council members had to face a reelection bid just a year later to get the city elections in sync with the rest of the state. All five council members faced reelection in 1958, and when the ballots were counted, there was one new city council member. William Camil had defeated Betty Wilson in District 3.

After the reelection, a new hurdle confronted the city council. In 1959, some disgruntled residents started a recall campaign against three city council members. These residents claimed that council members John Moreno, Foy Peak, and William Camil had mismanaged the city and its funds. Failing to get the required number of signatures in Foy Peak's district, only Moreno and Camil were on the recall ballot. City council members and their supporters believed that the L.A. County firemen through the Federated Firefighters Association financed the recall. They believed it was an attempt to get even for the city council's vote to end its contract with L.A. County Fire and start its own fire department. The recall attempt was unsuccessful, and the two council members retained their seats.

In 1960, Warren Ferguson resigned his position as city attorney. To fill this position, William Camil stepped down from city council and accepted Ferguson's former job. With the new vacancy in the city council, the council appointed Betty Wilson to fill the post. She served continually until she retired in 1997.

With the hurdles behind them, the city council and the residents of the city looked forward to the developing of Santa Fe Springs.

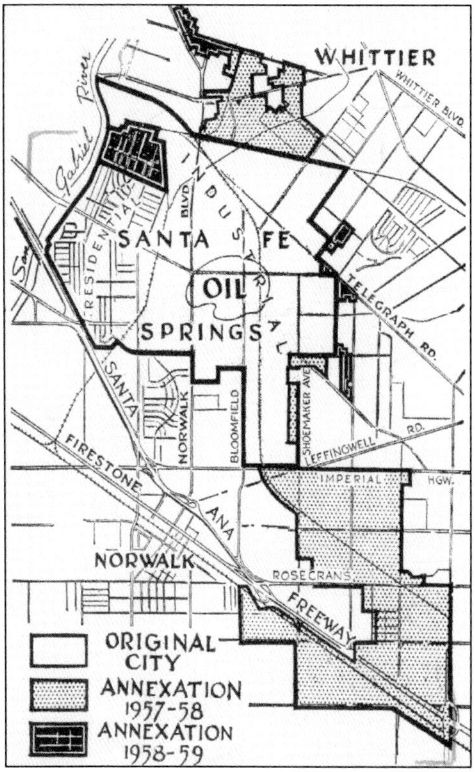

At the time of incorporation, the area of the city encompassed approximately five square miles. By the end of 1959, because of the annexation of adjacent lands, it reached 90 percent of its current size, as seen in this 1960 map from a report to city residents. By 1959, Santa Fe Springs had reached the size of a little less than eight and a half square miles. It reached its current size of just over nine square miles in 1979 after its last annexation. (Courtesy SFS Archives.)

It soon became apparent that the small building at the corner of Alburtis Avenue and Telegraph Road was inadequate (see page 105). So in 1958, the city leased a building at 9836 Jersey Avenue to be used for city hall staff. This larger building allowed room for the city manager and his directors to have offices. It also had a larger service counter for residents needing services and a council chamber that could seat 100 people. (Courtesy SFS Archives.)

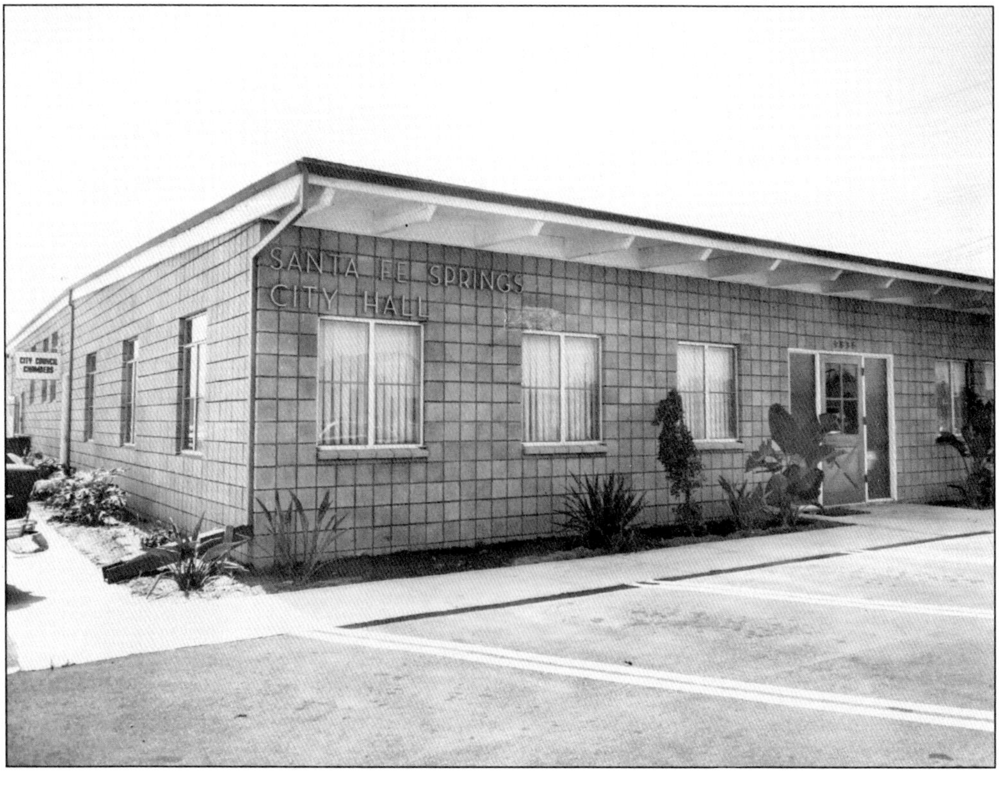

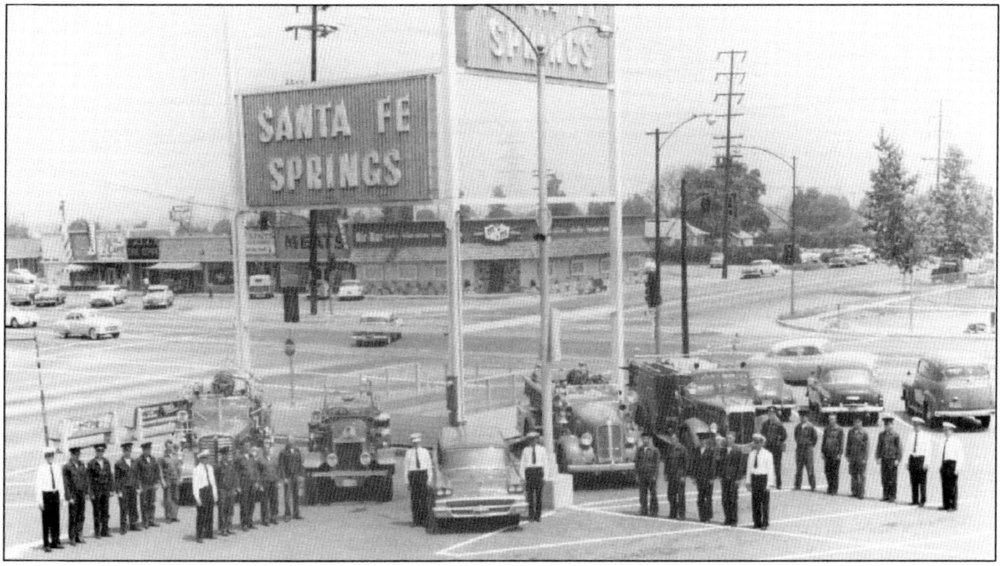

In 1958, the residents and city council, not satisfied with the quality of service provided by Los Angeles County Fire Department, voted unanimously to establish their own fire department. In this 1958 photograph, the new Santa Fe Springs Fire Department assembles at the corner of Telegraph and Orr & Day Roads. Directly behind them and across the street is the Mir Mar Restaurant, which would later become the Rim Ram. (Courtesy SFS Archives.)

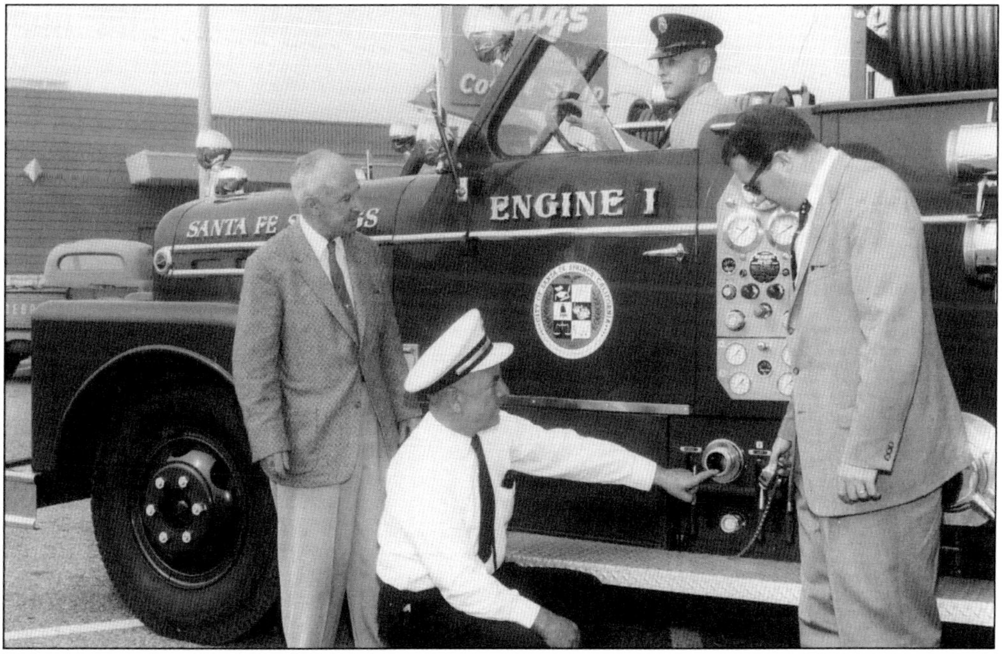

The newly formed fire department had no station, no equipment, and no chief. After months of struggles and court injunctions, the department was up and running under Fire Chief Elmer Gates, who served until 1970. Mayor William Emmens, pictured with Chief Gates and City Manager Meno Wilhelm on the right, inspects the recently acquired 1958 Seagrave fire engine, which the department still maintains to this day and which can be seen at many city events. (Courtesy SFS Archives.)

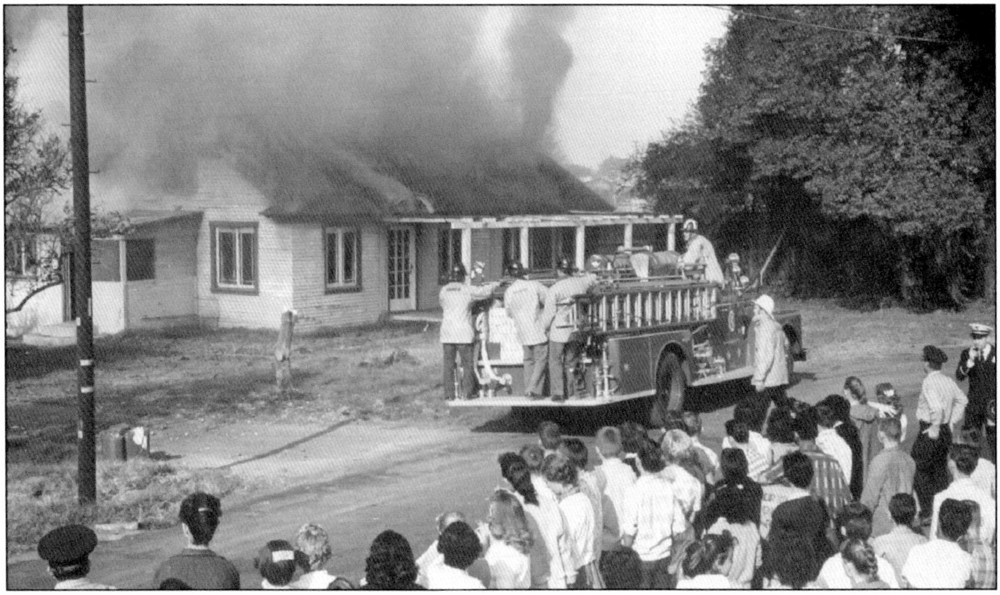

With the fire department established and equipped, the firefighters trained in preparation for emergencies. The city had many old houses that the city's building department had deemed undesirable. These houses were perfect for training, as seen in this 1959 photograph. With many hazardous materials in the industrial portion of the city, the department needed specialized skills and equipment. Rising to the challenge, the department has been nationally recognized for its excellence. (Courtesy SFS Archives.)

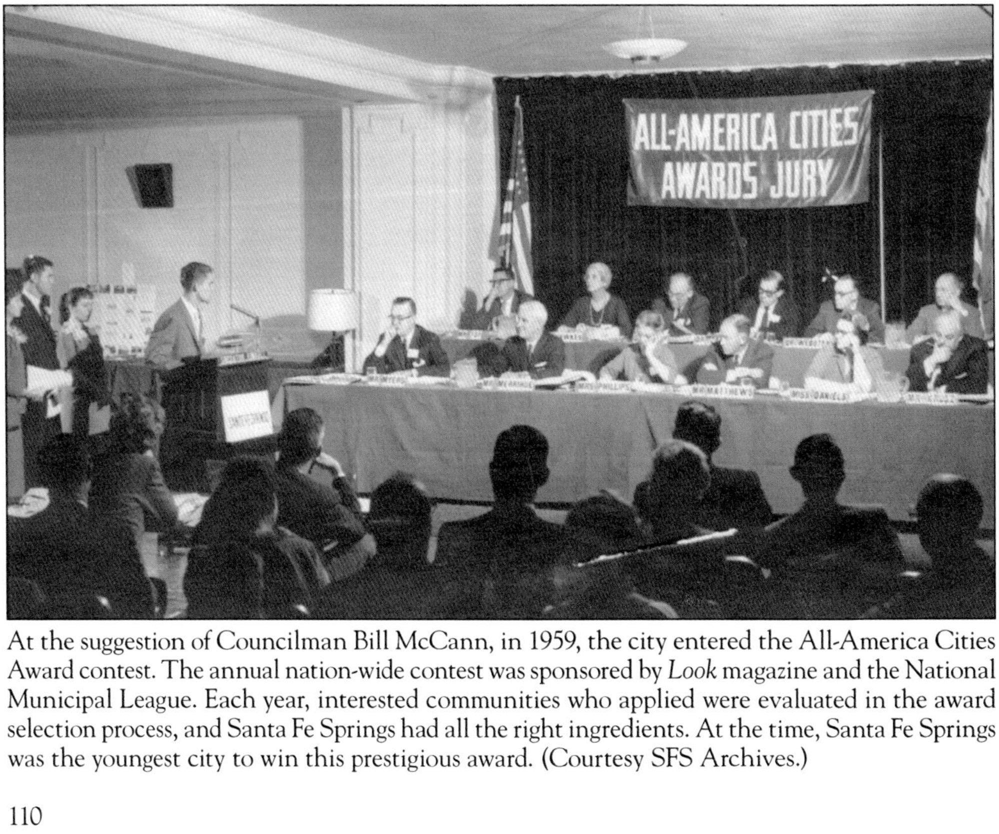

At the suggestion of Councilman Bill McCann, in 1959, the city entered the All-America Cities Award contest. The annual nation-wide contest was sponsored by *Look* magazine and the National Municipal League. Each year, interested communities who applied were evaluated in the award selection process, and Santa Fe Springs had all the right ingredients. At the time, Santa Fe Springs was the youngest city to win this prestigious award. (Courtesy SFS Archives.)

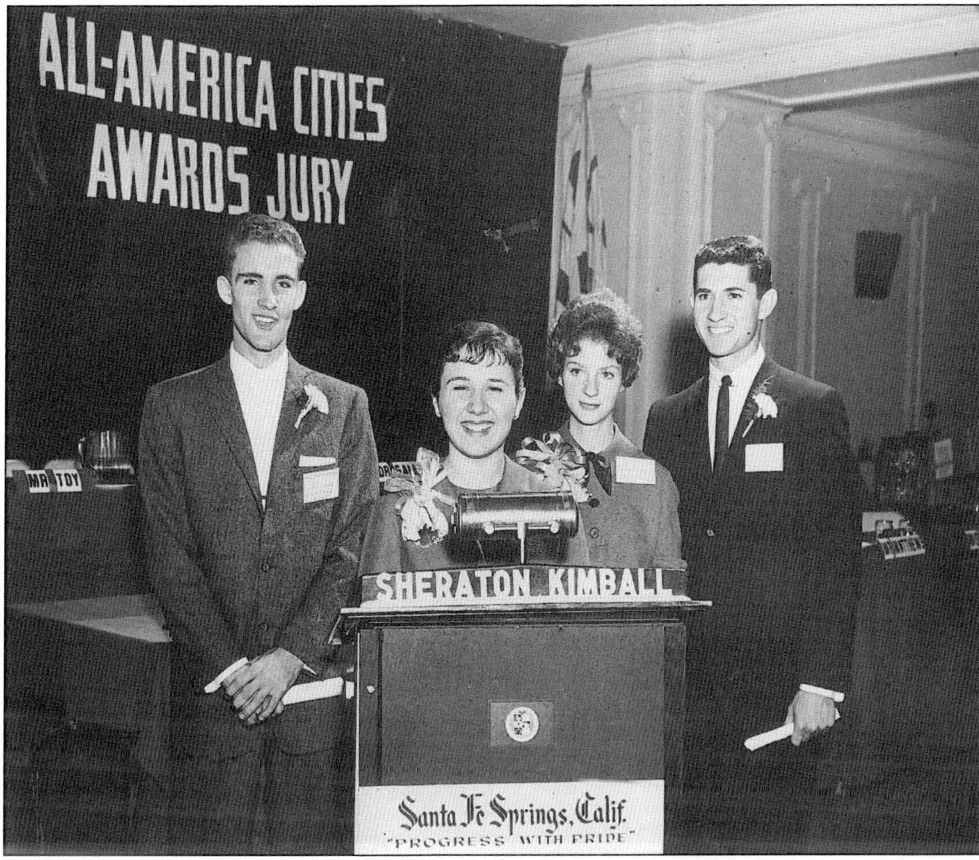

Ted Snyder, in charge of publicity for the city and a journalism teacher at Santa Fe High, was asked to help handle the application. Snyder picked four local high school students to give the presentation in Springfield, Massachusetts. Snyder and other city officials accompanied the students. Students making the presentation in 1959 are, from left to right, Steve Dickerson, Penny Yapelli, Kathleen Burton, and Barney Martinez. (Courtesy SFS Archives.)

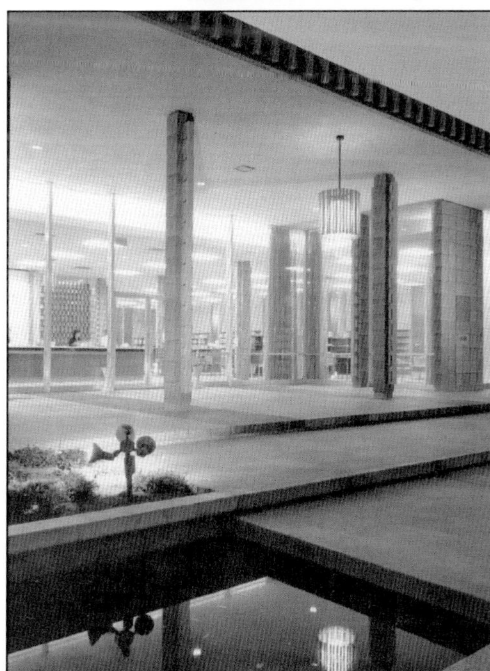

After the fire station was built, the city council approved the construction of the city library, pictured here at its 1961 opening. This beautiful building was designed by architect William Pereira and received the Southern California Chapter of the American Institute of Architects award for its excellence in architectural styling. The library was expanded in 1977 to its present size, and in 2010, it was renovated and updated. (Courtesy SFS Archives.)

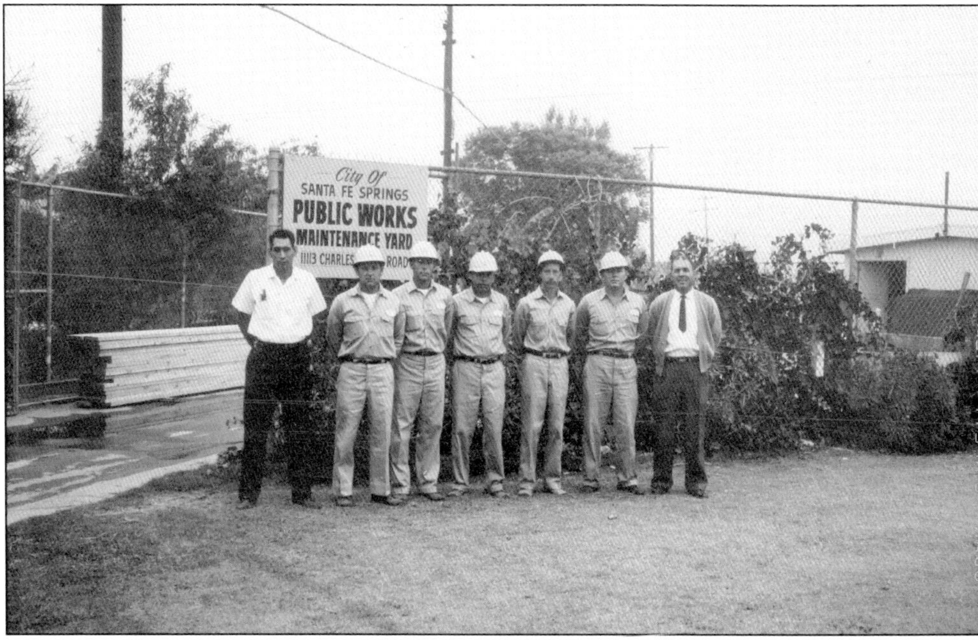

Almost immediately, the city council realized the need to establish a public works department. At first, there was just a handful of employees, and the city yard was located at the southwest corner of Los Nietos Park on Charlesworth Road. To this day, the City of Santa Fe Springs Public Works Department works tirelessly to maintain the city's streets and many parks and civic buildings in pristine condition. (Courtesy SFS Archives.)

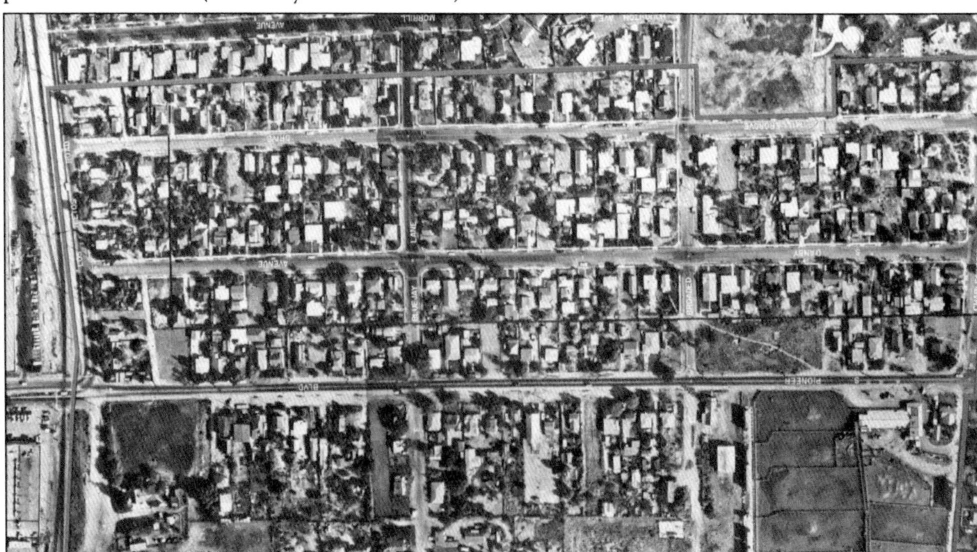

On October 27, 1958, shortly after the incorporation of Santa Fe Springs, the property between the San Gabriel River, Charlesworth Road, the Southern Pacific Railroad at Rivera Road, and the Santa Fe Railroad on the east was annexed to the city. This included Flood Ranch, pictured here in the early 1960s, a 65-acre Mexican American community of approximately 300 families, most of whom owned their property and had lived there for at least two generations. (Courtesy SFS Archives.)

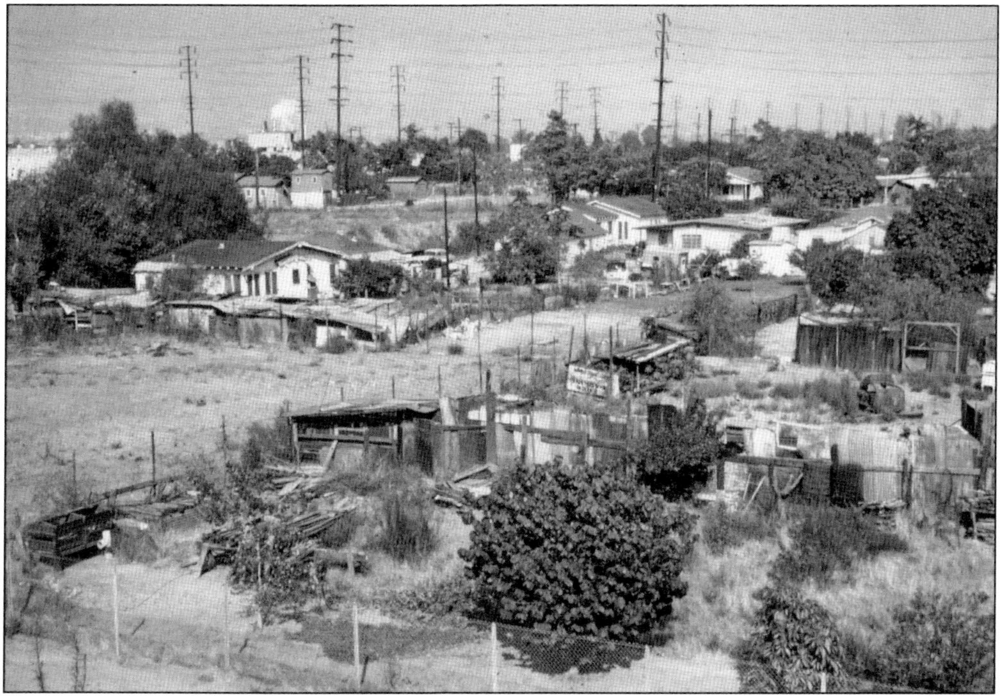

In 1962, the city council began considering the possibility of urban renewal in the Flood Ranch Community. Seen in this 1961 photograph are some of the homes between Pioneer Boulevard and the San Gabriel River. When word leaked of the city's plans, the Flood Ranch residents fiercely voiced their opposition. Remembering how residents were displaced in Chavez Ravine, the residents felt it was the city's way of kicking them out of the All-America City. (Courtesy SFS Archives.)

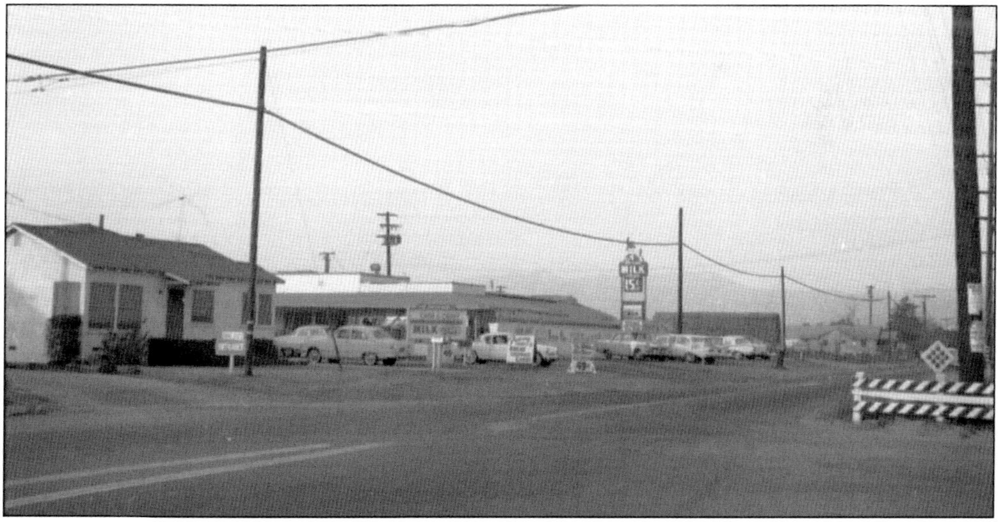

Van's Dairy had been a fixture in Santa Fe Springs since most residents could remember. Its founding date is not known, but it is visible in a 1945 aerial photograph of the Flood Ranch area. For decades, residents used the dairy to buy their milk and other dairy products. The construction of the San Gabriel River Freeway took the back half of the dairy in 1963, and urban renewal closed it down completely. (Courtesy SFS Archives.)

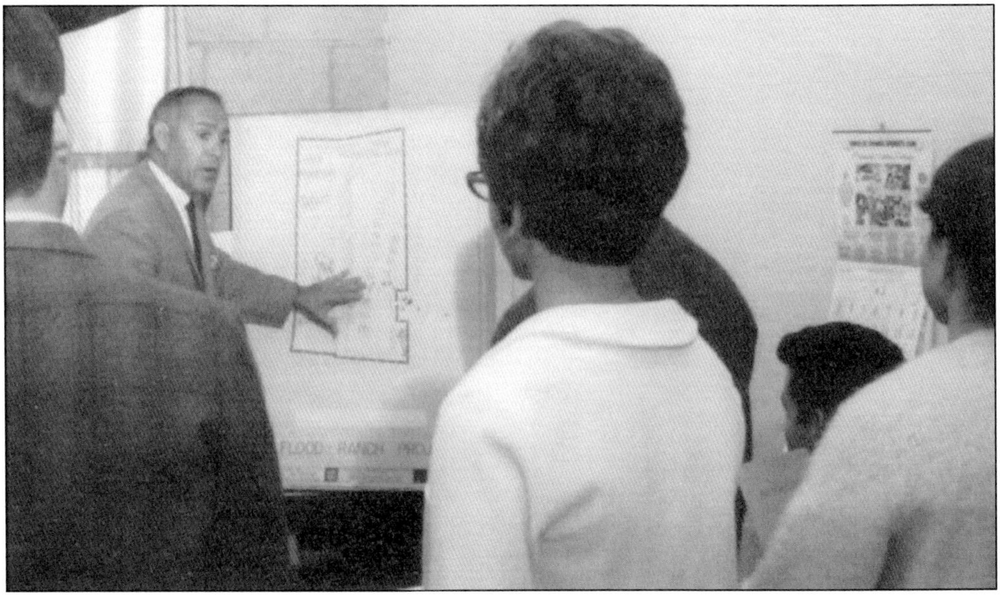

Public hearings began in 1963 as a result of community opposition to urban renewal. Massey Herrera, executive director of the city's redevelopment agency, meets with the community-formed Flood Ranch Improvement Association. A militant opposition to the plan arose in the small Mexican American community. Outside the meetings, picket signs could be seen reading, "I Will Fight for My Land," and, "When You Bring Your Bulldozers, Don't Forget to Bring Your Gun." (Courtesy SFS Archives.)

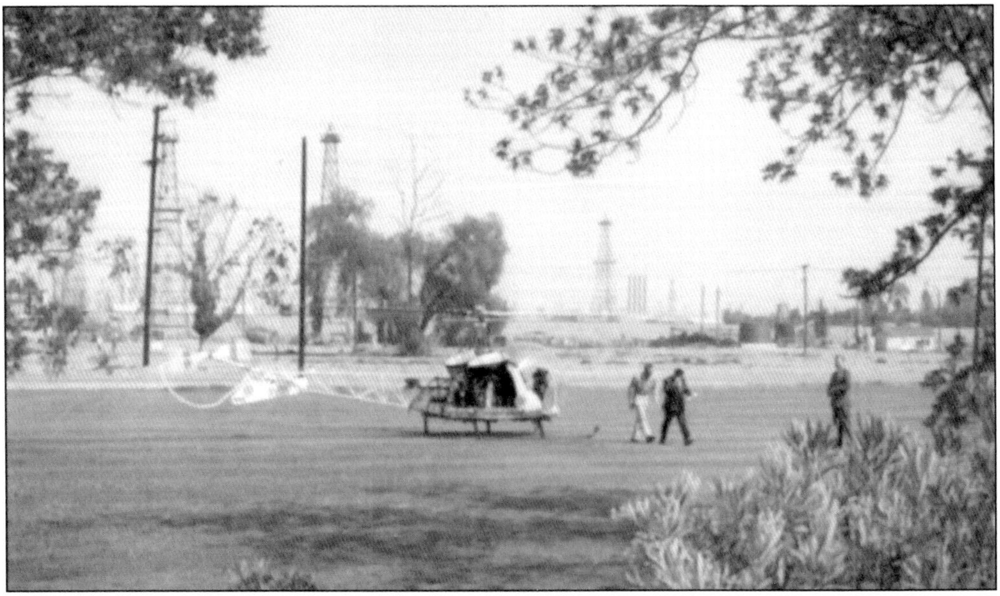

The Flood Ranch Improvement Association received assistance from attorney Robert Mitchell, pictured arriving by helicopter for a meeting. With the help of Mitchell, the city and the residents of Flood Ranch were able to reach a consensus. The community uniting in proactive involvement for its neighborhood was an unforeseen benefit of their ordeal. Two prominent organizations sprang up, the Club Cultural Mexicano and the Santa Fe Springs Coordinating Council. (Courtesy SFS Archives.)

One hundred and sixty-five homes were identified for rehabilitation. Self-financing, federally funded, low-interest loans and grants were available for homes being rehabilitated. Homes on Danby Avenue and Millergrove Drive were designated for this type of renewal. Homes impossible to rehabilitate, such as those west of and on Pioneer Boulevard, and those whose owners opted not to participate, were purchased by the SFS Redevelopment Agency. Here, the Cisnersos home was one of those slated for demolition. (Courtesy Cisneros Collection.)

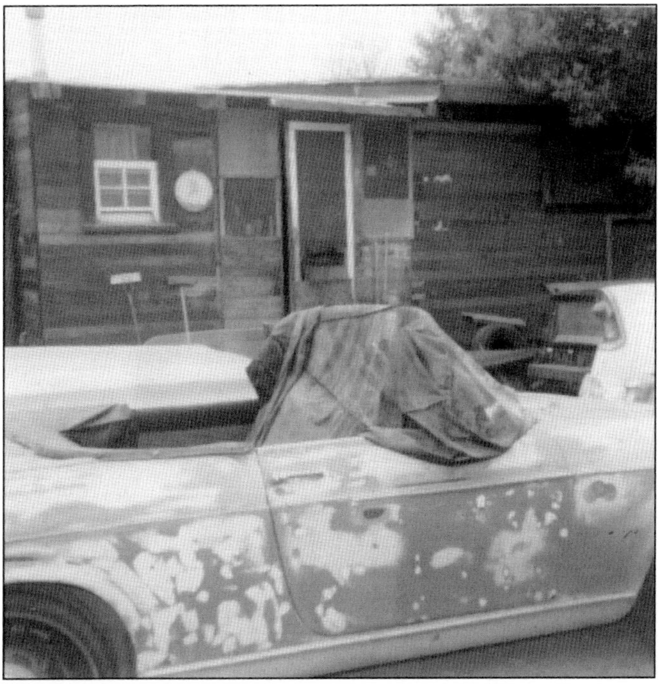

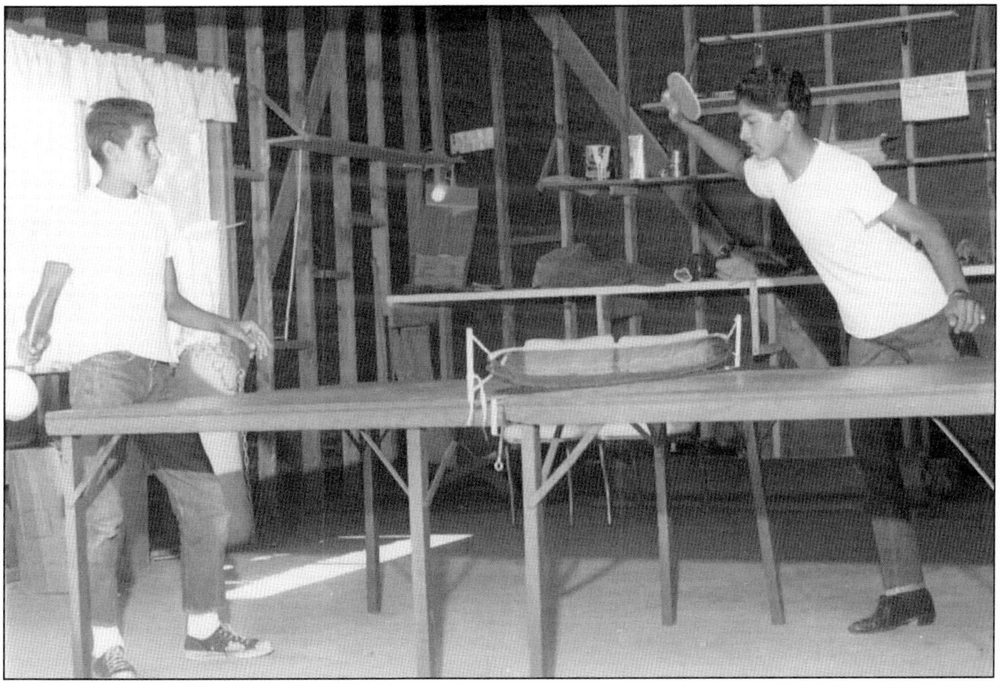

Residents of Flood Ranch established a community youth center in a vacant house on Millergrove Drive, and the city agreed to pay the rent. Volunteers, mostly women from the Flood Ranch community, staffed the center. Many neighborhood activities took place at this home, such as a well-baby clinic, counseling, sewing, and craft classes for children. Rito Leal and Mike Moreno play ping-pong in the garage of the youth center in this c. 1967 photograph. (Courtesy SFS Archives.)

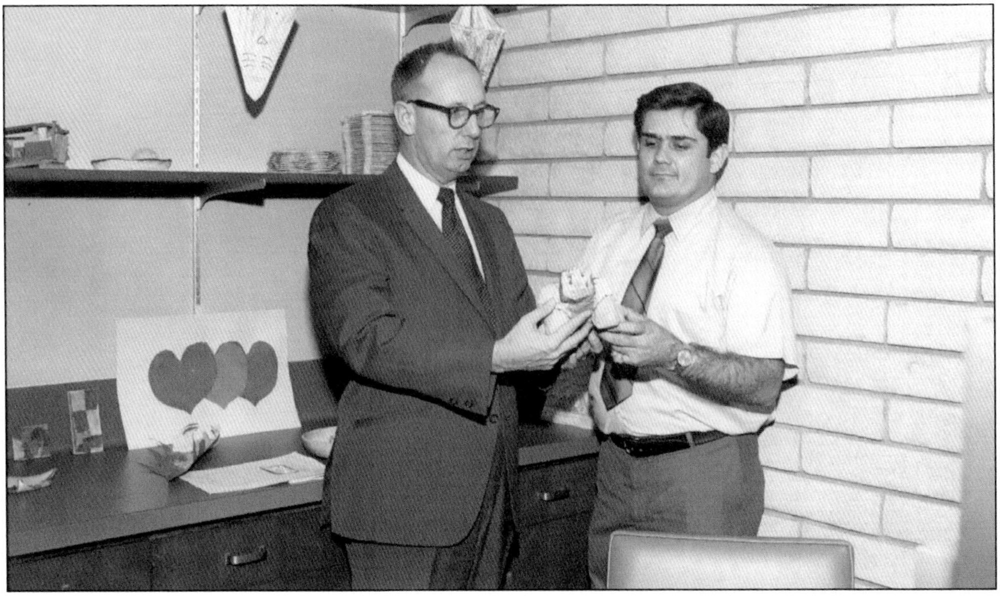

Councilman Bill McCann and Gus Velasco, director of the Neighborhood Center, are pictured at the center's 1969 opening-day ceremony. The new Neighborhood Center replaced the youth center in the little house on Millergrove Drive. Gus Velasco was hired as its first director, and shortly after, he hired Anna Price to assist him. The center became a national model for community centers and in 2011 was renamed the Gus Velasco Neighborhood Center in his honor. (Courtesy SFS Archives.)

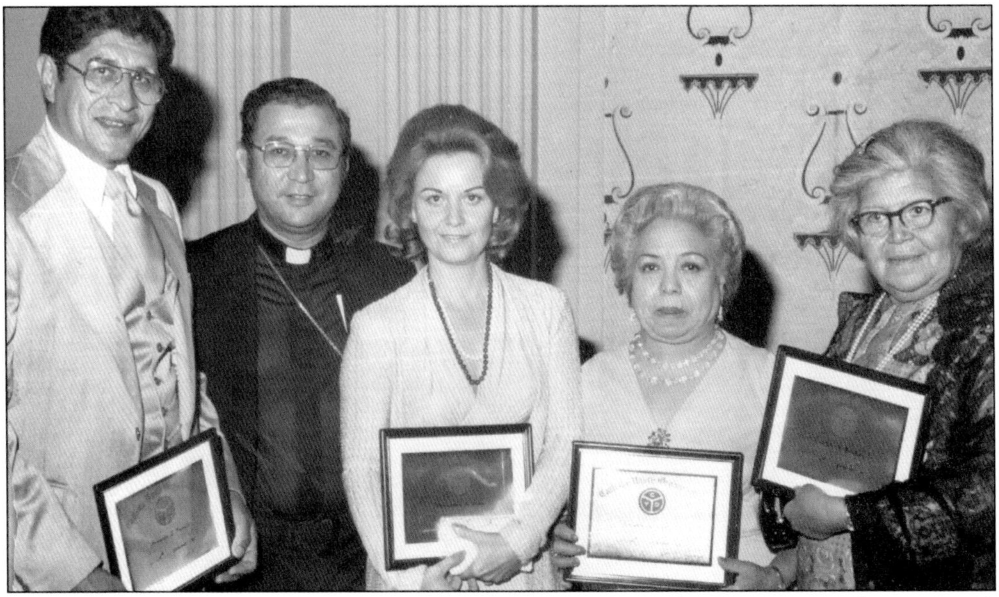

During a Fiestas Patrias celebration, local residents receive awards of recognition for their work with the Neighborhood Center. Pictured around 1969 are, from left to right, Armando Mora, an unidentified priest, Mercedes Diaz, Candelaria Corral, and Emilia Bustos. Corral, her husband, Gregorio Corral, and Emilia Bustos were among the driving forces behind the forming of the Club Cultural Mexicano (Mexican Cultural Club). It was a civic organization that provided activities and services for the community. (Courtesy Velasco family.)

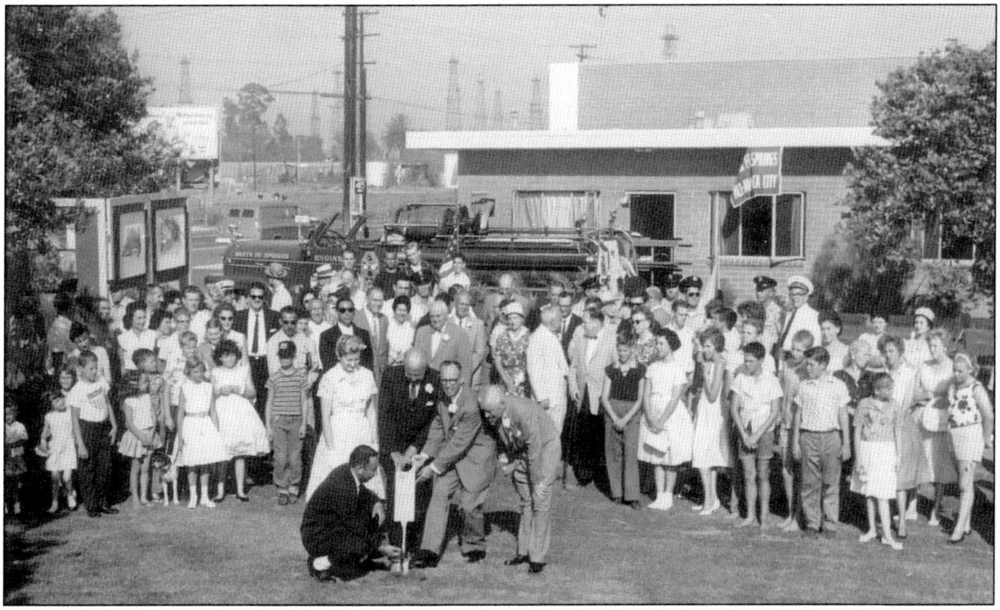

In 1958, the city had purchased five acres of land that it had chosen for the civic center site. Because the city paid cash, it was able to save an estimated $14,800. In this 1964 photograph of the ground-breaking ceremony are, from left to right, (standing, at the shovel) Betty Wilson, Bill Emmens, Bill McCann, and Foy Peak. Kneeling is John Moreno, who was a state assemblyman at the time. (Courtesy SFS Archives.)

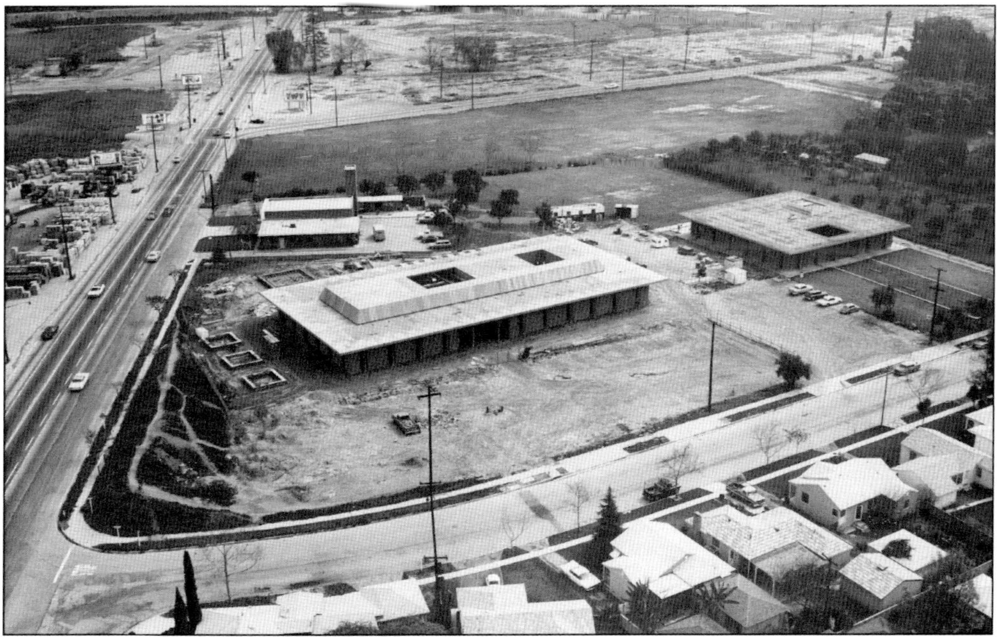

Santa Fe Springs was expanding rapidly, encompassing nine square miles by 1960 and with a population approaching 17,000. A functional city hall and city center were now essential. Construction for the new city hall began in 1966, two years after ground breaking. Pictured in 1966 is the new city hall nearing completion; it would open in 1967. The city hall was expanded on the south end to its current size in 1979. (Courtesy SFS Archives.)

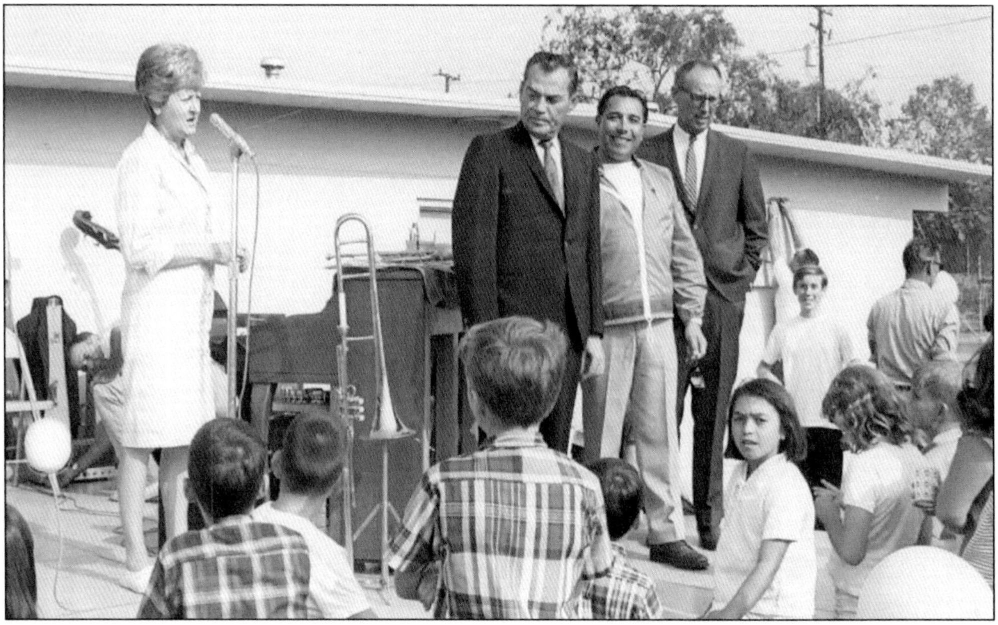

In October 1967, the new Santa Fe Springs Park was dedicated. It was located on 15 acres of land leased from the Southern California Edison Company and on land that was purchased by the city between the San Gabriel River and the 605 Freeway. At the dedication are, from left to right, council member Betty Wilson (at the microphone), Mayor Archie Beasor, council member Ernest Flores, and Mayor Pro Tem Bill McCann. (Courtesy SFS Archives.)

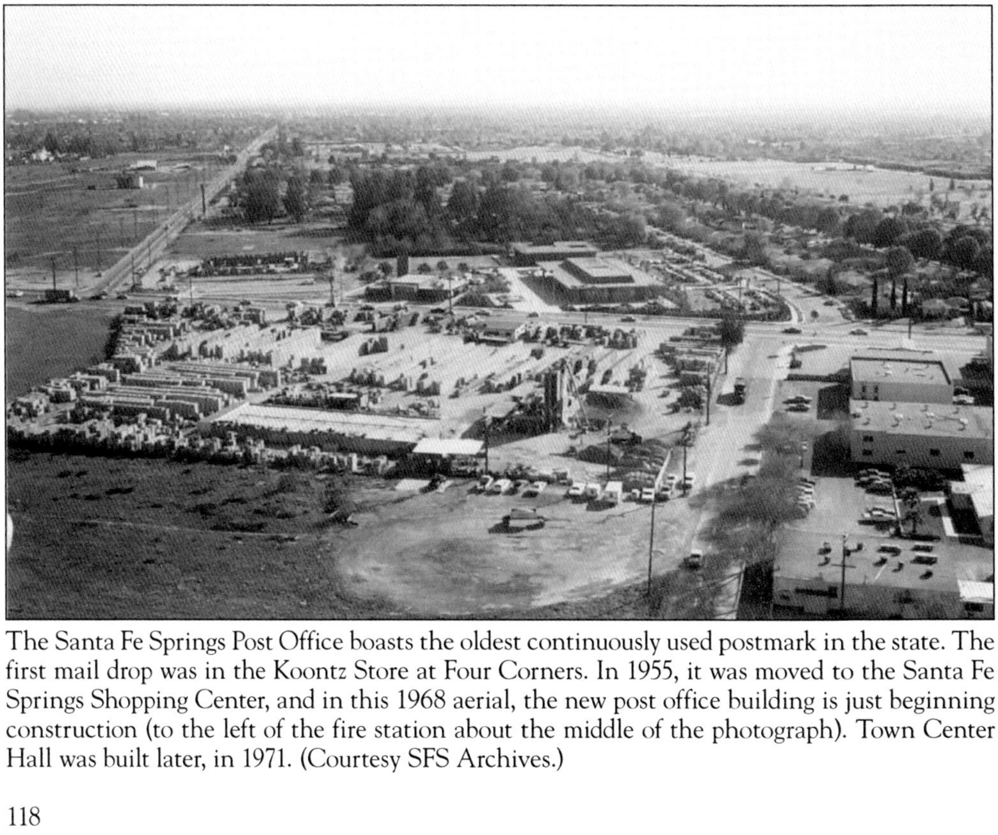

The Santa Fe Springs Post Office boasts the oldest continuously used postmark in the state. The first mail drop was in the Koontz Store at Four Corners. In 1955, it was moved to the Santa Fe Springs Shopping Center, and in this 1968 aerial, the new post office building is just beginning construction (to the left of the fire station about the middle of the photograph). Town Center Hall was built later, in 1971. (Courtesy SFS Archives.)

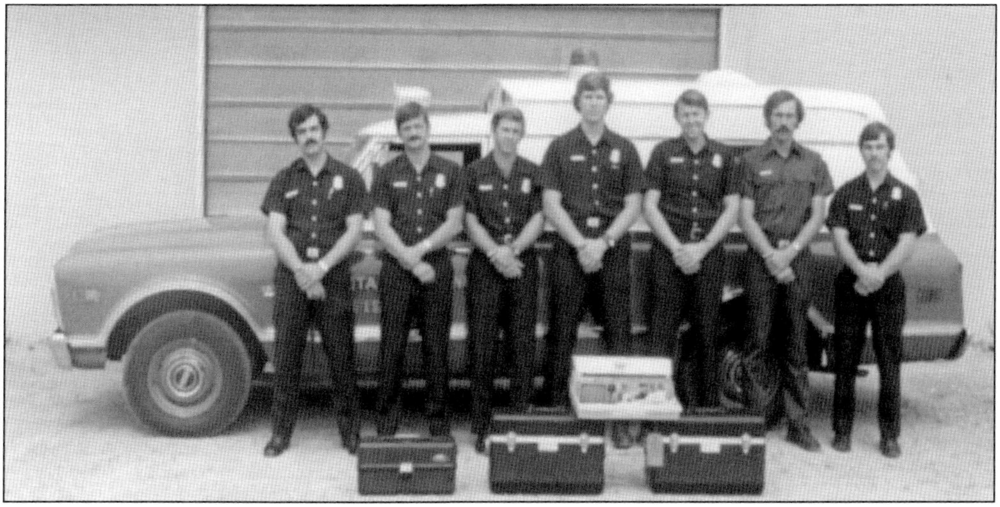

The Santa Fe Springs Fire Department had the goal of providing the best service available to the entire community it served. In this 1974 photograph, the city boasts one of the first paramedic units in the county. In 1972, there were only six paramedic units in three pilot programs in all of the United States. In the years ahead, the department would continue to expand its services. (Courtesy SFS Archives.)

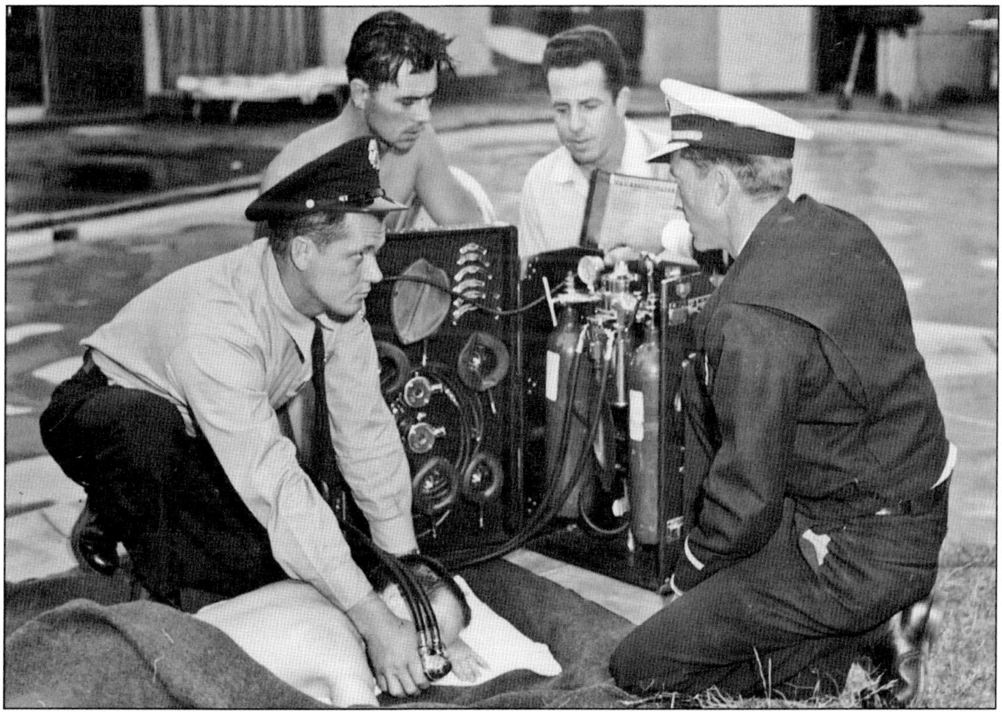

In this early 1960s photograph, members of the fledgling fire department practice medical emergency techniques. From its humble beginnings as a 30-man department, it would grow to its current 73-man force. The department now has four stations and is an "all-risk" emergency response provider, with specialty programs in emergency medical services, urban search and rescue, hazardous materials emergency response, environmental protection, and fire prevention. (Courtesy SFS Archives.)

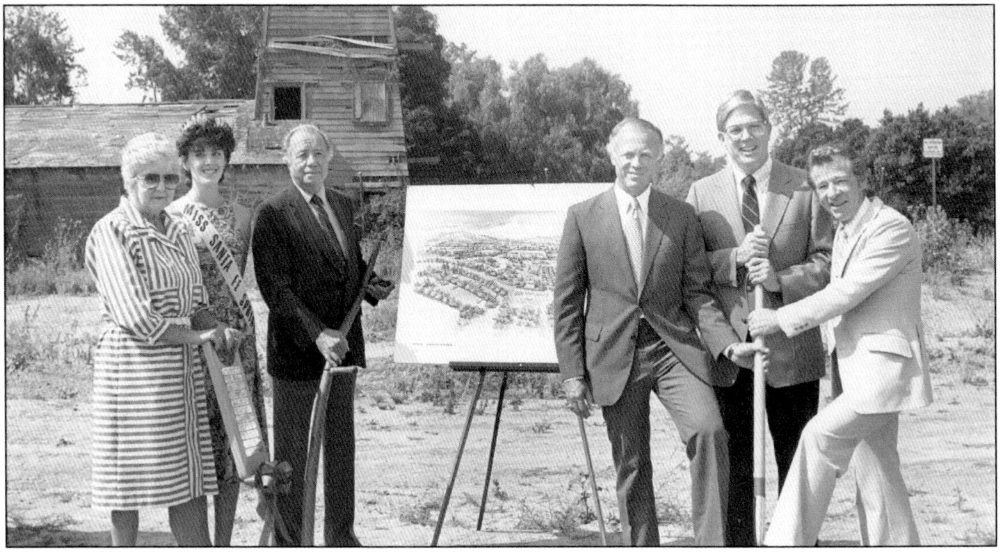

Fearing a historic landmark would be lost, members of the Rancho Santa Gertrudes Historical Society were led by Nadine Hathaway to lobby the city council to restore the Hawkins estate and turn it into a park. Pictured is the 1986 ground breaking with Miss Santa Fe Springs. From left to right are council members Betty Wilson and Larry Sandoval, Blair Armstrong of O'Donnell Brigham & Partners (park developer), and council members Albert Sharp and Ron Kernes. Heritage Park opened in 1988. (Courtesy SFS Archives.)

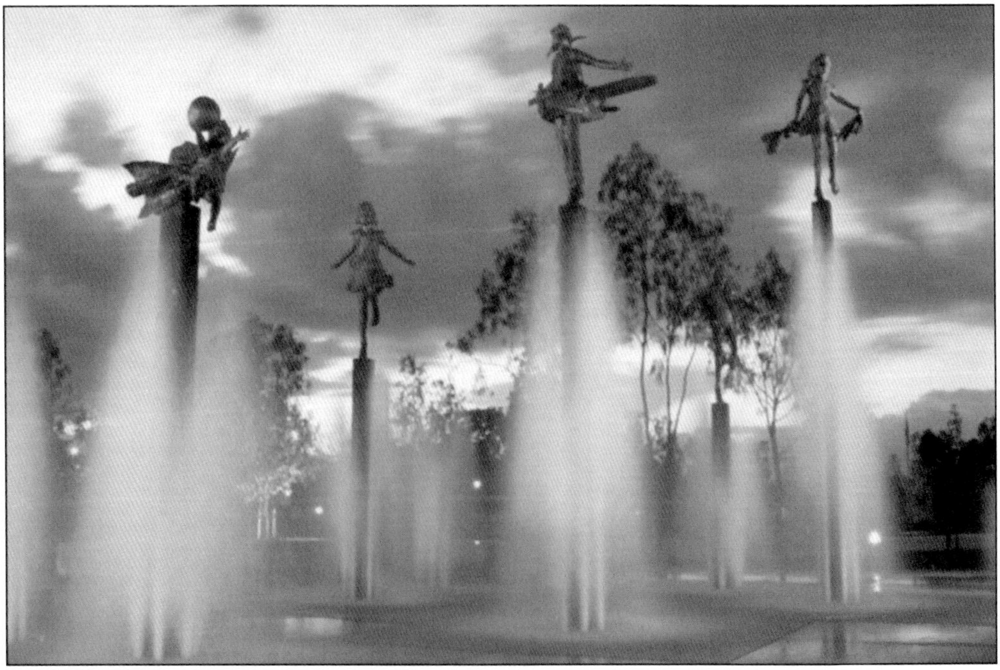

In 1988, the city formed the Heritage Art in Public Places Program. Its mission is to "Encourage the enhancement of life among residents through the acquisition and display of quality art." A portion of the program funds are used for grants to local schools to support art programs. *Soaring Dreams*, by Dennis Smith, is one of the many art pieces commissioned through the program that adorn the city. (Courtesy SFS Archives.)

Seven

Famous People and Events

Despite its small size, the city of Santa Fe Springs has been recognized by celebrities and is proud of the famous people who have come out of its small population.

US presidents, from Dwight D. Eisenhower to Gerald Ford and Ronald Reagan, have acknowledged the city with awards and proclamations. Dr. George Fischbeck, meteorologist and weatherman, helped rededicate Lakeview Park. Ed Asner, Emmy Award–winning actor, participated in the dedication of the Betty Wilson Center. When 24 Hour Fitness opened on Imperial Highway, Earvin "Magic" Johnson of the L.A. Lakers came out to promote health and physical well being.

Santa Fe Springs can boast of its own celebrities. Raul Rodriguez, nationally known for his award-winning Rose Parade floats, got his start in Santa Fe Springs. Joe Gibbs graduated from Santa Fe High School in 1959, where he was the star quarterback. He became head coach of the Washington Redskins and led them to three Super Bowl championships. Just before he retired from coaching, he started his own NASCAR team, Joe Gibbs Racing. Rodrigo "Rod" Barajas began his baseball career at Santa Fe High, earning first-team all-conference honors. He is a 2001 World Series champion with the Arizona Diamondbacks and is currently a catcher for the L.A. Dodgers. Another athlete is bantamweight champion Yonnhy Perez. He won his championship in 2009 against Joseph Agbeko. Yonnhy Perez dedicated this win to the city of Santa Fe Springs, where he lived and trained.

Santa Fe Springs proudly mentions its Olympians. Mark Kotsay won the bronze medal in men's baseball in the 1996 Olympics and is presently on the Milwaukee Brewers roster. Laura Berg earned gold medals in women's softball in the 1996, 2000, and 2004 Olympics. She also earned a silver medal in the 2008 Olympics. Laura had the reputation of being the team prankster, and when Pres. George W. Bush came to greet the team, Laura put a big chalk handprint on his back.

Santa Fe alumna Tamara E. Jernigan has been out of this world. A 1977 graduate from Santa Fe High, she became a scientist and NASA astronaut with five shuttle missions. Her last mission was on *Discovery* in 1999.

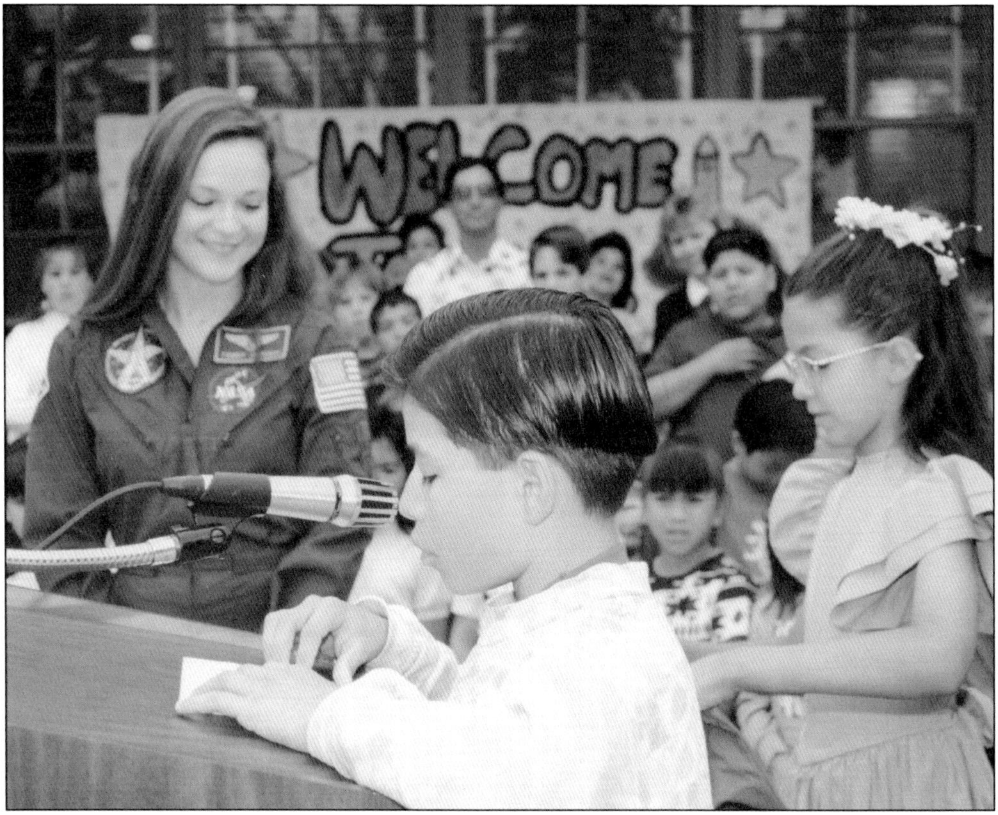

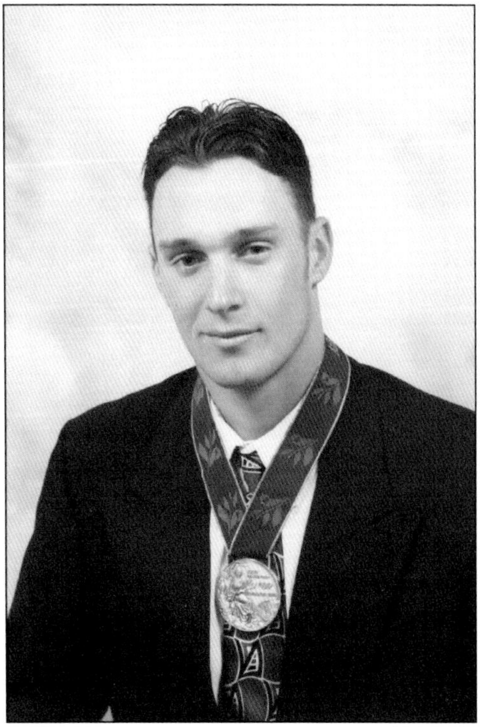

Tamara E. "Tammy" Jernigan, PhD, was born on May 7, 1959, in Chattanooga, Tennessee. After high school, Tammy received a plethora of degrees in physics, engineering science, and astronomy and a doctorate in space physics and astronomy. She became an astronaut in 1986, taking on various assignments and earning numerous awards during her career. She retired from NASA in 2001 to accept a position at Lawrence Livermore National Laboratory. Tammy is married to fellow astronaut Peter Wisoff. (Courtesy SFS archives.)

Mark Steven Kotsay was born on December 2, 1975, in Whittier, California. Mark attended Santa Fe High, where he excelled in football and baseball. In 1995, Kotsay won the Golden Spikes Award and was the Most Outstanding Player of the College World Series. The Florida Marlins called him to the Major Leagues in 1997. He batted a career best in 2004 with the Oakland A's, and as of 2011, he plays utility man with the Milwaukee Brewers. (Courtesy SFS archives.)

Laura Kay Berg was born on January 6, 1975, in Santa Fe Springs, California. Laura graduated from Santa Fe High and is a four-time All-American and one of only four women to win four Olympic medals in women's softball. She graduated from Fresno State and assisted there as softball coach when not training for the Olympics. She spent one year on the Los Angeles Police Department, then joined Oregon State's coaching staff in 2011. (Courtesy SFS Archives.)

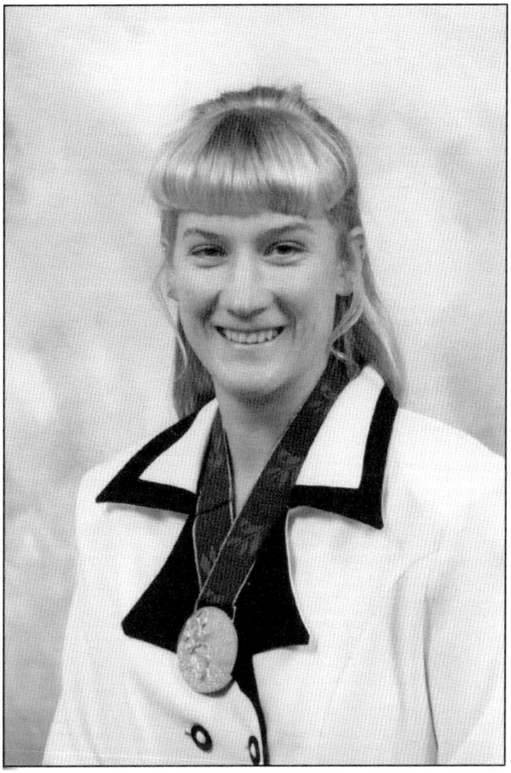

Raul R. Rodriguez graduated from Santa Fe High in 1961. Raul's career began at age 15, when he won City of Whittier's design contest for a Tournament of Roses Parade float. Since then, he has designed over 500 floats and earned more awards than any other designer. In this 1961 photograph, he discusses the City of Santa Fe Springs' first Rose Parade float with Joe Ramirez. He also designed the city's 50th Anniversary Rose Parade float in 2007. (Courtesy SFS Archives.)

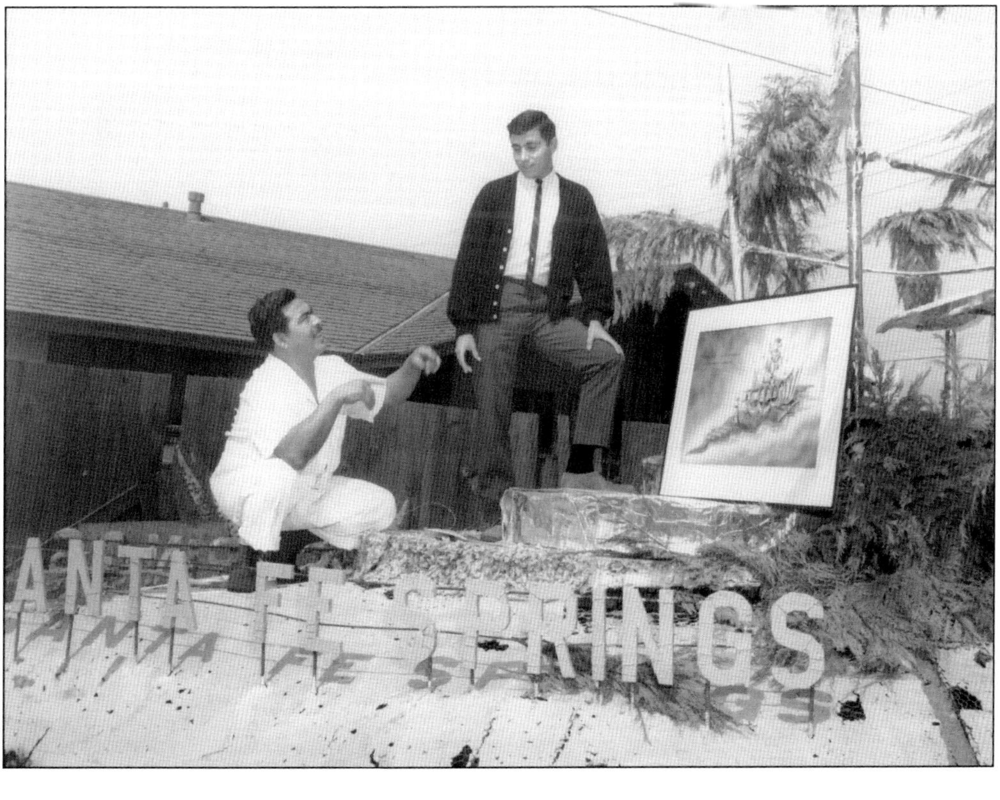

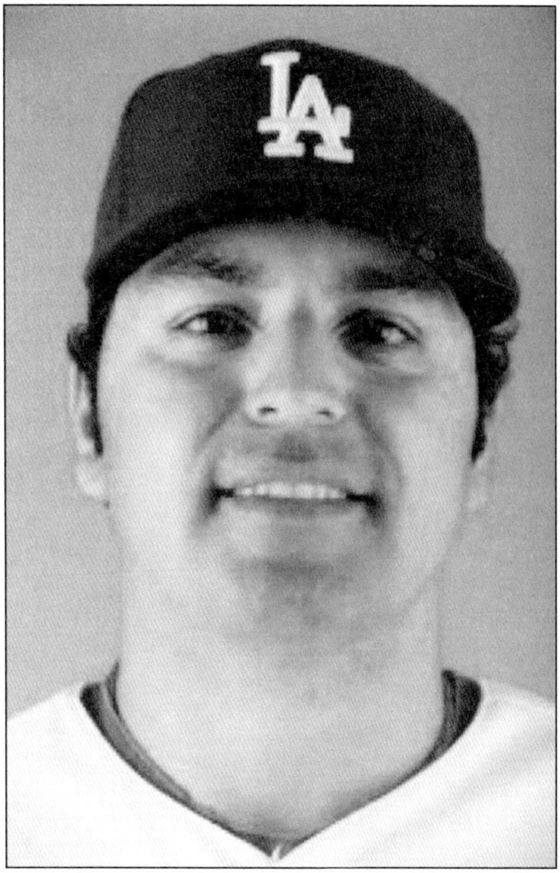

"Rod" Rodrigo Richard Barajas was born on September 5, 1975. Rod graduated from Santa Fe High School and Cerritos Community College. He made his Major League debut playing for the Arizona Diamondbacks in 1999, when he was named to the Texas League Post Season All-Stars. He became a World Series champion with the team in 2001. He was acquired by the L.A. Dodgers in 2010 and hit two doubles and a three-run homer in his first game. (Courtesy L.A. Dodgers.)

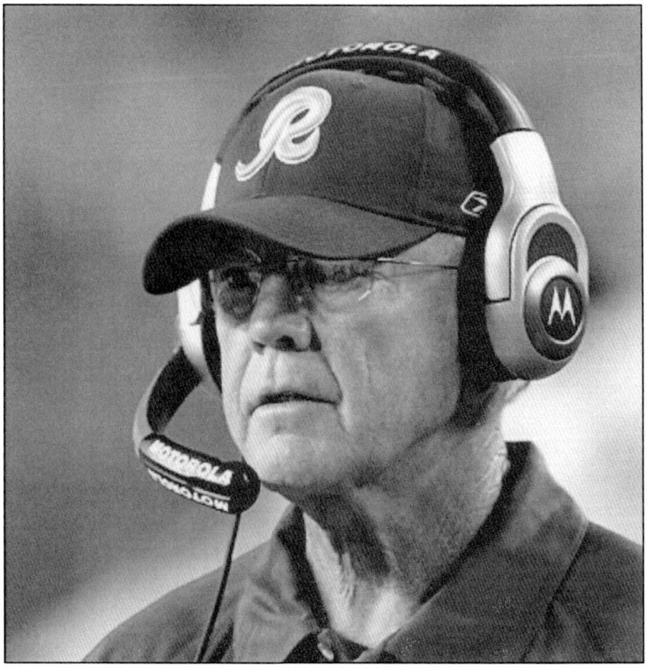

Joe Gibbs was born in Enka, North Carolina. Joe, a 1959 graduate of Santa Fe High, was the school's star quarterback and also lettered in baseball and basketball. He was involved in student government and was voted "most popular." He became the Washington Redskins' head coach in 1981 and was enshrined in the Pro Football Hall of Fame in 1996. He created the NASCAR team Joe Gibbs Racing in 1992 and is now a motivational speaker and author. (Courtesy nflbook.wordpress.com.)

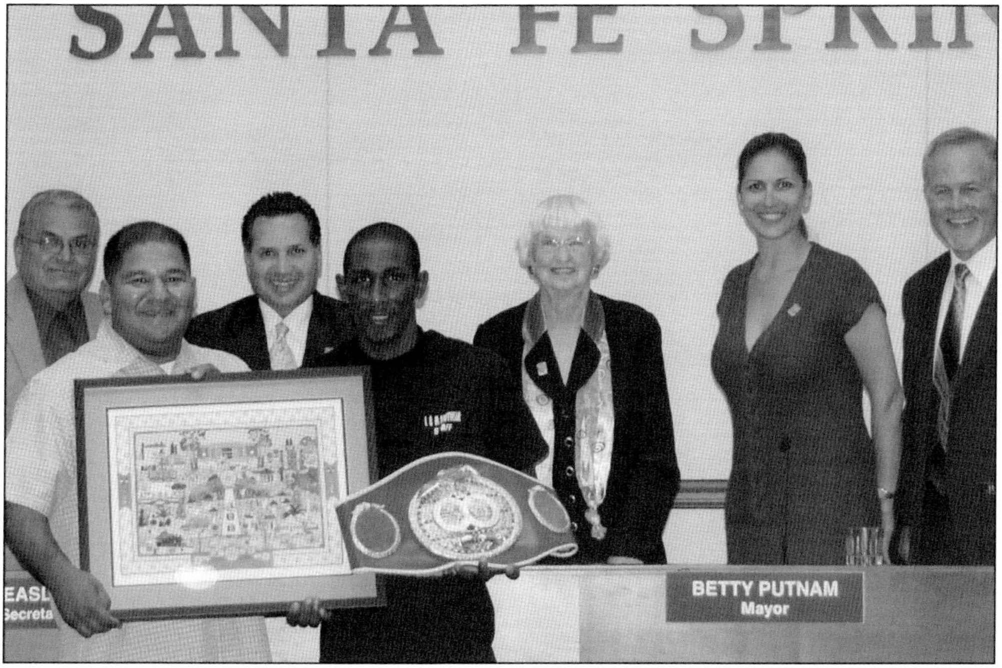

Yonnhy Perez was born on January 18, 1979, in Cartagena, Columbia. Yonnhy, a professional boxer who trains and lives in Santa Fe Springs, won the IBF Bantamweight Championship in Johannesburg, South Africa, in 2009. Yohnny and his trainer, Danny Zamora, made a presentation at the Santa Fe Springs City Council meeting before his bout in 2010 at the Staples Center in Los Angeles, where he successfully defended his title. (Courtesy SFS Archives.)

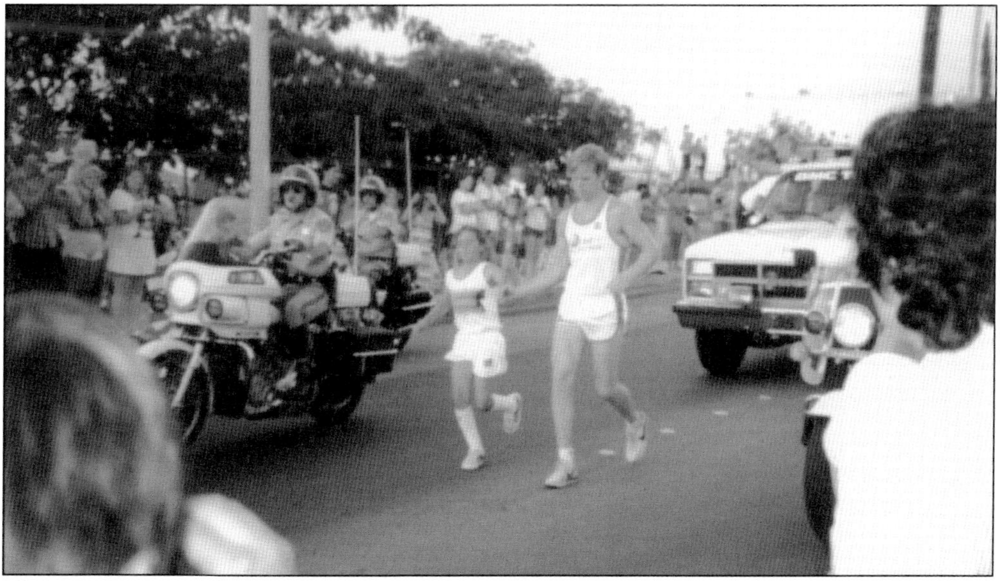

The 1984 Summer Olympics were held in Los Angeles, California. The torch started in New York and was carried by 3,616 runners through 33 states and covered over 9,320 miles before arriving in L.A. The route included Santa Fe Springs, the only time in its history. The torch headed west on Florence Avenue, where excited residents lined the streets and cheered as it went by. (Courtesy Oblea Collection.)

Bibliography

Bancroft, Hubert Howe. *History of California*. vol. I, III, IV, and V. San Francisco: The History Company, 1886.

Bartunek, Ann. *Pre-Incorporation Days*. Unpublished essay, 1960.

Bente, Vance G. *Test Excavation of LAn-1016aH: The Ontiveros Adobe, Santa Fe Springs, California*. Report submitted to the Redevelopment Agency, City of Santa Fe Springs, by Greenwood & Associates, March 1980.

California Spanish Archives, National Archives–Los Angeles Branch, Laguna Nigel, CA. Spanish Archives Translations, vol. 7, *Records of Unclassified Original Spanish Expedientes Relative to Land Claims*. Manuel Nieto to Pedro Fages, 1784, p. 172; Manuel Nieto to Pedro Fages, 1790, p. 171; Felipe Goycochea to Manuel Nieto, 8 March 1790, p. 171; Felipe Goycochea to Gov. Diego Borica, 28 April 1796, p. 165; Fr. Antonio Cruzado and Fr. Miguel Sanchez to Gov. Diego Borica, 25 April 1796, pp. 168, 169; Fr. Fermin Lasuen to Gov. Diego Borica, 6 May 1796, pp. 171–173.

Cleland, Robert Glass. *The Cattle on a Thousand Hills: Southern California, 1850–1880*. San Marino, CA: The Huntington Library Press, 1969.

Hathaway Ranch Museum. *The Life History of Jesse and Lola Hathaway*. 2009–2010.

Jensen, Marilyn. *The History of Santa Fe Springs, A Pictorial History*. Virginia Beach: The Donning Company Publishers, 1991.

McMurray, Mildred Dorland. *The Story of Our Community: Part II*. Unpublished essay, 1963.

Oblea, Larry F. *Biography of Manuel Nieto: Heritage Park Docent Notebook*. Santa Fe Springs: City of Santa Fe Springs, 1995.

Proceedings before the US Board of Land Commissioners, Case No. 404, "Rancho Los Alamitos," Letter from Pedro Fages to his superior officers in Mexico, 20 November 1784, pp. 52–53.

Robinson, Alfred. *Chinigchinich*. Santa Ana, CA: Fine Arts Press, 1933.

Santa Fe Springs Bicentennial Commission. *History in the Making*. 1975.

Santa Fe Springs Historical Committee. *The History of Santa Fe Springs*. 1979.

Snyder, Ted. My *Recollections of Incorporation*. Unpublished essay, 2006.

South Whittier School District Board of Trustees. *South Whittier School District, Harbor Box Co., and South Whittier School Controversy*. Unpublished essay, 1957.

About the Authors

The Santa Fe Springs Historical Committee is a close-knit group dedicated to using all available resources to collect factual and historical data as it is woven together with our American culture and thus into the fabric of the history of Santa Fe Springs. The committee advises the city council in historical matters and takes pride in making all of its resources available to schools in order to supplement any curriculum needed concerning the Santa Fe Springs area.

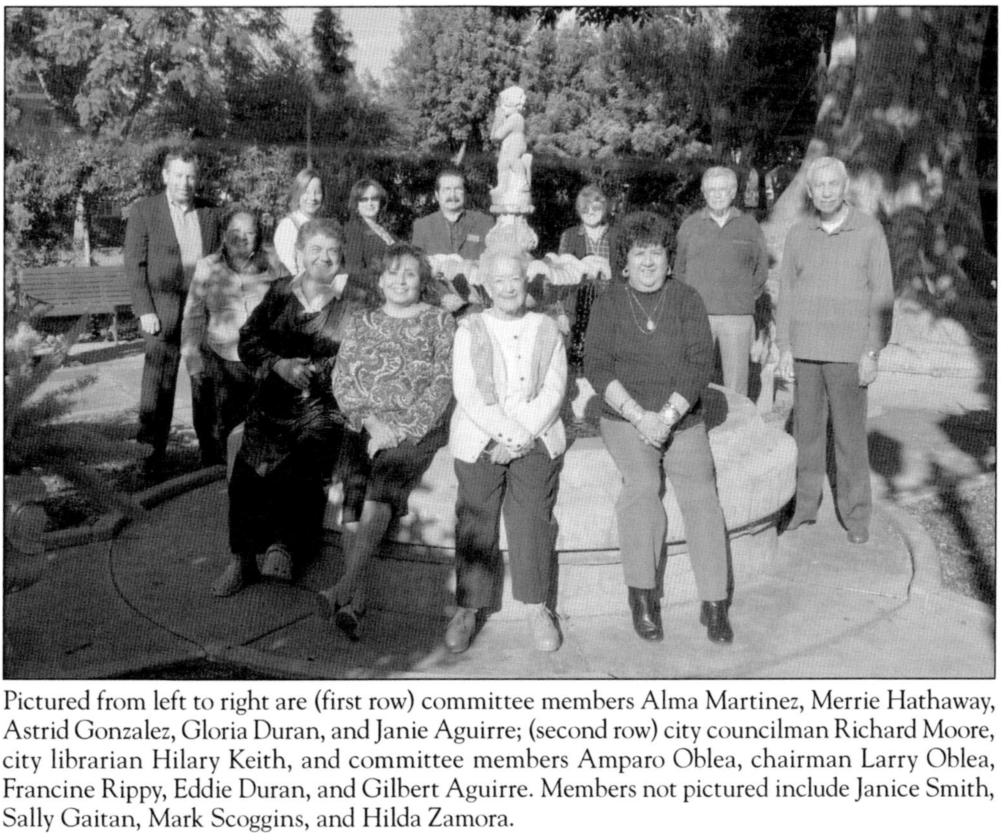

Pictured from left to right are (first row) committee members Alma Martinez, Merrie Hathaway, Astrid Gonzalez, Gloria Duran, and Janie Aguirre; (second row) city councilman Richard Moore, city librarian Hilary Keith, and committee members Amparo Oblea, chairman Larry Oblea, Francine Rippy, Eddie Duran, and Gilbert Aguirre. Members not pictured include Janice Smith, Sally Gaitan, Mark Scoggins, and Hilda Zamora.